THE
MINIMALIST
KITCHEN

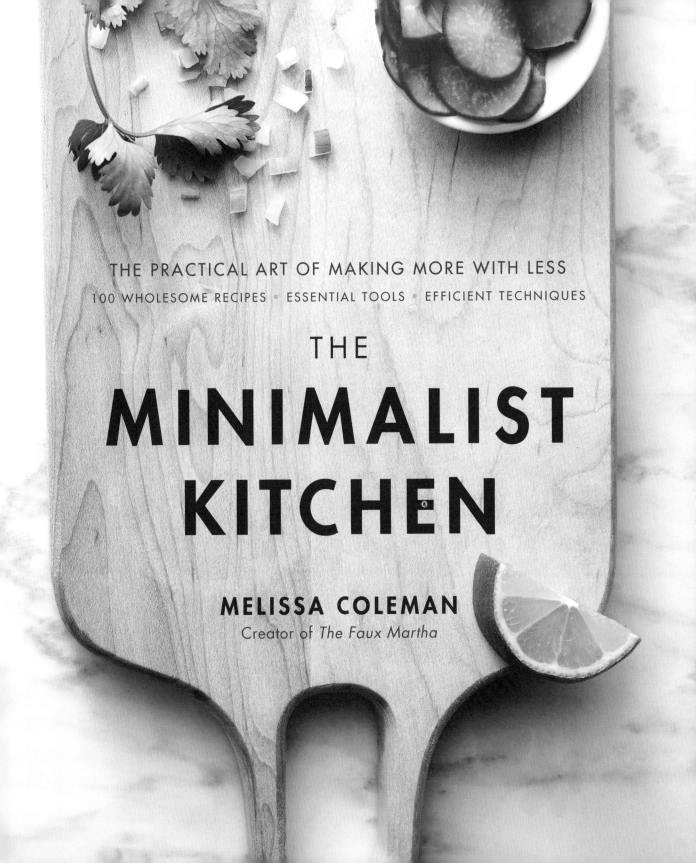

THE PRACTICAL ART OF MAKING MORE WITH LESS

100 WHOLESOME RECIPES · ESSENTIAL TOOLS · EFFICIENT TECHNIQUES

THE

MINIMALIST

KITCHEN

MELISSA COLEMAN

Creator of *The Faux Martha*

Design and Photography ©2018 by Time Inc. Books

Published by Oxmoor House, an imprint of Time Inc. Books
225 Liberty Street, New York, NY 10281

Senior Editor: Rachel Quinlivan West
Project Editor: Lacie Pinyan
Design Director: Melissa Clark
Photo Director: Paden Reich
Senior Designer: Allison Chi
Designer: Matt Ryan
Photographers: Caitlin Bensel, Jennifer Causey, Kim Cornelison,
   Greg DuPree, Alison Miksch, Scott Rounds
Prop Stylists: Mary Clayton Carl, Kay Clarke, Thom Driver,
   Mindi Shapiro
Food Stylists: Mary Claire Britton, Margaret Dickey, Anna Hampton,
   Karen Rankin, Diana Scanlon
Prop Coordinator: Audrey Davis
Test Kitchen: Paige Grandjean, Julia Levy, Callie Nash, Ivy Odom,
   Marianne Williams
Assistant Production Manager: Diane Rose Keener
Assistant Production and Project Manager: Lauren Moriarty
Copy Editor: Rebecca Brennan
Proofreader: Jacqueline Giovanelli
Indexer: Mary Ann Laurens
Fellows: Kaitlyn Pacheco, Holly Ravazzolo, Hanna Yokeley

ISBN-13: 978-0-8487-5526-3

Library of Congress Control Number: 2017932992

First Edition 2018

Printed in China

10 9 8 7 6 5 4 3 2 1

We welcome your comments and suggestions about Time Inc. Books.
Time Inc. Books
Attention: Book Editors
P.O. Box 62310
Tampa, Florida 33662-2310

Time Inc. Books products may be purchased for business or promotional use.
For information on bulk purchases, please contact Christi Crowley in the
Special Sales Department at (845) 395-9858.

To Hallie, who put a deadline on dinnertime—this is for you. This is for us. To prioritizing meals together and gathering around the table night after night.

Contents

8   Welcome

10   **CHAPTER 1** The Minimalist Kitchen

38   **CHAPTER 2** Breakfast

76   **CHAPTER 3** Main Dishes

122   **CHAPTER 4** Burgers, Wraps & Sandwiches

146   **CHAPTER 5** Soups & Salads

176   **CHAPTER 6** Sides

204   **CHAPTER 7** Drinks

226   **CHAPTER 8** Desserts

264   Seasonal Produce Guide

265   Metric Equivalents

266   Indexes

271   About the Author

272   Acknowledgments

Welcome

I MEAN IT, *welcome.* I hope you feel that as you flip through the pages of this book, which cover a topic that can sometimes generate feelings other than that. We'll decode the word minimalism in more detail in the pages that follow.

But first, *hi!* My name is Melissa. I am a former graphic designer by day and food blogger by night. I blog full time now at thefauxmartha.com. I spent years thinking about how my two loves—design and food—could possibly work together. All the while, I was blind to the fact that the two were constantly influencing one another. Design and food are the propane tanks fueling this book. I live with my husband, Kevin, and daughter, Hallie, in Minneapolis, MN. Kev (you can call him that, too) is a child psychologist who often gets called Doogie Howser (forever a baby face). We bounced around the states for his schooling and doctoral internship before firmly planting ourselves under the snowbanks of Minnesota, a state with heavy Nordic influence.

While building our house, we were forced to nail down our style in a couple words. At first, I declared our style modern until realizing it was actually minimal with cozy accents. This, too, is a common descriptor of Nordic homes, which practice *hygge,* loosely translated to mean cozy. *Hygge* (pronounced hoo-guh) is finding joy in the simplest of things, like the warm flicker of a flame or a 2 p.m. coffee break, especially during the dead of winter. It's creating a thoughtful rhythm to otherwise ordinary days. I hope that's what you find in the pages of this book. I hope the practice of creating and keeping a minimalist kitchen yields a kitchen that works and gets used. I hope, too, that it yields joy from gathering around the dinner table night after night. There's so much magic in this ancient, ordinary practice of eating together.

CHAPTER 1

The Minimalist Kitchen

THE MINIMALIST KITCHEN is as much of an art form as it is a practical cooking philosophy. From paring down your tools and ingredients, to building a successful pantry, to using efficient cooking techniques, this book will help make over the most complicated room in the house—the kitchen—so that dinnertime feels doable again.

Introduction

"HOW DO YOU DO IT EVERY DAY?" Kevin, my husband, asked. "Do what?" I asked. "Start with a blank document." I was a graphic designer then. Most workdays started with a ⌘+N, a new blank document.

In a lot of ways, that's what we're all doing every day—starting with a new blank document, trying to make something good, maybe even something great, out of the ordinary. Somehow though, we've made ourselves believe that creating something great has to be new and novel and different. It's exhausting. And even in the process of doing simple things like making eggs, I get stabbed by the strawberry de-stemmer in the catchall kitchen gadget drawer, a tool that's done more work stabbing me than it's done removing the leafy greens from the end of the strawberry. And that's when I'm presented with that problem again. There's too much—too many gadgets, an overflowing pantry, and the idea that in order for dinner to be great, it needs to be novel. If you're anything like me, you grab for the same things anyways—the spatula with the sharp edge, that trusty pasta recipe, and the rice that takes less than 20 minutes to cook. The rest is just taking up space.

So to answer his question I said, "There are a thousand tools in this design program, but I know a couple really well. Those are the ones I use over and over again. That's how I know how to create."

After moving to Texas in the fourth grade, I started playing soccer, playing right up until my freshman year of college. That's when a second knee surgery made me hang up my cleats. After watching a couple seasons, my mom learned that I played my best soccer when I was mad. Turns out, I do my best designing when I'm mad, too—when something doesn't work the way it should. I started taking it out on the kitchen, the most used yet inefficient room in the house. The strawberry destemmer was the first to go.

WHAT IS MINIMALISM?
"Pare down to the essence, but don't remove the poetry."

—LEONARD KOREN, *Wabi-Sabi for Artists, Designers, Poets & Philosophers*

Before we go any further, let's address the word minimalism. It sounds stodgy and austere, and sometimes it is. But, as Leonard Koren says, it's possible to pare down without removing the poetry, the beauty. In general, a minimalist lifestyle is marked by living with less. I like to think of it as living efficiently, keeping only the essentials. My husband likes to think of it as living lean. Minimalist living exists on a spectrum and can look extremely different for a family of one to a family of six, to a person just starting out, to a person 10 years in. In a lot of ways, it's like yoga—a practice. It's an ongoing, active practice that manifests itself differently over time. It's ongoing, too, in that you never quite arrive. Once you clean out the front of the drawer, you notice the back. In short, minimalism is the practical application of the idea that less is more.

WHAT IS A MINIMALIST KITCHEN?
If I had to guess, the kitchen is a problem area in your home, too. It's the most used room, always outfitted with a trail of crumbs, a pile of dirty dishes, disappearing spices, and a stack of half-empty pasta bags spilling over. A minimalist kitchen won't solve the trail of crumbs or the pile of dirty dishes. It's a kitchen after all. But it will solve the pasta bag issue, plus a multitude of other issues birthed from behind the doors of the kitchen cabinets.

This is going to sound silly, but I'd like to suggest that we've been thinking about the kitchen all wrong. It's a room, yes. But it's also the largest closet in the house. Closets are natural troublemakers. And within the greater kitchen closet ecosystem, there are several tiny systems at work—the gadget drawer(s), the small appliance cabinet, the refrigerator, and the pantry shelves. It's no wonder dinnertime feels impossible with the complex ecosystem of the kitchen.

So, what is a minimalist kitchen? Think of it as a capsule wardrobe. If you're unfamiliar with the term, a capsule wardrobe is a closet pared down to 30 or so essential clothing items. When rearranged, you can create 100 different outfits. Now, apply the wardrobe concept to the kitchen, and you have a capsule kitchen. It's outfitted with only the essential tools and ingredients used on a regular basis. The rest goes. As with a capsule wardrobe, once you pare down, you realize all the things you can make.

"

So, what's a minimalist kitchen? Think of it as a capsule wardrobe ... once you pare down, you realize all the things you can make ... in the case of this book, it's 100 recipes."

You can also think of a minimalist kitchen like this: In a design class in college, my professor used the sandbox analogy during a lesson on creating branding standards. If you put a child in a huge park and tell them to play, they might get a little lost and overwhelmed. But if you put them in the confines of a sandbox with a couple tools, they'll know how to play. When I was a designer, I gave myself a sandbox, too, using only the tools I knew well to create. For me, having too many choices is completely debilitating. Creating a minimalist kitchen is counterintuitive. You pare down so you can create

more. It's amazing the sheer amount of things you can make in a really good sandbox. In the case of this book, it's 100 recipes.

By the sound of it, you might think *The Minimalist Kitchen* is a book of 5-ingredient recipes, but even a book like that could make your pantry spill over. The recipes in this book vary from 3 to 20 ingredients and use the same handful of tools and ingredients but offer a wide range of flavors. With a well-stocked pantry, pared-down tools, efficient techniques, and maintenance grocery shopping, *The Minimalist Kitchen* creates space to cook. Practicing this method makes meal planning and cooking a doable chore. Because let's be honest—cooking is a whole lot like working out. If you want a homemade meal, you have to cook.

In the pages that follow, I'll break down the practical art of creating and keeping a minimalist kitchen.

A LITTLE ABOUT ME

Minimalism is my natural tendency, but it's something I've fought my whole life. It's not popular to want less when the American dream is to have more. I started wanting less when I realized the weight of more. More stuff comes with more responsibility. When I was too young to be purging my closet, I was purging my closet. In middle school, I hated buying yet another bottle of Cucumber Melon lotion to give as a birthday present, a bottle that would surely get lost next to the five other bottles of Country Apple in the bathroom cabinet. But I did it because that's what you did for your friends in seventh grade. In high school, I painted. And when I look back at my work, I was a reductionist. Always simplifying—using less colors and more negative space to tell the story. By college, I was studying graphic design. We were taught to communicate the essentials beautifully. I found a home and a normalcy in that. Postcollege, I worked as a designer by day and started blogging about food by night at thefauxmartha.com. In the early days, it was the highly styled and propped images that went viral on Pinterest. The most elaborate recipes usually got the most love. I loved looking at those images and recipes but could never reproduce them without sweating and getting mad.

My heart beats to efficiency—using the same measuring utensil throughout the entire recipe (see Italian Summer Salad, page 162, and Yogurt Shortcake, page 258) and only opening the fridge once before cooking a meal makes me so happy. This minimalist bent also makes me feel crazy some days. Does everything need to be efficient and just right? No. As with everything, I hope you see this philosophy for all its good and for all its flaws. I like to think of minimalism as a practice, because it needs constant refining. Rules that are too rigid will strip away the joy. Rules that are too loose will create an overflowing and frustrating kitchen. The magic is in the space between, or as Koren refers to it, the magic is in the poetry. And mastering that kind of magic takes continual practice.

For me, the kitchen became a big problem after becoming a mom. Dinner came with a set time and a new mouth to feed. I was working for myself as a designer and food blogger. Kevin was finishing up his doctoral work as a child psychologist, studying for boards, and teaching online classes at night. Busy was an understatement. Grocery shopping, meal planning, and cooking felt so overwhelming. I began to hate the kitchen. And I was a food blogger! I had always made everything from scratch, even if it took all weekend. "You'll change when you have a kid," they said. "You'll switch to boxes and drive-thrus." So we waited. But when she eventually arrived into our lives, I understood it all. They were right; I changed. But I wasn't willing to give up nourishing homemade meals and gathering around the dinner table every night, a practice my parents instilled in me.

As a designer who is happiest when things work, I took my fury to the kitchen. Everything made me mad—from the drawer that always stabbed me to the pantry that exploded upon opening. This room was broken. My options were to fix it or stop cooking altogether. If you're reading this book, you know how the story ends.

HOW TO BECOME A MINIMALIST

This section is a *very* basic primer on minimalism. And yet, if you're applying this philosophy to your kitchen, I imagine it will naturally spill over into other areas of your life—from your hall closet to your personal life.

The process of paring down can be emotional. Our possessions have high value even when they won't sell for more than a dollar on Craigslist. We end up with too much stuff from the natural accumulation of time, from kids, and from overbuying. And sometimes we end up with too much stuff for emotional reasons, making it even harder to get rid of. So before we jump into paring down the kitchen cabinets and pantry, it's important to acknowledge the potential invisible motives populating the home with too much stuff. (We'll talk more practically about creating good shopping habits in the pages to come. There's an art to that, too.) But here are some questions to keep in the periphery. They don't need overnight answers. In fact, think about them as ongoing questions to ask yourself. Why do I overbuy? When do I overbuy? Why do I have trouble getting rid of excess stuff?

So how do you become a minimalist? There's no exact answer, but simply put, you intentionally choose to live with less. When you start keeping less around in your physical space, you create space to notice more, and sometimes it results in noticing more about yourself. A byproduct of this practice is self-awareness. Minimalists are typically very aware of their good stuff and their bad stuff. I think there's a whole lot of beauty in that—of being able to sit with both. Which brings me back to Leonard Koren, "Pare down to the essence, but don't remove the poetry." The poetry is the humanity. If that extra bowl reminds you of your grandma, and brings joy every time you look at it, well then, don't remove the poetry. Minimalism is as much an art form as it is a practice. There are no prescriptions or perfect answers. And where it starts and stops in your life is a bit unpredictable. Let it be.

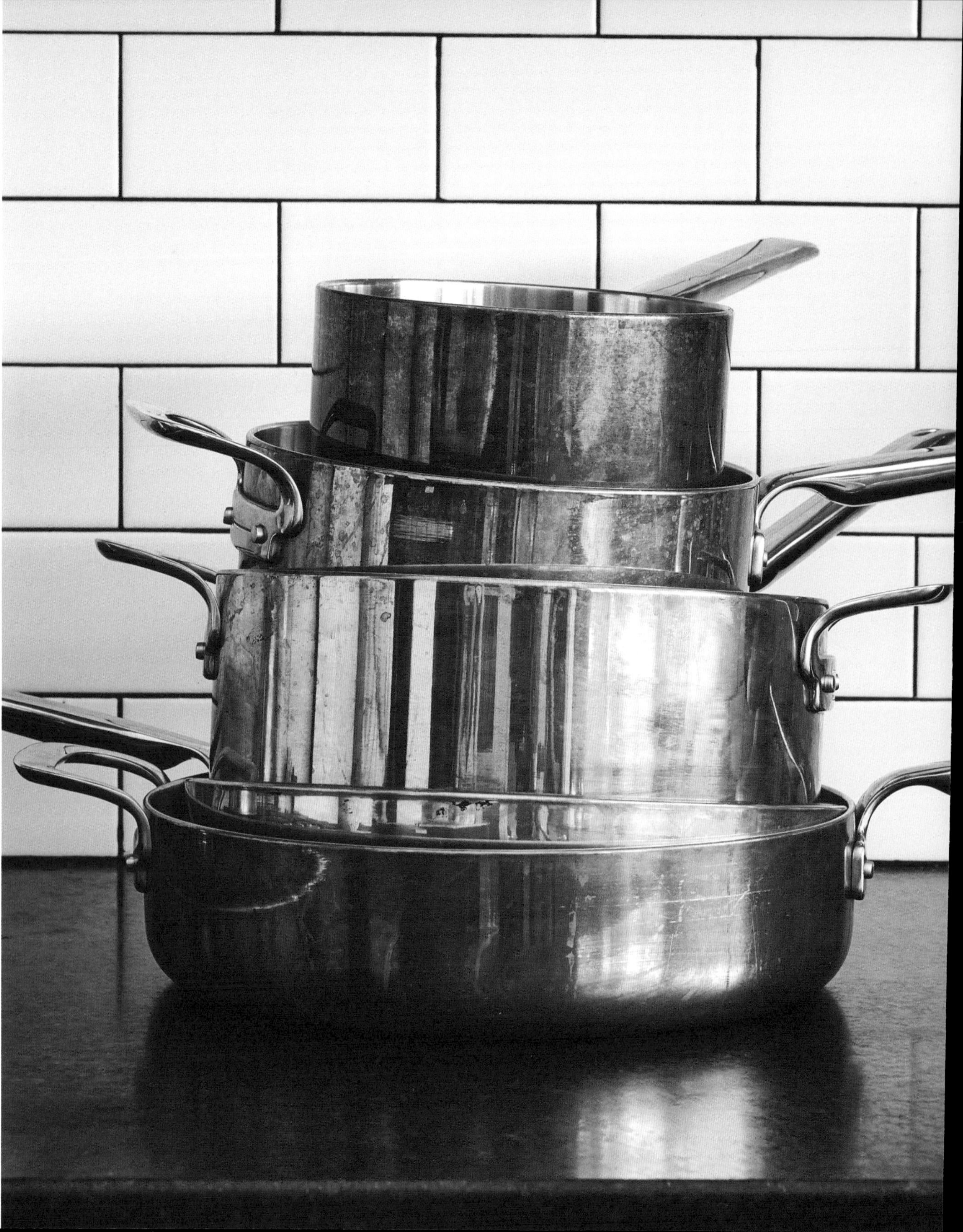

The Essential Tools

WHEN WE REGISTERED before getting married, we were budding minimalists, the kind of buds that look like a slight swell at the end of a branch, only visible if you're looking for it. We broke tradition and skipped registering for fine china and silver, but we scanned every other gadget. People love gadgets, so we got lots of them. At one point in my early adult life, I had four gadgets alone for garlic—two different types of garlic presses, a garlic roller for easy skin removal, and a stainless steel bar for rubbing the smell out of my hands afterwards. I only used one of the tools on occasion. The rest were just taking up space.

Space is precious in the kitchen. Somehow there's never enough of it even with plenty of it. But if you're anything like me, you probably reach for the same tools just like you reach for the same pair of jeans. What if you only kept the things you actually used? I started doing that. In fact, I'm still doing that.

A major overhaul is usually needed to kick-start these paring-down efforts. To do so, get rid of the things you don't have to think twice about, even if they're in mint condition. Then, let yourself slowly get rid of things as you notice their infrequent use. To practically do this, keep a storage bin in the basement or a closet. Fill it up with unused tools, even small kitchen appliances. After 3 months or once the bin is full, donate the items. This 3-month window will give you enough time to rescue a gadget if absolutely needed. Only once have I ever rescued an item from the bin. Everything else was just as forgotten as it was in the drawer. If you're having trouble figuring out what you actually use and what you don't, then try the dishwasher test. It sounds silly, but the next time it's running, look through your drawers. What's left? Looking at your kitchen this way will help you to see beneath the top layer.

Once you've pared down, consider adding dividers to your drawers. Even a pared-down kitchen gadget drawer can feel chaotic if it's not organized. I use inexpensive bamboo dividers to create contained spaces for tools in each drawer.

Let's build your kitchen sandbox, your capsule kitchen, your minimalist kitchen, using only the tools you need. So that when it comes time to cook dinner, you'll know exactly what to do. Or, at minimum, you'll be able to find the whisk.

VARIABLES TO KEEP IN MIND WHEN PARING DOWN

QUALITY. My dad always advised us to save up and buy quality products when possible. "When you buy the cheap product now," he said, "you'll end up replacing it, sometimes multiple times, spending the same amount or more than had you just bought the quality product." That's hard to do when you're just starting out. And sometimes, you just can't. But when you can, the payoff is almost always there.

QUANTITY. It's OK to have more than one of something. I bake quite a bit, so I keep two whisks and spatulas around so that I don't have to clean them mid-baking. As you pare down, it's important to consider the number of people in your family, too. Larger families, for example, may require two cast-iron skillets instead of one for efficiency's sake. Also, consider how often you run your dishwasher. You may need more than one spatula for that reason alone.

HOLIDAYS AND HOSTING. This can create a huge problem in kitchens. The occasional can often creep into the space of the everyday. I like to keep holidays and entertaining as simple as the everyday, using the same tools. If additional tools are necessary, store them separately as you would your holiday decorations.

THE JUNK DRAWER PHENOMENON. This phenomenon is crazy yet trustworthy. Once you clean out your junk drawer, it fills right back up. I've given myself over to having one junk drawer. I think we all need a space in our home to have a mess, a place to be human. So give yourself a space to keep a small, contained mess. But as you pare down the rest of the kitchen, be mindful of this phenomenon. The issue of too much starts at the store. And the empty space doesn't always need filling.

RECIPES. Consider the recipes you make on a regular basis, and keep the tools around needed to make them. As I've pared down over the years to accommodate the recipes I make every day, the following list is what I'm left with. It's also the same list that made this book. Use it as a guide, not a prescription, keeping in mind the variables. Every home is different and your needs may change over the years, too. Every 6 months or so, take inventory of your tools, and add to the giveaway bin as needed.

COOKING PANS

10-INCH CAST-IRON SKILLET

Cast-iron skillets are inexpensive workhorses in the kitchen that produce a flavor no other pan can produce. When well cared for, they'll last longer than a lifetime. I use mine almost daily. Over time, cast-iron skillets develop a natural nonstick surface from normal usage. Though most skillets come preseasoned, I have the best luck with new pans after adding a couple thin layers of oil. To do so, rub a light coat of neutral oil on the interior of the pan, wiping away any excess. Cook over medium-low for about 10 to 15 minutes. The black of the skillet should look matte, not shiny. Using too much oil will create a shiny, sticky, hard-to-clean mess. If starting with a brand-new pan, give it the oil treatment every other time after using until you have a trustworthy surface, and then repeat the process when you notice food sticking more often. To wash, use hot water and dry completely with a paper towel, including the bottom, to keep rust from forming. Use mild soap only if necessary. If soap is needed, that's a good indicator, too, that your surface needs a little oil maintenance.

For quick cleaning, pour water into the hot pan (a couple tablespoons). The steam from the hot water pulls up the stuck-on bits. Once most of the water has burned off, carefully wipe the insides down with a paper towel. If using this method, be careful of the heat the steam gives off. I've used a 10-inch skillet throughout the book. You'll also see mention of a cast-iron griddle. The larger cooking surface is more efficient for cooking larger amounts of food at one time (like fajitas or pancakes). You should note: Cast-iron cookware can scratch glass cooking surfaces, so be careful when working on a glass stovetop.

DUTCH OVEN

A 6-quart Dutch oven is another lifetime investment. It's also the tool used to cook large pieces of meat, like the Dutch Oven Whole Chicken (page 106) or the Humble Chuck Roast (page 118). Dutch ovens are cast-iron pans coated in enamel. They're incredible heat conductors. And, when using the heavy lid, they turn into efficient slow cookers, too, creating tender, fall-apart meat. Dutch ovens also double as stockpots.

STAINLESS-STEEL COOKWARE SET

Cookware sets are often sold with more pots than you actually need. If you do buy a set, go with a 10-piece set at most. I recommend stocking a small 8-inch and a large 10-inch skillet, a large 4-quart sauté pan, and a small 2-quart and large 4-quart saucepan. (What's the difference between a sauté pan and a skillet? A sauté pan has tall, straight sides whereas a skillet has curved, shorter sides.) I prefer stainless steel–lined pans for everyday cooking. But for eggs, I stock a 10-inch ceramic-coated nonstick skillet. To clean tough messes on stainless-steel pans, or to shine up the exterior, use Bar Keepers Friend (or a similar product). A good set of stainless-steel pans should last you a lifetime. Nonstick pans, however, tend to have a shorter life span. If you want to be an ultra minimalist, you can skip adding another skillet to your lineup, using your cast iron exclusively. You can also use a Dutch oven as a stockpot. For long-term preservation, hand wash all your pots and pans.

BAKING PANS

BAKING DISH

Baking dishes (also called casserole pans) are most commonly sold in glass or ceramic. I've used both over the years but prefer enamelware baking dishes for a variety of reasons. They're beautiful pans. Storagewise, they stack inside one another and weigh very little. They perform very well and clean up even better. If any staining occurs, use Bar Keepers Friend (or a similar product) to clean.

SHEET PAN

Also called a jelly-roll pan or a half-sheet pan. I use aluminum, commercial-grade baking sheets. If they're strong enough to endure a restaurant kitchen, they're strong enough for the home kitchen. For easy storage, keep two of the same baking sheets. When you're in need of a nonstick baking surface, line the baking sheet with parchment paper or a reusable silicone baking mat (like a Silpat). I keep my baking sheets permanently lined with a Silpat for easy storage. If you often bake small batches, consider keeping a quarter sheet around, too. In general, choose lighter colored pans as dark pans tend to cause overbrowning.

COOLING RACK

I'm not incredibly particular about cooling racks, though I do have one requirement: The rack needs to also fit inside a baking sheet. It's great for storage but also works well for keeping waffles crisp in the oven after cooking or for containing drizzle messes from icing scones.

MUFFIN TIN

Like the baking sheet, I stock a 12-cup aluminum, commercial-grade muffin tin. For easy muffin or cupcake removal, use parchment liners.

CAKE PAN

The recipes in this book use an 8-inch round aluminum cake pan. I prefer the slightly smaller size to the more traditional 9-inch pans, as it produces a taller cake with more proportionate cake slices. If using a 9-inch cake pan, reduce the baking time. For easy cake removal, line the bottom of the pan with parchment paper.

TART PAN

Unless you're a devoted pie maker, pies can be difficult to make look as beautiful as they taste. A good tart pan will change your pie-making life. The fluted edges make it naturally beautiful. No crimping involved. I recommend a 10-inch removable-bottom tart pan with at least a 2-inch height. The extra height gives peace of mind when pouring in a filling, whether making a quiche (like the one on page 69) or Roasted Banana Cream Pie (page 253), while the removable bottom makes for the easiest removal. For the best pie-making results, keep a set of pie weights or dried beans around as well to weigh the crust down while baking.

GADGETS

CAN OPENER

Find a small manual can opener that cuts a smooth edge rather than a sharp one.

VEGETABLE PEELER

The two most common vegetable peelers are the swivel peeler and the Y peeler. Use what feels most comfortable to you.

BOX GRATER

OXO, one of my favorite kitchen brands for their smart, functional products, sells a deconstructed box grater that works amazingly well. It looks and operates a bit like a mandoline with four different grating adapters—coarse grater, medium grater, straight slicer, and julienne slicer. It stores completely contained as well. I prefer the OXO Grate and Slice Set to a traditional box grater. Whenever a thinly sliced, shredded, or julienne vegetable is called for, I use this tool. It's so efficient.

CUTTING BOARD

I prefer polyethylene plastic cutting boards, as they are nonporous, unlike wood cutting boards, and require zero maintenance. I keep two boards, a small and a large. Tip: Use one side of your board exclusively for meats and the other for produce. Write a small "M" or "V" with a marker near the handle or edge of the board.

SMALL APPLIANCES

HIGH-POWERED BLENDER

Next to my cast-iron skillet, this is my second most used kitchen tool. It's the other workhorse of the kitchen, doubling as a blender and food processor. From smoothies and sauces to falafels and Dutch babies, our high-powered blender gets used daily. But unlike the cast-iron skillet, the high-powered blender is an investment, one worth saving up for. A good one will last you years, whereas an inexpensive one will get replaced again and again. (Our Vitamix is 10+ years old.) Look for a high-powered blender with a one-piece container, meaning the blade can't screw off from the basin. We keep two containers—a small one (32 ounces) for everyday use and a large one (64 ounces) for bigger batches. If I had to choose one, I'd go with the smaller container. If you don't have a high-powered blender, you'll find alternatives in the recipes for using other appliances (or sometimes simply a bowl and whisk).

MIXER

I prefer a stand mixer over a hand mixer, but either will work. Stand mixers come in multiple sizes. Buy the size that fits your everyday needs. If you're a smaller family, a mini stand mixer is the perfect size. If you're cooking for a large family, consider buying a professional series, or land somewhere in between with the traditional size.

TOASTER

When purchasing a toaster, consider your family size. A two-slot toaster is great for a smaller family. For larger families, consider one with more slots.

KNIVES

CHEF'S KNIFE, PARING KNIFE, BREAD KNIFE

Like cookware sets, knives are sold in sets with way more than you actually need or use. All you really need is a good chef's knife for everyday chopping, a paring knife for smaller chopping, and a serrated bread knife for crusty breads or even meats. For long-term preservation, hand wash only.

COOKING UTENSILS

SILICONE SPATULA

I like my silicone spatulas to have a sharp edge for scraping all the stuck-on bits from the sides of the bowl. I also prefer spatulas that are coated in one material, producing a single seam, for ease of cleaning. Use heat-resistant silicone spatulas on nonstick pans instead of metal as metal can damage the nonstick coating.

STURDY METAL SPATULA

Keep a sturdy metal spatula for flipping burgers or removing cookies from the baking sheet. This tool can also double as a bench scraper for cleaning the counter after rolling out pie dough or for carefully scraping off stuck-on bits from the cast-iron skillet.

COOKING SPOONS

Look for metal or wood spoons. (Note: Wood spoons require more care. They'll need to be conditioned with mineral oil and should never sit in water.) Wood spoons age beautifully when well cared for. Metal spoons, while not as beautiful, function extremely well but should not be used on nonstick surfaces.

TONGS

I prefer tongs that have an open and close mechanism for narrow drawer storage.

COLANDER

I keep two metal colanders. A large one for pasta and a small one for everyday use—like rinsing berries or a can of beans—which I keep permanently in my kitchen sink.

STEAMER BASKET

Buy a simple stainless steamer basket that can fit inside your large saucepan for steaming vegetables. For storage, a folded-up steamer basket nestles perfectly inside a colander.

BAKING UTENSILS

MEASURING SPOONS
A set of metal measuring spoons will last a lifetime. Plastic tends to warp over time, which is a bit untrustworthy for baking.

MEASURING CUPS
Like the measuring spoons, a set of metal measuring cups will last a lifetime. A glass liquid measuring cup is another necessary tool. Look for a 2- or 4-cup basin.

WOODEN ROLLING PIN
A wooden rolling pin will last you a lifetime and age beautifully. The fat from butter and oil naturally conditions the wood. It also doubles as a meat mallet.

MIXING BOWLS
Buy a set of bowls, either enamel, stainless steel, or glass, that nestle inside each other for easy storage.

WHISK
Look for durable stainless-steel whisks. In true fashion, I keep a small and a large whisk.

MASON JARS
Mason jars are all over our kitchen. I use the larger jars to store dried goods in the pantry and the smaller jars for storing leftovers in the fridge, for making dressings and sauces, as well as for making mixed drinks. Buy wide-mouth Ball jars if you can, as the wide opening is much more user-friendly.

SPRING-RELEASE SCOOPS

Spring-release scoops are most commonly used to scoop ice cream. But they are efficient little tools for portioning out things like cookie and falafel dough. I keep a small 2 teaspoon-sized spring-release scoop (0.3-ounce scoop/#60 scoop) and a large 4 tablespoon-sized spring-release scoop (2-ounce scoop/#16 scoop). You'll see exact mention of these tools throughout.

NONESSENTIALS BUT RECOMMENDED
OIL SPRAYER

I'm pretty picky about my oils. Rather than keeping canned cooking spray around, I use an oil sprayer so that I can manually add my oil of choice. You'll notice the phrasing "neutral oil" used throughout. I like to stock an oil that is both stable at high heat and neutral tasting, which is what I also use in my oil sprayer.

BUTTER WARMER

We opted to forgo installing a microwave in our house for space issues. It oftentimes means we have to get a pan dirty for reheating, but the food is always so much better when reheated this way. I use an enamel butter warmer (which looks like a tiny saucepan) multiple times a day—whether for melting butter for a recipe or for reheating pasta.

TORTILLA WARMER

For the amount of tortillas we eat, we keep a cloth tortilla warmer around. You'll see this in the recipe directions, too, but the best way to heat tortillas is to lightly char them over a gas flame (or on a hot skillet if you're using electric), and then cover to steam. To cover, we place the hot tortillas in the cloth warmer to soften and steam to perfection. This can be done with a plate and towel, too. If you eat a lot of tortillas, an inexpensive tortilla warmer is worth keeping around.

MEAT THERMOMETER

It's really easy to over- or undercook meat. I was good at doing both until I bought an instant-read meat thermometer. This tiny, single-use gadget gets so much use in my kitchen. It's a great teacher, too. Feel the meat when the thermometer says it's done and commit that feeling to memory.

MEAT MALLET

Chicken cooks faster and more evenly when it is pounded thin and is the same thickness throughout. (You can use a rolling pin if you don't have a mallet.) We also use it to crush things like peppermint and nuts.

KITCHEN SHEARS

Keep a pair of shears (scissors) specifically for the kitchen so there's no cross-contamination with everyday household tasks. Kitchen shears are also efficient tools for cutting and trimming raw meat.

MICROPLANE

Keep this around for easy citrus zesting or grating nutmeg. You can also zest citrus by using a sharp chef's knife to skim off the top layer just above the white pith. Then, chop finely.

SALAD SPINNER

When handling large leafy greens (like kale or romaine) a salad spinner is an efficient tool for cleaning and drying, and requires zero paper towels. It's great, too, for revitalizing wilted greens. If your leaves are looking a bit limp, fill the salad spinner with cold water, ice, and the greens. Let sit for 10 minutes to crisp back up. Drain the water and ice, and spin to dry.

AP FLOUR

BREAD FLOUR

Wheat Pastry Flo

MEAL

OAT FLOUR

POWDERED SUGAR

UNSWEETENED
COCOA POWDER

TURBINADO

N SUGAR

1:2 ratio
20 MINUTES

How to Build a Minimalist Pantry

26

YOU CAN CLEAN OUT your clothes closets, add storage bins, fold or hang your clothes in a certain way, and it works. The closet stays fairly clean and organized with very little maintenance. But the pantry is another kind of closet beast. It's a beast because there are constantly things coming in and out and often multiple people using it. Pantries are known for being full of half-eaten bags of stale chips and nearly empty boxes of pasta. When left alone, they don't work well.

Food management in general is challenging, even more so during the busy work week. It takes forethought and planning. Do I have enough pasta and eggs to get us through the week? Keeping a well-stocked pantry and refrigerator is a game changer for everyday cooking. When stocked well, you don't have to think about it. You can just count on it.

In order to create an efficient pantry, a new set of rules is necessary. Implementing the system will feel as clunky as trying out a recipe for the first time. But as soon as you get into the rhythm (which won't take long), you'll begin calling these rules habits and offering to make over your neighbor's pantry.

DEVELOP A SYSTEM

Think of your pantry like a small restaurant. Inventory is constantly coming in and out. You've got limited shelving and a bunch of employees (family members) ranging in age. Hire a boss (you), and create a user-friendly pantry system to meet your inventory needs. Then, communicate the system to the employees. A successful system is developed from understanding the personal habits of all employees and creating proactive, intuitive solutions. At first, it's important that the boss enforce the system for it to take hold. We'll break down the practical details in the following pages. Use this section as a guide, and make changes according to your lifestyle. The system will vary from kitchen to kitchen.

THINK OF EVERYTHING IN YOUR PANTRY AS AN INGREDIENT

From a box of cereal to sliced almonds—treat each item as an ingredient. This helps to give the pantry system context and saves time, money, and mental energy when shopping. Some ingredients can be restocked from shopping the bulk bins at the store, which is typically less expensive due to the lack of packaging. Otherwise, become brand loyal and/or buy the same exact ingredients every time. No two brands of canned chickpeas, for example, are exactly the same. Find your favorite, and stick with it. This loyalty takes the guesswork out of cooking, too. You'll know exactly how the ingredient performs.

GIVE YOURSELF PARAMETERS

It's OK not to stock every ingredient from the grocery store. In fact, it's wise to give yourself parameters for the pantry, which will also help guide the recipes you can make. So build your pantry system around what you can feasibly maintain. We stock one type of short-grain pasta, one type of 20-minute brown rice, one type of tortilla chip, etc. Consider dropping your number of spices down to about 20, especially if you rarely use the other 10 (see page 30 for more about spices). What about those pesky cereal boxes? Create a rule. For our family of three, we stock two types of cereal at a time—a box my daughter picks out and muesli. It may seem counterintuitive, but too many options can lead to decision-making paralysis while also creating storage problems. Rules give us context to create.

BUY CLEAR CONTAINERS

Store-bought food comes in boxes and bags that are designed to look good on the shelf at the store, but they don't translate well to the home pantry. You can't see the interior contents, they look disorderly on the pantry shelf, and once opened, they don't keep food fresh. Buy clear containers to store your dry goods. We use OXO Pop Containers, which come in a variety of sizes for stocking larger amounts of food like pasta, rice, chips, cereal, and oats. We also use quart-sized wide-mouth Ball jars for smaller things like nuts, seeds, and dried fruits. Using clear containers makes it easy to see what's in stock and what needs refilling. It also makes it easy to find what you're looking for. Rebuild your spice cabinet, too, using a set of clear glass containers (see page 30 for more guidance on spices).

A pantry overhaul can be expensive. Do a little at a time as budget permits. When buying containers, think about functionality. Will it keep food fresh? Will it fit on the pantry shelf? Is it easy to use? Will a hand fit inside? If using Ball jars, swap out the less convenient, two-piece metal lids for one-piece plastic lids, also made by Ball. It's a cheap upgrade.

ADD SCOOPS

Add permanent scoops for ease to the containers that require scooping (like rice, flour, or sugar).

LABEL THE CONTAINERS

It's important to label similar-looking ingredients, like dried cranberries and dried cherries. Add cook times and ratios to the labels, too, where necessary. For example, the label on my rice container says 1:2 (1 part rice to 2 parts water) and 20 minutes (for the cook time). Help yourself out as much as possible to make weeknight cooking breezier.

ADD BINS

Even after overhauling your pantry, you may find puddles of random small things—like kid snacks, liquid sweeteners, sprinkles, and leavening powders. They can often make shelves look cluttered. And clutter seems to welcome clutter. To solve this problem, add small bins to collect those items. Typically, I use clear containers for visibility, but in this case, I recommend hiding the clutter as long as the bins are well categorized. We keep one for kid snacks (located on a shelf they can reach), one for leaveners and liquid sweeteners (like honey), and one for sprinkles and chocolates.

CATEGORIZE SHELVES

Make sure your shelves make sense. With multiple people using the pantry, an intuitive system is imperative. We have a canned goods shelf, a baking shelf, a breakfast shelf, a grains shelf, a snack shelf, a dried nuts and fruit shelf, etc. The more intuitive, the more likely the pantry will stay organized. Also, consider keeping your storage depth shallow, even if you have extra-deep shelves. Out of sight (hidden) is often out of mind. To handle overflow, designate an unused shelf, either a top or bottom shelf (or a closet shelf), for backup inventory. Shop from the overflow shelves first before adding the item to the grocery list. We buy quite a bit in bulk for the price break, like oats, sugar, and nuts. We also keep extra condiments on hand (like soy sauce and olive oil) to keep from running out mid-recipe. Shopping in bulk doesn't sound like a minimalist practice. But in the kitchen, it's also just as important to consider efficiency and cost.

ADD IT TO THE CALENDAR

There's a common misconception that if you organize and clean really well one time, you'll never have to do it again. As with most things in life, the pantry requires ongoing maintenance. But if you put a successful infrastructure in place, it's really easy to maintenance clean. Four times a year or so, set a reminder on your calendar to take inventory of the pantry. What's not working? Does a shelf need rearranging? Should you buy a couple more containers? An efficient workflow needs ongoing tweaking.

KNOW THE RULES SO YOU CAN BREAK THEM WELL

When you slim down your pantry, it gives you room (literally) to break the rules here and there. Maybe you buy a box of Peppermint Oreos at Christmastime or maybe you decide to start buying pistachios. A tidy pantry will give you space to explore a little. Notice your habits. Is this a one-time purchase? Then let it be. Is this an ongoing purchase? Then give it a permanent space in the pantry by adding a new jar or replacing an item that doesn't get used.

How to Stock a Minimalist Pantry

KEEP A LIST

As soon as you think of something, write it down. This is a habit worth developing and one that took me a very long time to develop. Over- or under-buying will kill a pantry. I use a list-keeping app on my phone, Wunderlist, to keep separate lists for every store we shop. My husband can see and contribute to the list as well, so either person can do the shopping. If you're extra efficient, you can even manually arrange the shopping list to the flow of the store.

SHOP YOUR LIST, NOT THE STORE

This is my number one rule. A list is no good unless you use it, right? It's important to note, a minimal pantry starts at the store, not at home. Be mindful of what you're buying. If you notice yourself getting bored with the same old things, find a positive way to meet that need. Maybe it's going out to eat to get something special. Or, maybe you introduce a new rule—buy one spontaneous thing a month. Again, know the rules so you can break them.

BREAK UP SHOPPING

Grocery shopping is one of my least favorite tasks, and yet it has to be done on a weekly basis. To make it more manageable, I break up shopping into two categories—pantry/bulk shopping and weekly maintenance shopping. About once a month, I shop in bulk for the pantry, using the list we've been maintaining. About one to two times a week, I make quick maintenance trips to the grocery store to pick up fresh produce and other perishables. As you consider shopping in bulk, keep a couple things in mind. If an item is shelf-stable, do you have a designated spot to store the excess so that it doesn't crowd the everyday? If perishable, can you consume it before it goes bad? If not, consider buying in smaller portions from a traditional grocery store.

Waste from buying in bulk can cancel out the cost savings.

RESTOCK THE PANTRY WHEN YOU GET HOME

As soon as you get home from the store, restock the pantry by emptying store-bought boxes and bags into the designated pantry containers. If you're anything like me, later rarely happens.

STOCK THE FRIDGE SMARTLY

Sometimes I forget to address the fridge. Because when you have a well-stocked pantry, a meal plan, and only do minor grocery shopping for fresh produce and other perishables one to two times a week, the fridge handles itself pretty well. In the pages that follow, we'll talk about what to keep stocked in the fridge versus what to buy on an as-needed basis. Like the pantry, give yourself parameters here, too. I find meal planning to be the most helpful for keeping the fridge from going wild.

By design, the fridge comes with its own set of flaws. Some are too small, others are too deep, and very few are just right. I think we often assume that more space is always better. Sometimes, in the case of really small refrigerators, this is true. But in the case of most, there's often too much space. Like deep pantry shelves, deep fridge shelves are places for food to go to get lost. Extra space often begs to be filled. So if you have deep fridge shelves, consider only using the full depth when absolutely needed in an effort to keep visibility high. Stock amounts you're able to consume before expiration, and don't be afraid to have empty spots in the fridge. When (and if) you find yourself in the market for a new fridge, I'd recommend a counter-depth fridge, which is more shallow than the traditional fridge. It has just enough space.

How to Build a Minimalist Spice Cabinet

MOST SPICE CABINETS look like well-collected libraries. Libraries age well, but spices do not. Like all living food, spices have an expiration date. Eventually, they reach a point when they no longer taste like themselves. As with the pantry, spice cabinets need parameters, too. There was a time when my collection was out of control. I think I had every spice sold at the grocery store, whether I used it or not. It seemed like the right thing to do. After years of inefficiently (and angrily) picking up every spice in the cabinet before finding the right one, I made over the spice cabinet. I keep around 20 spices now, the ones I actually use. The rest were taking up space (and most likely expired).

NARROW DOWN YOUR SPICES TO A MANAGEABLE AMOUNT

Stock only what you use on a regular basis. To know which ones you use most often, look no further than the ones in the front row or the half-empty jars. There's no right or wrong answer on which spices to stock, but rather, notice your spice-using habits. To your right is the list used to season the recipes in this book. In that list, you may notice the absence of two commonly stocked spices—garlic powder and onion powder. Since I always keep the fresh versions stocked, I don't keep them in powder form. On the other hand, I keep dried varieties of herbs I often like to buy fresh for the many occasions when my fresh herbs have either gone bad or I'm without. To swap fresh herbs with dry, you'll need one-third the amount. Dried herbs are more concentrated in size than fresh.

Consider kosher salt and whole peppercorns freebies. Store salt in a cellar on the counter for ease of use while cooking, and keep pepper in a mill for fresh grinding.

STORE SPICES IN CLEAR SPICE CONTAINERS FOR VISIBILITY. You can buy spice jars online or in stores. Add shaker covers to the spices you find yourself shaking rather than measuring.

ADD LABELS. Because cumin and cinnamon look too close for comfort.

RESTOCK SPICES FROM THE BULK BINS AT THE STORE. This method tends to be cheaper, as you're not having to pay for packaging and can control the amount purchased.

STORE SPICES IN A SINGLE LAYER. Whether flat in a drawer or tiered in a cabinet, make sure all spices are visible at once for efficient retrieval.

The Spices I Keep Stocked

- ☐ Ground chili powder
- ☐ Ground coriander
- ☐ Ground cumin
- ☐ Ground curry powder
- ☐ Ground smoked paprika
- ☐ Ground turmeric
- ☐ Ground cayenne pepper
- ☐ Lemon pepper
- ☐ Red pepper flakes
- ☐ Dried basil
- ☐ Dried cilantro
- ☐ Dried oregano
- ☐ Dried rosemary
- ☐ Dried thyme
- ☐ Bay leaves
- ☐ Ground cardamom
- ☐ Ground cinnamon
- ☐ Ground cloves
- ☐ Ground ginger
- ☐ Whole nutmeg
- ☐ Sesame seeds
- ☐ Poppy seeds

The Ingredients

AS MENTIONED in The Pantry section, I break up shopping into two categories to make it more manageable—pantry shopping and weekly maintenance shopping, which you'll find mirrored in the lists below. Pantry shopping is typically done in bulk, about once a month. The term pantry used here is both literal and figurative. The pantry consists of all permanently stocked ingredients, even those ingredients sitting on the counter and in the fridge. Weekly shopping, on the other hand, is done one to two times per week and is dependent upon meal planning and seasonal availability. Crossover between the two lists when shopping is very common. Let it be.

Something worth noting: The stocked fridge produce listed is durable, lasting up to three weeks in the fridge when stored in a produce bag, and typically tastes like itself year-round. These are ingredients you can count on. You'll notice an asterisk next to items that I purchase in bulk. For ingredients that are pantry-stable but not sold in bulk, I buy in multiples at the grocery store, enough to fill my pantry containers full.

NOTE: When considering shopping in bulk, a seemingly maximalist practice, reference "Categorize Shelves" (page 27) for more guidelines.

Stocked

DRINKS
- ☐ Bourbon
- ☐ Tequila
- ☐ Vodka
- ☐ Orange liqueur
- ☐ Red wines
- ☐ Green tea
- ☐ Pale beer

Stocked

PANTRY
GRAINS
- ☐ Short-grain pasta (like fusilli)*
- ☐ 20-minute brown rice*
- ☐ Soba noodles
- ☐ Quinoa
- ☐ Old-fashioned oats*
- ☐ Panko
- ☐ Steel-cut oats

CANNED GOODS
- ☐ Canned black beans*
- ☐ Canned chickpeas*
- ☐ Fire-roasted tomatoes*
- ☐ Coconut milk*
- ☐ Chicken stock*
- ☐ Chipotles in adobo
- ☐ Tomato paste*

CHIPS
- ☐ Sweet potato tortilla chips*
- ☐ Pita chips*
- ☐ Wheat crackers

BAKING
- ☐ Unbleached all-purpose flour
- ☐ Whole-wheat pastry flour
- ☐ Organic fine-ground cornmeal
- ☐ Organic cornstarch
- ☐ Aluminum-free baking powder
- ☐ Baking soda
- ☐ Cream of tartar
- ☐ Chocolate chips
- ☐ Cacao nibs
- ☐ Pure vanilla extract
- ☐ Almond extract
- ☐ Unsweetened cocoa powder

SWEETENERS
- ☐ Brown sugar
- ☐ Granulated sugar (pure cane sugar)
- ☐ Turbinado (coarse) sugar
- ☐ Powdered sugar
- ☐ Honey
- ☐ Agave nectar

NUT BUTTERS
- ☐ Peanut butter
- ☐ Almond butter

NUTS, SEEDS, LEGUMES, DRIED FRUITS, AND TOPPINGS
- ☐ Raw sliced almonds
- ☐ Raw pecans
- ☐ Roasted cashews
- ☐ Roasted peanuts
- ☐ Raw pepita seeds
- ☐ Roasted sunflower seeds
- ☐ Hemp seeds
- ☐ Chia seeds
- ☐ Dried ancho chiles
- ☐ Dried lentils
- ☐ Dried cranberries
- ☐ Dried tart cherries
- ☐ Dried currants or raisins
- ☐ Large flaked unsweetened coconut
- ☐ Unsweetened coconut shreds
- ☐ Bee pollen
- ☐ Raw pistachios

OIL AND VINEGAR
- [ ] Olive oil*
- [ ] Neutral oil (one that is both high-heat stable and neutral in flavor)
- [ ] Balsamic vinegar
- [ ] Red wine vinegar
- [ ] White wine vinegar
- [ ] Rice vinegar
- [ ] Apple cider vinegar
- [ ] Distilled white vinegar*

FRIDGE
CONDIMENTS
- [ ] High-quality mayonnaise
- [ ] Pure maple syrup*
- [ ] Dijon mustard
- [ ] Ketchup
- [ ] Soy sauce
- [ ] Sesame oil
- [ ] Hoisin sauce
- [ ] Sriracha
- [ ] Harissa
- [ ] Tahini
- [ ] BBQ sauce
- [ ] Thai red curry paste
- [ ] SAF instant yeast*

PRESERVED PRODUCE
- [ ] Sun-dried tomatoes in oil
- [ ] Jarred pepperoncinis
- [ ] Jarred jalapeños
- [ ] Kalamata olives
- [ ] Jams

DAIRY
- [ ] Whole milk*
- [ ] Heavy cream*
- [ ] Plain whole-milk yogurt

- [ ] Butter*
- [ ] Eggs*

PRODUCE
- [ ] Whole carrots
- [ ] Bell peppers
- [ ] Box of mixed greens
- [ ] Limes
- [ ] Lemons
- [ ] Oranges
- [ ] Green onions

HERBS
- [ ] Cilantro
- [ ] Curly parsley
- [ ] Ginger

CHEESE
- [ ] Parmesan
- [ ] Cheddar
- [ ] Cotija

TORTILLAS
- [ ] Whole-wheat tortillas
- [ ] Corn tortillas

FREEZER
- [ ] Peas
- [ ] Edamame
- [ ] Tart cherries
- [ ] Wild blueberries
- [ ] Wild Alaskan salmon*

STOCKED COUNTER PRODUCE
- [ ] Garlic
- [ ] Sweet onions
- [ ] Red onions
- [ ] Bananas
- [ ] Avocados*

Weekly

SEASONAL FRIDGE
PRODUCE
- [ ] Red cabbage ☀ 🍁
- [ ] Asparagus 🌱
- [ ] Kale 🌱 🍁 ❄
- [ ] Arugula 🌱
- [ ] Radishes 🌱 ☀
- [ ] Mushrooms 🌱 🍁 ❄
- [ ] Sprouts or microgreens 🌱 ☀ 🍁 ❄
- [ ] Spinach 🌱
- [ ] Zucchini ☀
- [ ] Organic corn ☀
- [ ] Broccoli 🌱 🍁
- [ ] Brussels sprouts 🍁 ❄
- [ ] Collard greens ☀
- [ ] Cauliflower 🌱 🍁
- [ ] French green beans ☀
- [ ] Jalapeños ☀
- [ ] English cucumbers ☀
- [ ] Apples 🍁 ❄
- [ ] Blueberries ☀
- [ ] Strawberries 🌱 ☀
- [ ] Grapes ☀ 🍁
- [ ] Rhubarb 🌱
- [ ] Kiwi 🌱 ❄
- [ ] Clementines 🍁 ❄
- [ ] Grapefruit 🌱 ❄

HERBS
- [ ] Basil ☀ 🍁
- [ ] Mint 🌱 ☀
- [ ] Thyme 🌱 ☀ 🍁
- [ ] Sage ☀ 🍁

KEY
🌱 Spring   ☀ Summer   🍁 Fall   ❄ Winter

CHEESE
- [ ] Gruyère
- [ ] Mozzarella
- [ ] Mascarpone
- [ ] Ricotta

ANIMAL PROTEIN
- [ ] Chicken breast
- [ ] Whole chicken*
- [ ] Chuck roast
- [ ] White fish
- [ ] Butcher-cut bacon
- [ ] Breakfast sausage
- [ ] Deli ham

SEASONAL COUNTER PRODUCE
- [ ] Tomatoes ☀
- [ ] Potatoes 🌱 🍁
- [ ] Sweet potatoes 🍁
- [ ] Butternut squash 🍁 ❄
- [ ] Watermelon ☀
- [ ] Pineapple 🌱
- [ ] Peaches ☀
- [ ] Apricots ☀
- [ ] Plums 🌱 ☀ 🍁

FREEZER
- [ ] High-quality vanilla ice cream
- [ ] Organic corn

CHOCOLATE
- [ ] White chocolate bar
- [ ] Dark chocolate bar

*PURCHASED IN BULK

MENU
/21 - 5/27
odle Bowls
Noodle Soup
+ Asian kale Salad
asta
Pizza + Sangria
en Tinga + Margs
Mi Salad

The Recipes

WE'VE SAID GOODBYE to unused kitchen tools, made over the pantry, narrowed down our ingredients, and refined our shopping method. Before jumping into cooking, there are a couple things to know about how best to use these recipes.

THE MINIMALIST KITCHEN RECIPE ANATOMY

The recipes in this book are vegetable forward, made with wholesome, unadulterated ingredients (like butter, cream, milk, yogurt, and unbleached flour), and use a mix of both meat- and plant-based proteins. You'll find familiar flavors and ingredients with modern updates. The recipes themselves flow with the natural rhythm of the week. Look for ingredient-specific tips and seasonal swaps to keep these tried-and-true recipes relevant the whole year long, as well as minimalist tips offering recipe-specific advice.

To help determine which recipes to make when, you'll see tags like MAKE AHEAD , WEEKDAY , and WEEKEND .

Make Ahead tags are on recipes where it's absolutely necessary to prep in advance and on recipes where it's more efficient to prep in advance. If you're anything like me, you'll hate the idea of having to think ahead. But when large chunks of your meal are ready in your fridge, you'll eventually give yourself over to this practice. This idea is not new. Restaurants are known for large-batch cooking and prepping in advance. That's what makes them so efficient. I've used both methods throughout the book to make cooking feel more doable, especially during the week. I typically prepare the make-ahead recipes on weekends or whenever I have an extra chunk of time.

Weekday recipes are quick to prepare. More often than not, the hands-on time is the same as the total time, meaning the meal is ready in the same short time it takes to prepare. These recipes are heavily reliant on a well-stocked pantry while also integrating fresh produce from quick weekday shopping.

Weekend recipes take a bit longer to prepare— more components and more chopping. You'll find these recipes to be a bit more celebratory and communal in nature, as weekends are. Many of the recipes in the breakfast and dessert chapters are firmly planted in this category. If you have extra time during the week, don't be afraid to make these recipes then.

You'll also find icons of the major appliances used in each recipe at the end of the method.

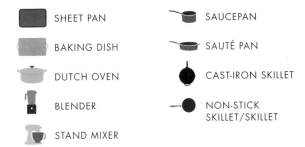

SHEET PAN

BAKING DISH

DUTCH OVEN

BLENDER

STAND MIXER

SAUCEPAN

SAUTÉ PAN

CAST-IRON SKILLET

NON-STICK SKILLET/SKILLET

A NOTE ABOUT PROTEIN

I grew up thinking that meat was the only way to get protein in your diet. But in an effort to lower our grocery bill while my husband was in graduate school, we cut meat out of everyday cooking. I learned a lot about plant-based proteins during that time. I still rely heavily on them throughout the week, as they are quick cooking and extremely affordable. It was the efficiency of plant-based proteins, too, that inspired the make-ahead, large-batch meat recipes for the book. These recipes are meant to be made in advance and sit ready in the fridge for the week or in the freezer for whenever.

See Dutch Oven Whole Chicken (page 106) and Humble Chuck Roast (page 118). Though these recipes are good on their own, the magic is in the fact that they can completely transform into a new recipe. The same chicken that's used in the Chicken Salad Remix (page 169) is also used in the Chicken Tinga Tacos (page 114). And the same beef that's used in the Beef Tacos with Chimichurri (page 117) is also used in the Quinoa Bibimbap Bowls (page 88). Efficiency never tasted so good.

FOLLOW YOUR GUT

A pastry chef once disclosed to me that so many chefs use the same basic pastry recipes. "They're all taught the classics," she said. "The same scone recipe will look different in every kitchen though. The brand of butter will make a difference. Your oven. Your technique. There are so many variables at play," she said. I think that story is relevant to the recipes in this book and any recipe you try. Your kitchen has a personality worth getting to know.

In general, when making a recipe for the first time, expect it to take a bit longer as you familiarize yourself with it. It's like driving to a new place. The first drive is always the longest.

And when a recipe enters your kitchen, let it become yours. Add more salt if the flavor tastes flat or a splash of vinegar if it needs a zing. Trust your gut and know your appliances, tools, and ingredients well so you can adjust as needed. Something I often say—marry a recipe. If not this one, then another one. I'd like to leave you with that. Make these recipes yours. Notice what works in your kitchen and what doesn't. Keep the good things and get rid of the rest. Just like your pantry and bedroom closet.

MEAL PLANNING

There's something romantic about forgoing a plan and skipping a list. I learned to cook that way. But then I became a working mom. Dinner had a precise time, my memory barely worked, and grocery shopping felt like the weightiest chore next to thinking up meal ideas. At 5 p.m., you'd often find me staring at the pantry, hoping inspiration would strike (or that dinner would fall through the popcorn

ceilings). My relationship with dinnertime stayed on the rocks for years until I channeled my angry designer brain towards the problem. To start with, I had to give up this romanticized way of cooking. And then, I had to give myself over to meal planning.

At the start of the week, I make a dinner schedule. Even with a book full of weekday recipes and a life immersed in food, meal planning is still my least favorite chore. Which often makes me ask the question—is all this effort worth it? My parents gave us a homemade dinner around the table every night, even on nights when soccer practice ran until 8:30 p.m. This ancient practice of gathering around the dinner table, especially during the week, can feel a lot like working out. The process is a chore but the payoff is worth every effort. That, too, must be the poetry Koren is talking about.

To practically meal plan, I write out a week's worth of dinners on the old vintage chalkboard in our dining room. This method works for me. If meal planning is something you want to give yourself over to as well, find a method that works for you, and make sure you can see the plan—whether it's on your dining room wall or taped to the inside of a common pantry door.

HELPFUL TIPS FOR MEAL PLANNING

- Start by taking inventory of the fridge from the week before. Look for perishable produce, leftover sauces, quick-pickled vegetables, or previously prepared frozen food to use up first. (You'll find guidance for this in the index as well as in the recipes.)
- Double up when possible. For example, make a double batch of pesto for two meals. Make a double fajita recipe for burrito bowls later in the week. Or make extra rice one meal so that you can make Fried Rice (page 101) days later.
- As mentioned above, keep a set of reliable recipes. The ones that follow are ours.
- If you're having trouble generating ideas, ascribe to a rhythmic dinner schedule like Meatless Monday, Taco Tuesday, Pasta Wednesday, etc. As noted throughout the book, rules are not bad; they give you parameters to create.

	SPRING	SUMMER	FALL	WINTER
MONDAY	Family-Style Chicken Caesar Salad	Pesto Garden Pasta *(make extra pesto for Friday)*	Creamy Chicken Noodle Soup *(use Dutch Oven Whole Chicken from the fridge/freezer)*	Quinoa Bibimbap Bowls *(use Humble Chuck Roast from the freezer + make extra pickled vegetables)*
TUESDAY	White Wine Spring Pasta	Chicken Gyros with Tzatziki	Chickpea Tikka Masala *(make extra rice for Thursday)*	Thai-Spiced Rice Bowls
WEDNESDAY	Pan-Fried White Fish + green beans or Caramelized Roasted Carrots	BBQ Black Bean and Quick Slaw Tacos	Sun-Dried Greek Pasta	Quick Vodka Sauce Pasta
THURSDAY	Takeout Cashew Chicken	Soba Bowls with Peanut Sauce	Fried Rice	Roasted Chickpea Bánh Mì Salad *(use leftover pickled vegetables from Quinoa Bibimbap Bowls)*
FRIDAY	Diner Burgers + Garlicky Potato Wedges *(make burger sauce ahead of time)*	Chicken Pesto Sandwiches	Chicken Tinga Tacos *(use Dutch Oven Whole Chicken from the fridge/freezer)*	Crispy Pizza with Caramelized Onions *(make the onions in advance)*
SATURDAY	Open-Faced Sweet Potato Tortas *(use leftover beans to make tostadas for breakfast)*	Maple-Soaked Salmon + Lentil Lettuce Wraps *(use up extra cabbage from Wednesday's tacos)*	Quinoa Chili	Ancho-ladas
SUNDAY	Baked Falafel Pitas with Tahini Sauce *(make pickled onions ahead of time)*	Chipotle-Garlic Chopped Salad *(make dressing ahead of time)*	Butternut Pasta *(roast butternut squash ahead of time)*	Beef Tacos with Chimichurri *(use Humble Chuck Roast from the freezer)*

37

CHAPTER 2

Breakfast

COME THE WEEKEND, breakfast is a thing of celebration around here. We skip brunch lines, wear whatever we want, and make long-winded breakfasts at home. More often than not, I prepare some variation of a pancake—Swedish, American, or Dutch. We eat around the dinner table and stay awhile. But during the week, we eat efficiently by way of overnight oats or eggs and toast at the kitchen counter. Either way, we never skip breakfast. Some say it's the most important meal; it's just our favorite.

Had I written this recipe a year ago, I would have told you to "be gentle" every other sentence. It's what every good biscuit maker said. But if you turn down the volume, you'll notice them kneading, folding, and rolling out the dough multiple times. The real key to making good biscuits at home is using as little flour as possible. But folds, turns, kneads, and layers are a must for mile-high results. And then there's jam. We've gotten into making quick jams, especially when our fridge is overflowing with fruit. It preserves the life by a couple weeks. Quick jams are known for being a bit loose. Let them be. Use leftover jam (or make a double batch) for the semifreddo (page 228).

Biscuits with Bourbon-Blueberry Quick Jam `WEEKDAY`

HANDS-ON: **20 MIN.**   TOTAL: **35 MIN.**
YIELDS: **8 (2½-INCH) BISCUITS AND ½ CUP JAM**

QUICK JAM	BISCUITS
1½ cups fresh blueberries	¼ cup cold unsalted butter
Scant ¼ cup granulated sugar	⅔ cup cold whole milk
1 tablespoon bourbon	⅓ cup cold heavy cream
1 teaspoon lemon juice	2 cups unbleached all-purpose flour, plus more for shaping
	1 tablespoon aluminum-free baking powder
	1 teaspoon kosher salt

MAKE THE JAM. In a small saucepan, combine all of the jam ingredients. Bring to a simmer; cook for about 8 minutes, swirling every so often. The berries will begin to burst and the mixture will slowly thicken. To keep this jam on the looser side, it is ready when it barely coats the back of a spoon. The jam will thicken a bit as it cools. Store covered in a glass jar. This can be made 4 weeks in advance.

MAKE THE BISCUITS. Preheat the oven to 425°F. Line a baking sheet with parchment paper or a Silpat. Set aside.

IN A LIQUID MEASURING CUP, measure out the milk and heavy cream. Set aside.

IN A MEDIUM BOWL, stir together the flour, baking powder, and salt with your largest fork. Cut the butter into skinny shreds (as if you were cutting thin slices of cheese) and toss them into the flour mixture to coat. Using your hands, quickly break apart the flour-covered butter into pea-sized pieces. Make a well in the center of the flour mixture and pour in the liquid mixture. (Don't rinse out the measuring cup just yet. You'll need the remaining liquid mixture later.) Using the fork, gently stir together until a shaggy mass forms.

TURN THE DOUGH OUT onto a lightly floured surface. Add a bit of flour to your hands to keep the dough from sticking. Press the dough into a rectangle (about 8 x 5 inches). Use enough flour to keep things from sticking and no more. Using a metal spatula or sharp knife, cut the dough in half and stack the two. Repeat 5 more times. (You'll have a total of 6 cuts.) Press the dough out until about 1 inch thick. Using a 2½-inch biscuit cutter, press straight down without a twisting motion to cut out the biscuits. For larger biscuits, use a 3-inch biscuit cutter for a yield of 5. Place the biscuits close enough on the prepared baking sheet that they rub shoulders while baking. Stack the leftover dough making sure to keep the layers parallel. Gently press out again and cut until most of the dough has been used.

USING THE TINY BIT OF LIQUID left in the measuring cup (add a little cream if the cup is dry), lightly brush the tops of the biscuits. Bake for 13 to 15 minutes until the tops are golden and the sides look baked through. Serve warm with the jam.

NOTES

To reheat, preheat the oven to 350°F. Place a damp paper towel on the top of the biscuits and wrap them completely with foil. Bake until warm. The damp towel keeps the biscuits from drying out.

MINIMALIST TIP

If you don't stock a round
cookie or biscuit cutter,
make square biscuits and
cut with a sharp knife or
metal spatula.

With the addition of fresh lemon and ginger, these scones are bright and floral, fit for breakfast, brunch, or an afternoon snack. They are just dry enough to land themselves in the scone category, with plenty of fat to keep them flavorful and moist. They're also a great scone base. (See the notes for variations.) The method here is the same friendly method used for the biscuits (page 40), the galette crust (page 242), and the puff pastry (page 233). It's friendly for the sheer fact that no special pastry tools are required. When you find success with one, it can be applied to the others.

Lemon-Ginger Scones `WEEKEND`

HANDS-ON: **5 MIN.**   TOTAL: **45 MIN.**
YIELDS: **12 SCONES**

WET
½ cup heavy cream
1 large egg
1 large egg yolk

DRY
1 cup unbleached all-purpose flour
1 cup whole-wheat pastry flour
⅓ cup granulated sugar
1 tablespoon aluminum-free baking powder
½ teaspoon kosher salt
1 tablespoon grated lemon zest, packed

1 tablespoon peeled minced fresh ginger, packed
6 tablespoons cold unsalted butter

GLAZE
½ cup powdered sugar
2 teaspoons lemon juice
1 teaspoon heavy cream

GARNISH (OPTIONAL)
Hemp seeds
Pepita seeds

LINE A BAKING SHEET with parchment paper or a Silpat. Set aside.

IN A LIQUID MEASURING CUP, whisk together all of the wet ingredients. Set aside.

IN A LARGE BOWL, whisk together all of the dry ingredients except for the butter. Cut the butter into skinny shreds (as if you were cutting thin slices of cheese) and toss them into the flour mixture to coat. Using your hands, quickly break apart the flour-covered butter into pea-sized pieces. Make a well in the center of the flour mixture and pour in the wet mixture. (Don't rinse out the measuring cup just yet. You'll need the remaining liquid mixture later.) Using a large fork, stir until the dough just comes together.

PLACE THE DOUGH on a counter or the prepared baking sheet; press together to form a shaggy mound. Press out to a 6-inch square; cut in half. Place the lingering crumbs on top of one of the dough halves and stack with the other. Press out and repeat the process 3 to 4 more times until all the crumbs are accounted for. Press the dough out into a 6-inch square, about 1 inch thick. Cut in half, and then into thirds the other direction, creating 6 rectangles. Cut each rectangle on the diagonal, creating 12 triangles. Using a sturdy spatula, loosen the scones from the counter and place evenly apart on the prepared baking sheet. Place in the freezer.

MEANWHILE, PREHEAT THE OVEN TO 425°F. Once preheated (about 10 minutes), remove the scones from the freezer. Using the remnants of cream in the measuring cup, lightly brush the tops. Bake for 15 minutes or until the sides are firm to the touch.

PLACE THE SCONES ON A COOLING RACK. Once cooled, stir together all of the glaze ingredients in a small bowl. Drizzle the scones with the glaze and sprinkle with the seeds, if desired. Allow the glaze to harden before serving, about 10 minutes. Store the scones in a ziplock bag that's slightly opened for up to 2 days.

NOTES

Feel free to omit the lemon, ginger, and glaze. Dried fruit and nuts incorporate well into these scones. Use ½ to ⅔ cup total. If using fresh fruit, freeze it first (or use prefrozen fruit) so that it doesn't explode as you incorporate it into the dough. To do so, wait until the last cut, stack, and roll. Gently press half of the frozen fruit into the bottom layer of dough. Stack the other layer. Press out the dough and gently press the remaining fruit into the top. Cut the scones and follow the recipe as directed.

I thrive on efficiency. For these muffins, I set the crumble ingredients out at the beginning to give the butter enough time to soften. But I don't actually assemble the crumble until just before topping the muffins. It also means I only have to wash my hands once. This makes me crazy, but it's the same crazy that fuels the pages of this book. My hope is that these types of tips will make your kitchen more efficient and more enjoyable. This muffin recipe has become my base over the years. It's not too sweet, plenty moist, and, like all bakery-made muffins, it has a substantial crumb. You might be surprised at the addition of the fresh thyme. I tried it once at a bakery and fell in love. I think you might, too. We prefer these muffins best when made the night before.

Berry Bakery Muffins MAKE AHEAD

HANDS-ON: **15 MIN.** TOTAL: **45 MIN.**
YIELDS: **9 MUFFINS**

CRUMBLE
¼ cup unbleached all-purpose flour
2 tablespoons packed brown sugar
1½ tablespoons unsalted butter, diced
Pinch of kosher salt

WET
½ cup unsalted butter
⅓ cup plain whole-milk yogurt
¼ cup packed brown sugar
¼ cup pure maple syrup
1 large egg

1 teaspoon fresh thyme leaves (optional)
½ teaspoon pure vanilla extract

DRY
1 cup unbleached all-purpose flour
½ cup whole-wheat pastry flour
1½ teaspoons aluminum-free baking powder
¼ teaspoon baking soda
¼ teaspoon kosher salt
1 cup fresh berries (blackberries, raspberries, blueberries)

PREHEAT THE OVEN TO 400°F. Line a muffin tin with parchment liners.

ASSEMBLE THE CRUMBLE. Place all of the crumble ingredients together in a small bowl (do not combine). Set aside.

BEGIN PREPARING THE WET INGREDIENTS. In a small saucepan, melt the butter on low until half melted. Set aside to continue melting and cooling.

PREPARE THE DRY INGREDIENTS. In a large bowl, whisk together all of the dry ingredients except for the berries. Fold in the berries, and set aside.

ONCE THE BUTTER HAS COOLED, whisk in all of the remaining wet ingredients until evenly combined. Add the wet mixture to the dry mixture, and stir until just combined. Using a 4 tablespoon-sized spring-release scoop (2-ounce scoop/#16 scoop), evenly distribute the batter in the prepared tin. Using your hands, mix together the crumble until a loose cohesion forms. Top the muffins with the crumble. Bake for 18 to 22 minutes or until a light press of the center springs back. Allow to cool completely before storing. Store in a loosely covered container, allowing just a little air to get in, for up to 4 days.

NOTES

You can also use this recipe to make quick breads. Pour the batter in a 9 x 5-inch parchment-lined loaf pan, and bake at 400°F for 40 to 50 minutes or until the center is firm. Tent with foil once the top is golden, about 20 minutes. Like the muffins, this loaf is best after an overnight rest.

MINIMALIST TIP

For quick prep, use small berries that don't require chopping. Frozen wild blueberries work well, too.

When you put these rolls in the oven on Saturday morning, you'll question my authority to speak on such things. Before baking, the rolls look the same as they did the night before when you stuck them in the fridge—small. But after a 10-minute bake in the oven, wrapped in foil to steam, they will bloom and double in size. It's magic. So please, trust me, and sleep in a little longer. I should also mention, I've never been a huge fan of morning rolls. They make me crash. These rolls have just enough sugar, utilizing the orange, blueberries, and cardamom to accentuate the sweetness level.

Blueberry-Orange Breakfast Rolls MAKE AHEAD

HANDS-ON: **40 MIN.**   TOTAL: **12 HR.**   YIELDS: **8 ROLLS**

DOUGH
Make-Ahead Yeast Rolls (page 202)

2 tablespoons granulated sugar

FILLING
⅓ cup granulated sugar

¼ cup unsalted butter, room temperature

Zest from 1 orange (about 2 tablespoons)

½ teaspoon cardamom

⅛ teaspoon kosher salt

1 cup frozen wild blueberries

GLAZE
2 ounces mascarpone

1 tablespoon orange juice

½ cup powdered sugar

THE DAY BEFORE SERVING, make the Make-Ahead Yeast Rolls, adding an additional 2 tablespoons of sugar to the wet ingredients. Follow the recipe up until the initial rise. Once doubled in size (2 to 3 hours), prepare these rolls.

MAKE THE FILLING. Place all of the filling ingredients except the blueberries in a small bowl (do not combine). Set aside.

ROLL OUT THE DOUGH to a 16 x 10–inch rectangle, using flour only if necessary to keep the dough from sticking. Mix the filling together with your hands or a spoon. Distribute chunks of the filling evenly around the dough. Using the back of a spoon, spread the mixture to the edge of three sides of the dough,

leaving a 1-inch border along one long side of the dough. Sprinkle the frozen blueberries evenly on top of the butter mixture, lightly pressing into the dough. Beginning with the long side that has the mixture spread to the edge, tightly roll the dough. Pinch the seam of the log closed. If the log is thicker in the middle, gently tug it out so the thickness is even throughout, still maintaining a 16-inch length. Cut the log into 8 equally sized rolls. Carefully place the rolls in an 8-inch round pan or a 12 x 10–inch enamel baking dish (or similar-sized glass or ceramic dish). Cover tightly with foil and place in the fridge for 8 hours or overnight.

THE MORNING OF, remove the pan from the fridge, leaving the foil in place, and preheat the oven to 350°F. Bake for 10 minutes covered tightly with foil. (Rolls will double in size.) Remove the foil and bake an additional 20 to 30 minutes. Check between rolls for doneness.

MEANWHILE, MAKE THE GLAZE. In a small bowl, whisk the mascarpone and orange juice until smooth. Add the powdered sugar, whisking until smooth. Add an additional squeeze of orange juice if necessary to come together. Drizzle over the rolls and serve warm.

NOTES
We prefer frozen wild blueberries in this recipe for their smaller size. We keep a bag in our freezer and top oatmeal in the off-season. You can substitute fresh blueberries. Just be sure to lightly chop before using.

I make these pancakes for my husband. He's team fluffy, and I'm team wheat. But wheat pancakes have a reputation for being dense and bitter. When I set out to write this book, I took an informal survey on the use of wheat flour in the kitchen. About half swore it off vehemently and the other half proclaimed their deep love for wheat pastry flour. After picking up a bag of it, I switched out all my regular wheat flour for wheat pastry flour. It makes a shocking difference. It's light without a trace of bitter. I've used it throughout the book. Even in the puff pastry! I hope you'll give it a chance and pick up a bag, too. If not, it's an equal exchange for all-purpose flour. P.S. Don't skip the orange zest if you can help it.

Fluffy Multigrain Pancakes

WEEKEND

HANDS-ON: **30 MIN.**   TOTAL: **40 MIN.**
YIELDS: **12 TO 14 PANCAKES**

WET
¼ cup unsalted butter
1½ cups whole milk
1 large egg
1 teaspoon grated orange zest (optional)
½ teaspoon pure vanilla extract

DRY
1 cup unbleached all-purpose flour
½ cup whole-wheat pastry flour

1 tablespoon granulated sugar
2 teaspoons aluminum-free baking powder
½ teaspoon baking soda
½ teaspoon kosher salt

PREPARING AND SERVING
Neutral oil cooking spray
Pure maple syrup, warmed
Seasonal fruit

BEGIN PREPARING THE WET INGREDIENTS. In a small saucepan, melt the butter on low until half melted. Set aside to continue melting and cooling.

PREPARE THE DRY INGREDIENTS. In a medium bowl, whisk together all of the dry ingredients. Set aside.

ONCE THE BUTTER HAS COOLED, whisk all of the remaining wet ingredients into the cooled butter until evenly combined. Pour the wet mixture into the dry mixture, whisking until only small lumps remain in the batter. Allow the batter to rest for about 10 minutes.

MEANWHILE, PREHEAT THE OVEN to 250°F and heat a 10-inch cast-iron skillet or griddle on medium-low. Just before cooking, lightly spray the surface with the cooking spray, and stir the batter gently a couple times more to incorporate. Using a 4 tablespoon-sized spring-release scoop (2-ounce scoop/#16 scoop), about ¼ cup, add the pancake batter to the pan. The pancake is ready to flip once bubbles begin to appear on the surface. Flip and allow the pancake to continue cooking undisturbed. Stack the pancakes on a baking sheet. Place them in the preheated oven to keep warm as you make the rest of the pancakes. Serve with pure maple syrup and seasonal fruit of your choice.

NOTES

There are two keys to making great pancakes—a good recipe and perfecting the heat of the skillet. Too low of heat will keep the pancakes from rising to their full potential, leaving a gummy, uncooked texture. Too high of heat will cause the exterior of the pancake to burn before the insides cook through. Of course every stovetop and every pan is different, so it will take a bit of trial and error to achieve the perfect pancake. As I often say, marry a recipe, and then adjust to make it work best in your kitchen. If using cast iron, know that it keeps heat really well. By the end of cooking, I've typically reduced the heat on my skillet to accommodate the heat wave.

INGREDIENT TIP

Freeze pancakes for later. Place the pancakes in a single layer on a baking sheet, and freeze them until solid (about 30 minutes). Then stack the frozen pancakes in a freezer-safe ziplock bag. This process keeps the pancakes from freezing to each other. Toast in the toaster to reheat.

MINIMALIST TIP

Turn this recipe into waffles by omitting the baking soda and using an additional ¼ cup whole-wheat pastry flour (¾ cup total). Pour ½ cup batter at a time into a waffle iron and cook over medium-high. It will yield six 6-inch round waffles.

Swedish Pancakes are the pancakes of Sweden and Minnesota (home to many Nordic Americans). They're much like a crepe without the overnight rest and a touch thicker. I like my pancakes thin and my husband likes his fluffy. This is one pancake recipe we don't fight over, as long as there's tart lingonberry jam in the fridge. If you can't find this jam anywhere else, you'll be sure to find it at Ikea. We stock it exclusively for these pancakes. Side note: This is one of the only recipes that touches our nonstick skillet outside of eggs.

Swedish Pancakes `WEEKEND`

HANDS-ON: **30 MIN.**   TOTAL: **30 MIN.**
YIELDS: **10 TO 12 PANCAKES**

PANCAKES	TOPPINGS
3 tablespoons unsalted butter	Lingonberry jam (or other tart jam)
2 cups whole milk	Plain whole-milk yogurt
3 large eggs	Pure maple syrup, warmed
1 cup unbleached all-purpose flour	
½ teaspoon kosher salt	

PREPARE THE PANCAKES. In a small saucepan, melt the butter on low until half melted. Set aside to continue melting and cooling.

ADD THE MILK AND EGGS to a high-powered blender. Blitz on medium speed until the mixture has doubled in size, about 20 seconds. Add in the cooled melted butter, flour, and salt. Blitz again for another 10 to 20 seconds. All the flour should be evenly incorporated. Scrape down the sides, if necessary, and blend again. Set aside. (If you don't have a high-powered blender, you can combine these ingredients using a bowl and whisk.)

PREHEAT A 10-INCH NONSTICK SKILLET on medium-high for about 5 minutes, giving the batter time to rest. Once the pan is hot, hold the pan slightly off the burner and pour about ¼ cup of batter into the center of the pan, swirling the pan around several times until the bottom of the pan is evenly coated and the batter stops moving, as you would a crepe. Return the pan to the burner, and cook until the edges begin to brown and the pancake is golden, about 1 to 2 minutes. Using a very thin spatula, carefully peel around the edges to separate the pancake from the pan, and then slide the spatula halfway under the pancake. Flip quickly and let the pancake finish cooking, about 30 seconds more. Slide off onto a plate. Repeat until all the batter has been used.

TO SERVE, fill with the lingonberry jam and roll or fold into fourths as you would a crepe. Top with the yogurt and maple syrup.

NOTES

It's not uncommon for the first pancake to completely flop as you adjust your heat to get it just right. Just take it as a gentle nudge to snack while cooking. If your pancakes are ripping, turn the heat up a bit more. Tiny rips when flipping will patch as they cook on the other side.

If you study this recipe, you'll find a nice ratio. For every one egg, there's a tablespoon of butter, ¼ cup flour, and ¼ cup milk. How you handle the sugar and salt is up to you. But I've found the best flavor when using a good amount of each due to the fact that Dutch babies don't soak up maple syrup in the same way spongy American pancakes do. Something to note: Dutch babies need warm eggs. A quick rest in a bowl of warm water will do the trick. These pancakes are perfect for holding seasonal fruit or stewed tart cherries, which are always in season since they're sold almost exclusively frozen or dried. Read more about tart cherries in the Almond–Tart Cherry Crisp recipe (page 234). For garnishing, we raid the pantry for all the natural sprinkles, like hemp seeds and pepita seeds, for an extra pretty presentation.

Blender Dutch Baby WEEKEND

HANDS-ON: **15 MIN.** TOTAL: **35 MIN.**
YIELDS: **3 TO 4 SERVINGS**

DUTCH BABY

3 large eggs

3 tablespoons unsalted butter

¾ cup unbleached all-purpose flour

¾ cup whole milk

1 to 2 tablespoons granulated sugar

½ teaspoon kosher salt

½ teaspoon pure vanilla extract

STEWED TART CHERRIES (OPTIONAL)

1 cup frozen tart cherries

Heaping 1 tablespoon granulated sugar

TOPPINGS

Plain whole-milk yogurt

Pure maple syrup, warmed

Pepita seeds

Hemp seeds

Unsweetened coconut shreds

MAKE THE DUTCH BABY. Place the eggs in a bowl of warm water to bring to room temperature quickly, about 5 minutes. This is an important step to get the most lift in the Dutch baby.

PREHEAT THE OVEN TO 425°F. Add the butter to a 10-inch cast-iron skillet; place the pan in the oven until the butter is melted and bubbly but not burned.

MEANWHILE, IN A HIGH-POWERED BLENDER (see notes for method without blender), blend the eggs on medium-high for about 5 seconds until bubbly. Add the remaining Dutch baby ingredients to the blender, and pulse on low until just combined, about 5 seconds more.

ONCE THE OVEN HAS PREHEATED and the butter has melted, remove the pan and immediately pour the batter into the prepared pan. Return the pan to the oven, and bake for 13 to 15 minutes. Turn oven off, then allow the pan to sit in the oven for 5 minutes more. This will help the Dutch baby to keep its structure out of the oven.

MEANWHILE, IF DESIRED, make the stewed tart cherries. Combine all the stewed tart cherries ingredients in a small saucepan. Cook on low for about 10 minutes or until the juice from the cherries can lightly coat the back of a spoon. Place in a shallow bowl for serving. This can be done ahead of time and reheated.

REMOVE THE DUTCH BABY FROM THE OVEN. Cut into wedges. Top with a dollop of yogurt and a spoonful of the stewed tart cherries. Lightly drizzle with the warmed maple syrup, and add toppings as desired.

NOTES

To make this recipe without a blender, stir together the flour, sugar, and salt in a medium bowl, and set aside. In a small bowl, whisk the eggs until fluffy. Whisk in the milk and extract until combined. Slowly pour the egg mixture into the flour mixture, and mix until just combined.

INGREDIENT TIP

To bring eggs to room
temperature quickly,
submerge them in a bowl
of warm water for about
5 minutes.

WE MEET AGAIN

Schedules are complicated. Even still, we make every effort to gather over breakfast and dinner. The taste of food is enticing enough to draw me back to the table (or kitchen counter). But if I'm being honest, I love the social aspect of food most. Food is just a really good reminder to gather and slow down for 10 minutes, even on the high-stress days. Lean on the Soaked Overnight Oatmeal during the busy weekdays, and if you must, pack it to go.

55

Despite the appearance of the breakfast chapter, we eat a ton of oats during the week, alternated with eggs and toast. Our favorite warm oatmeal comes from Megan Gordon's book, *Whole-Grain Mornings*. It's called The Very Best Oatmeal for good reason. It is. I hope you check out her book for that recipe alone. And while you're flipping through, dog-ear the granola, too. When we're not eating warmed oatmeal, we eat it soaked and chilled, much like muesli. If you've never had soaked oatmeal before, the ease of it (and texture) will blow your mind. The night before, soak the oats. By morning it's softened but not mushy. Soaked oatmeal comes alive from the toppings and a generous dollop of yogurt. Raid your fridge and pantry, topping with the best seasonal fruit or dried fruit. This breakfast is perfect for on-the-go or at-the-table.

Soaked Overnight Oatmeal

MAKE AHEAD   WEEKDAY

HANDS-ON: **5 MIN.**   TOTAL: **8 HR.**   YIELDS: **2 SERVINGS**

SOAKED OATS

1 cup old-fashioned oats

2 tablespoons steel-cut oats (optional)

About ¾ cup whole milk (see instructions)

TOPPINGS

Dollop of plain whole-milk yogurt

Generous drizzle of honey, pure maple syrup, or brown sugar to taste

Handful dried or fresh fruit

Unsweetened coconut shreds

Slivered almonds

Pepita seeds

THE NIGHT BEFORE, PREPARE THE SOAKED OATS. Place the oats in a large mason jar with a lid. Pour in the milk, just enough to barely cover the oats. Cover and refrigerate overnight (or up to 5 days).

THE MORNING OF, ADD THE TOPPINGS AS DESIRED. Yogurt is a must in my book. Taste and add more sweetener if necessary.

NOTES

My favorite combination, which only comes together when the bananas on the counter are perfectly ripe, is with diced bananas, diced Granny Smith apple, dried currants (or raisins), dried cranberries, yogurt, and brown sugar. For another flavor variation, try adding a drop of almond extract to the oats as they soak.

57

I've made a lot of pans of baked oatmeal, and this might be my favorite, mostly because of the coconut. Coconut is an ingredient that turns a lot of people off. It used to turn me off, too. I grew up on cloyingly sweet coconut shreds that never seemed to break down no matter how long you chewed. Unsweetened coconut is a completely different ingredient and so satisfying. It's slightly sweet on its own. We keep multiple forms around—large shreds, flaked, and coconut milk. Typically, I buy full-fat everything, but when it comes to coconut milk, I buy light for its even texture. Something to note: Straight out of the oven, this baked oatmeal is a delicious slab of beige. To make it extra pretty, dig through your pantry and top it with all of the garnishes. I've listed our favorites below.

Banana-Coconut Baked Oatmeal `WEEKEND`

HANDS-ON: **10 MIN.** TOTAL: **25 MIN.**
YIELDS: **4 TO 5 SERVINGS**

WET

2 tablespoons unsalted
   butter

⅔ cup light coconut milk

⅓ cup pure maple syrup

1 ripe banana

1 large egg

DRY

2 cups old-fashioned oats

1 teaspoon aluminum-free
   baking powder

½ teaspoon cinnamon

½ teaspoon kosher salt

⅛ teaspoon cardamom

Grate of fresh whole
   nutmeg

GARNISH (OPTIONAL)

Large flaked unsweetened
   coconut

Plain whole-milk yogurt

Banana slices

Chopped nuts

Pepita seeds

Hemp seeds

Bee pollen

PREHEAT THE OVEN TO 375°F.

BEGIN PREPARING THE WET INGREDIENTS. In a small saucepan, melt the butter on low until half melted. Set aside to continue melting and cooling.

PREPARE THE DRY INGREDIENTS. In a 12 x 10–inch enamel baking dish (or similar-sized glass or ceramic dish), stir together all of the dry ingredients inside the pan. Set aside.

IN A HIGH-POWERED OR REGULAR BLENDER, combine all of the wet ingredients, including the melted butter, and blend on medium-low until just combined. Pour the wet mixture over the dry mixture in the baking dish, and stir well to combine. Wipe down the exposed sides of the pan, if needed. Bake for 13 to 15 minutes or until a light press in the center bounces back. Serve warm. Add garnishes as desired.

NOTES

If you prefer your coconut and nuts toasted, add them to the baked oatmeal in the last 5 minutes of baking.

INGREDIENT TIP

Store leftover coconut milk in a glass jar for up to 2 weeks in the fridge. Use it in the Soba Bowls with Peanut Sauce (page 91), Blueberry-Coconut Smoothie (page 214), and Thai-Spiced Rice Bowls (page 152).

MINIMALIST TIP

Skip using an extra bowl and stir together the oatmeal mixture directly in the baking dish. I prefer enamel bakeware for both its natural beauty and its easy cleanup. See The Essential Tools section (page 19) for in-depth information.

INGREDIENT TIP

This is the perfect
sandwich to use up
leftover ham from
the holidays.

This classic sandwich is a favorite of Kev's. You'll often find it on a lunch or dinner menu, but I've always thought it belongs on the brunch menu. So that's where I'm putting it. Feel free to eat it anytime of the day. This sandwich is a savory-sweet combo cooked like French toast, eaten like a sandwich. It's traditionally dipped in jam, but I've liberally slathered it on both interior slices of the bread for easy eating. Use raspberry jam or another tart variety, like lingonberry jam from the Swedish Pancakes (page 51). With the leftover Gruyère, make the Crispy Pizza with Caramelized Onions (page 80). My daughter, Hallie, and I prefer straight up French toast. Once we're done making his sandwich, we add a couple more eggs to the dish, a splash of milk, plus a little cinnamon and vanilla to make ours. Everyone is happy.

Monte Cristo Breakfast Sandwich `WEEKEND`

HANDS-ON: **10 MIN.** TOTAL: **10 MIN.**
YIELDS: **2 SANDWICHES**

SANDWICH

4 slices of deli ham

4 slices of challah (½-inch thick)

Raspberry jam (or other tart jam)

4 to 6 thin slices of Gruyère

2 large eggs

Splash of whole milk

1 tablespoon salted butter

GARNISH (OPTIONAL)

Powdered sugar

MAKE THE SANDWICH. Heat a 10-inch cast-iron skillet over medium. Add the ham and pan-fry to heat through, about 2 minutes.

MEANWHILE, ASSEMBLE THE SANDWICHES. The sandwich will stack like so: bread, jam, ham, cheese, jam, bread. To do so, spread the raspberry jam over 1 side of each bread slice. Top half of the bread slices with enough cheese to cover the bread, and then top with the cooked ham. Sandwich together with the remaining slices of bread. Set aside.

IN A SHALLOW DISH, whisk together the eggs and a splash of milk until evenly combined. Dunk both sides of the sandwiches in the egg mixture, as if you were making French toast. Heat the pan over medium heat. Add the butter to the pan. Once melted, cook the sandwiches until golden on the bottom, about 2 minutes, and then flip. Using a spatula, smash the sandwich. Cook again until golden and the cheese is melted.

GARNISH THE SANDWICH. Remove the sandwiches from the pan. Cut in half and lightly sprinkle with the powdered sugar, if desired.

NOTES

If your cheese doesn't melt before the bottoms cook, remove the sandwiches from the pan and cover with a bowl or lid to steam them for a second. The heat from the cooked ham will also help with the melting process.

There's a lesson in these eggs. And the lesson is that food continues to cook long after you turn off the heat. If you cook eggs over the heat until done, they'll be overdone by the time you plate them. I know. I did that for eight years of our marriage, so eggs became the one thing Kev made exclusively. Until I landed on this method. And when I did, he handed me the torch, which looks a whole lot like our silicone spatula.

The Very Best Scrambled Eggs

HANDS-ON: **5 MIN.**   TOTAL: **5 MIN.**
YIELDS: **3 TO 4 SERVINGS**

6 large eggs	¼ teaspoon kosher salt
1 tablespoon whole milk	A couple cracks of pepper
½ tablespoon salted butter	(optional)

HEAT A 10-INCH NONSTICK SKILLET over medium. In a bowl, whisk together the eggs and milk until well combined. Once the pan is warm, add the butter. Pour the eggs where the melted butter pools. Using a silicone spatula, keep the eggs moving and semi-clumped together, flipping the eggs as you would a pancake to cook all sides. If the eggs stick, try increasing the heat slightly. If the eggs bubble, try decreasing the heat slightly.

Once the eggs appear to be soft scrambled, wet, and glossy, remove the pan from the heat. Sprinkle with the salt. Continue to stir the eggs, breaking up any large mounds into smaller pieces, until they reach the perfect hard scrambled consistency. Serve immediately. Add pepper as desired.

NOTES

A quality nonstick skillet is key to making good eggs. We went through a lot of bad ones before investing in a really good nonstick ceramic skillet. For the most part, only eggs (and the Swedish Pancakes on page 51) touch our nonstick skillet, which keeps it in top working condition. Next to a good pan, finding the right heat can make or break your eggs. Too low of a heat will keep a thin layer of eggs stuck to the bottom of the pan. Too high of a heat will give your eggs a hard, browned shell. The perfect heat is when no scrambled egg is left behind on the pan. It should basically clean itself. Play around with the heat to find your perfect heat notch.

INGREDIENT TIP

Eggs, compared to other fresh produce, have a long life in the fridge. If you consume as many as we do, consider buying them in bulk for the cost savings.

62

MINIMALIST TIP

For a quicker morning prep time, chop the vegetables the night before, and store covered in the fridge.

The Evergreen Frittata, like so many of the recipes in this book, is meant to be made year-round. The base will remain the same while the toppings and vegetables change from season to season. Though, I mostly cook it for the two longest produce seasons—summer and winter. This recipe is written for summer. See "Winter Sautéed Vegetables" for a winter alteration.

The Evergreen Frittata   `WEEKEND`

HANDS-ON: **15 MIN.**   TOTAL: **30 MIN.**
YIELDS: **4 TO 6 SERVINGS**

SUMMER SAUTÉED VEGETABLES	BASE
2 teaspoons olive oil	8 large eggs
¾ cup diced zucchini	¼ cup whole milk
¾ cup chopped red bell pepper	2 tablespoons chopped fresh basil
½ cup sliced sweet onion	¼ teaspoon kosher salt
Heaping ¼ teaspoon kosher salt	A couple cracks of pepper

TOPPING

Scant ¼ cup feta

4 grape tomatoes thinly sliced longways

PREHEAT THE OVEN TO 350°F.

MAKE THE SAUTÉED VEGETABLES. Heat a 10-inch cast-iron skillet over medium. Once the pan is warm, add the oil, zucchini, bell pepper, onion, and salt. Sauté for about 7 minutes or until the vegetables are tender, stirring occasionally. Taste and add more salt if necessary.

MEANWHILE, MAKE THE BASE. In a medium bowl, whisk together all of the base ingredients until well combined. Pour the egg mixture into the pan over the sautéed vegetables, stirring gently to make sure the vegetables are evenly distributed. Top with the feta and tomato slices.

PLACE THE PAN IN THE OVEN to finish cooking, about 10 to 15 minutes or until set. Turn on the broiler, and allow the frittata to lightly brown under close watch. If your frittata balloons under the heat of the broiler, fear not. It will relax as it cools.

NOTES

If you're using a smaller skillet, increase the baking time. If you're using a larger skillet, increase the recipe.

Winter Sautéed Vegetables

HEAT A 10-INCH CAST-IRON SKILLET over medium. Once the pan is warm, add 2 teaspoons olive oil and ¾ cup sliced red onion. Sauté for about 2 minutes, stirring occasionally. Stir in ¾ cup sweet potato cut into ½-inch cubes, ¼ cup water, 2 teaspoons fresh thyme leaves, and a heaping ¼ teaspoon kosher salt. Cover and steam for 2 to 3 minutes. Once the potatoes are just barely fork tender, remove the lid and stir in ¾ cup chopped kale. Cook for a minute more to soften the kale. Taste and add more salt if necessary. Prepare the base as listed above, omitting the basil. Pour the base mixture over the winter sautéed vegetables, and top with ¼ cup grated Gruyère (or the cheese of your choice) just before the frittata heads into the oven.

HOW TO HYGGE

Hygge (hoo-guh) is the Danish word loosely translated to mean cozy. The practice of minimalism is greatly enhanced with a layer of hygge; in fact, it's needed. Find things that make you feel happy and incorporate them into the everyday, like pour-over coffee, freshly cut flowers, enamel mugs, and linen towels. Come winter, I make a 2 p.m. cup of coffee to brighten a sleepy, cold afternoon. Self-care doesn't have to be extravagant or costly.

67

Add this recipe to the special-occasion list. It's not quick like a frittata, and you probably won't be making it every weekend. But I think it's good to have a quiche recipe in your Rolodex. Like a lot of recipes in this book, there are components that can and should be made ahead of time, like the crust. This particular quiche is a thing of beauty—a tall flaky pastry that extends above the canary yellow eggy custard, spotted with bright green shreds of fresh spinach and patches of orange cheddar. You can see now why I had to include it.

Fresh Spinach Quiche

`MAKE AHEAD` `WEEKEND`

HANDS-ON: **30 MIN.**   TOTAL: **1 HR., 5 MIN.**
YIELDS: **6 SLICES**

CRUST
1 premade Galette Crust
(page 242)

FILLING
2 teaspoons olive oil
½ cup diced sweet onion
2 cups baby spinach leaves,
chiffonade

Heaping ¼ teaspoon kosher
salt plus a pinch, divided
½ cup mascarpone or
cream cheese
½ cup whole milk
5 large eggs
A couple cracks of pepper
1 cup shredded cheddar
cheese

THE NIGHT BEFORE (so you can sleep in), bake the premade crust (also known as blind baking). Start with the premade disk, and roll the dough out on a lightly floured surface to 14 inches in diameter. (If using frozen dough, thaw completely in the fridge prior to rolling.) Fold the dough in quarters and transfer to a 10-inch removable bottom tart pan with a 2-inch height. Unfold and center within the pan. Trim excess, if needed. Place the pan in the freezer, and chill for 10 minutes.

MEANWHILE, PREHEAT THE OVEN to 425°F. Before baking, prick the bottom and sides of the dough with a fork to keep from bubbling. Line the dough with parchment paper and fill with pie weights. Place the pan on a baking sheet, and bake for 15 minutes. Remove the parchment and pie weights, and bake for 3 minutes more. Remove from the oven and allow to sit out at room temperature overnight.

THE MORNING OF, MAKE THE FILLING. Preheat the oven to 350°F. Heat a 10-inch cast-iron skillet over medium. Once the pan is warm, add the oil and onion. Cook for 3 minutes or until tender. Stir in the spinach and pinch of salt, and sauté 1 minute more or until the spinach is just barely wilted. Set aside.

IN A HIGH-POWERED or regular blender, blend the mascarpone and milk on the lowest speed until smooth. Add the eggs, salt, and pepper and blend on low again until evenly combined. Pour in the prepared pastry shell. Gently stir in the shredded cheese and sautéed spinach mixture. The filling will be about half the height of the crust.

BAKE FOR 30 TO 35 MINUTES or until the eggs are set. Let stand for 5 minutes before slicing.

69

NOTES

To add 2 strips of bacon, forgo the olive oil and cook the bacon first until crispy. Remove from the pan and place on a paper towel. Then continue with the recipe as written by sautéing the onion and spinach in the bacon fat. Crumble or chop the bacon, and add into the final egg mixture just before baking.

INGREDIENT TIP

Chiffonade is the French word for cutting thin slices of leaves, typically used in the context of basil. In the case of this quiche, I've cut the spinach in the same way. Stack a handful of leaves together, roll, and thinly slice.

MINIMALIST TIP

Buy a 10-inch removable bottom tart pan that has a 2-inch height. See The Essential Tools section (page 19) for more details. This will remove worries of a filling overflow, burned pie edges, and a shrinking crust. Even if (when) the crust shrinks a bit, you have room to spare. When it's serving time, the removable bottom makes it far easier to cut and remove the slices. This pan just works.

This recipe might be one of the theses of the book—how to turn leftovers into an entirely new meal. Leftovers have a bad rap, except when they taste like this. By using up premade refried black beans, pickled veggies, and Ancho-lada Sauce, this tostada takes on a new life of its own. This is the beauty of putting in work earlier in the week—a weekday breakfast that tastes like the weekend. Of course, you could just sleep in on the weekend and wake up to this, too.

Breakfast Tostada

MAKE AHEAD   WEEKDAY   WEEKEND

HANDS-ON: **8 MIN.**   TOTAL: **8 MIN.**
YIELDS: **1 TOSTADA**

TOSTADA

1 tablespoon neutral oil

1 large egg

1 corn tortilla

¼ cup leftover Refried Black Beans (page 186) or canned

GARNISH

¼ avocado, sliced

2 tablespoons Quick-Pickled Red Onions (page 145) or Quick-Pickled Radishes and Carrots (page 88)

1 tablespoon leftover Ancho-lada Sauce (page 109) or store-bought

Pinch of alfalfa sprouts (optional)

Fresh cilantro leaves

Crumbled cotija

Lime wedge

MAKE THE TOSTADA. Heat a 10-inch nonstick skillet over medium-low. Once the pan is warm, add the oil. Crack the egg where the oil pools, using a silicone spatula to pull in the whites of the egg. If the whites of the egg begin to bubble, turn the heat down further or pull the pan off the heat for a second.

Cook for 1 minute, and then spoon the oil in the pan over the whites of the egg until cooked through. Carefully remove the egg from the pan. Set aside.

ADD THE CORN TORTILLA to the leftover oil in the same pan. Turn the heat up to medium, and fry the tortilla for about 2 minutes on each side until toasted. In another corner of the pan, reheat the refried black beans until warm.

TO SERVE, place the pan-fried tortilla on a plate, and top with a shmear of refried black beans. Garnish with the avocado slices, the sunnyside egg, pickled vegetables, Ancho-lada Sauce, alfalfa sprouts, if desired, cilantro, and cotija. Give it a fresh squeeze of lime, and serve immediately.

NOTES

Optional add-in: Use up leftover cooked bacon in the freezer from the Bacon-Veggie-Tomato Wraps (page 132). Reheat the bacon with the beans, crumble it, and use it on top of the tostada.

INGREDIENT TIP

You'll notice cotija cheese used throughout the book. I love it for two reasons—a little goes a long way and it doesn't require dirtying a grater.

INGREDIENT TIP

With leftover Ancho-lada Sauce, make Ancho-ladas (page 109) or the Breakfast Tostada (page 70).

Chilaquiles are a bit like breakfast nachos, but lighter on the cheese. Here, I coat and cook tortilla chips in an enchilada sauce until slightly softened, and then top them with sunnyside eggs and a fiesta of bright garnishes. It's a beautiful breakfast skillet meant to be served family style. If you don't already have some sitting in the fridge, make a batch of the Ancho-lada Sauce (page 109) the night before for quick brunch prep.

Chilaquiles

`MAKE AHEAD` `WEEKDAY` `WEEKEND`

HANDS-ON: **18 MIN.**   TOTAL: **18 MIN.**
YIELDS: **3 SERVINGS**

GARNISH
¼ cup finely diced red onion

2 tablespoons chopped fresh cilantro

2 to 3 radishes, thinly sliced

1 avocado, diced

1 lime, cut into wedges

Sprinkle of crumbled cotija

Sprinkle of kosher salt

SUNNYSIDE EGGS
2 tablespoons neutral oil

3 large eggs

FILLING
1 cup premade Ancho-lada Sauce (page 109) or store-bought

4 cups sweet potato tortilla chips (or corn tortilla chips)

PREPARE THE GARNISHES. Set aside.

MAKE THE EGGS. Heat a 10-inch nonstick skillet over medium-low. Once the pan is warm, add the oil. Crack the eggs into separate corners, using a silicone spatula to pull in the whites of the eggs. If the whites of the eggs begin to bubble, turn the heat down further or pull the pan off the heat for a second. Cook for 1 minute, and then spoon the oil in the pan over the whites of the eggs until cooked through. Carefully remove the eggs from the pan. Set aside.

MAKE THE FILLING. Heat a 10-inch cast-iron skillet over medium-high. Once the pan is warm, add the Ancho-lada Sauce. Stir the sauce to evenly heat it. Gently stir in the chips until evenly coated in the sauce. Cook for 1 to 2 minutes to slightly soften. Remove from the heat.

TO SERVE, top the coated chips with the eggs and garnishes. Sprinkle with salt as needed. Serve family style straight out of the cast-iron pan.

This is not the mushy egg casserole of your youth. Maybe it's the addition of the kale. Or maybe it's the fact that this casserole is actually a strata. The crusty bread classifies it as such, also pulling it out of the mushy casserole category, making it more than tolerable. It's delicious. Start with the very best breakfast sausage from the meat counter and bakery-quality crusty bread (even better if it's leftover from dinner). Every ingredient counts. Assemble the night before serving for easy morning prep.

Not Your Mom's Egg Casserole

MAKE AHEAD   WEEKDAY   WEEKEND

HANDS-ON: **20 MIN.**   TOTAL: **9 HR.**
YIELDS: **4 TO 6 SERVINGS**

SAUSAGE MIXTURE
1 pound breakfast sausage
4 cups chopped kale
4 cups cubed or torn crusty bread (like sourdough, baguette, or ciabatta)
1 cup shredded cheddar cheese

EGG MIXTURE
2 cups whole milk
6 large eggs
1½ teaspoons kosher salt
½ teaspoon cracked pepper

GARNISH
1 sprig fresh thyme

THE NIGHT BEFORE SERVING, assemble the casserole. Prepare the sausage mixture. In a 10-inch cast-iron skillet over medium-high, cook the sausage, stirring until browned. Stir in the kale, and cook for 2 minutes more. Place the sausage-kale mixture in a 12 x 10–inch enamel baking dish (or similar-sized glass or ceramic dish). Add the cubed bread and cheese to the dish. Toss to combine.

PREPARE THE EGG MIXTURE. In a medium bowl, whisk together all of the egg mixture ingredients until combined. Pour evenly over the sausage mixture. Cover and refrigerate overnight.

THE MORNING OF, PREHEAT the oven to 350°F. Bake for 35 to 40 minutes or until the eggs are set. Garnish with fresh thyme.

74

CHAPTER 3

Main Dishes

THIS CHAPTER, in some ways, is the crux of the book. These recipes are the practical application of the minimalist kitchen cooking philosophy. They are designed to fit within the natural cadence of the week, with options for weekday and weekend cooking. I've found the most success with dinnertime when I prepare a bit in advance. For that reason, you'll notice many of the recipes have make-ahead components. If I had a dream for this chapter, it would be that dinnertime feels doable again. Because gathering around the dinner table feeds more than just your belly.

I fell in love with my husband over a sizzling skillet of vegetable fajitas. We served them at our rehearsal dinner. And if I could do it all over again, this would be the meal at our wedding. This recipe, these fajitas, are a stone in our Stonehenge. Use vegetables that are in season, choosing at least one meaty vegetable, like broccoli, cauliflower, or thick-cut zucchini. Use your favorite store-bought salsa. Something smoky or roasted is nice here. If you're pressed for time, sliced avocados work well in place of the guac. Be sure to sip on a Single-Serving Margarita (page 221) while chopping away. Recompose this meal into burrito bowls by swapping tortillas for rice.

Summer Veggie Fajitas `WEEKEND`

HANDS-ON: **1 HR.**   TOTAL: **1 HR.**   YIELDS: **4 SERVINGS**

GUACAMOLE

2 avocados, diced

1 clove garlic, minced

1 tablespoon jarred or fresh chopped jalapeños

1 tablespoon lime juice

1 tablespoon chopped fresh cilantro

¼ teaspoon kosher salt

¼ teaspoon cumin

VEGGIES

2 cups sliced green bell pepper (about 1 large pepper)

2 cups sliced red onion (about 1 onion)

2 cups broccoli, cut into small florets (about 1 head)

2 tablespoons olive oil

1 teaspoon kosher salt, divided

2 cups halved and sliced zucchini (about 1 to 2 zucchini)

1 cup fresh or frozen corn kernels

BLACK BEANS

2 (15-ounce) cans black beans, drained and rinsed

1 cup water

1 clove garlic, minced

¾ teaspoon kosher salt

¾ teaspoon cumin

¾ teaspoon dried oregano

1 bay leaf

FAJITAS

12 to 15 (6-inch) corn tortillas

Shredded Monterey Jack or crumbled cotija

Salsa of choice

MAKE THE GUACAMOLE. In a serving bowl, combine all of the guacamole ingredients. Set aside. If you're making it ahead of time, press a piece of plastic wrap directly on the surface of the guacamole and refrigerate for up to 8 hours.

PREPARE THE VEGGIES. Heat a 10-inch cast-iron skillet or griddle over medium-high. Once the pan is warm, add the pepper, onion, broccoli, oil, and

½ teaspoon of the salt; sauté for 5 minutes, tossing the vegetables occasionally with tongs. Adjust the heat as needed. If using a skillet versus a griddle, cook the vegetables in batches.

MEANWHILE, COMBINE all the black bean ingredients in a small saucepan. Cook over medium heat for about 10 minutes.

AFTER 5 MINUTES OF SAUTÉING the vegetables, add the zucchini, corn, and the remaining ½ teaspoon of salt. Sauté for 8 minutes more. The veggies are ready when they're slightly tender and charred. Taste and add more salt if necessary.

TO SERVE, warm the tortillas. Place directly over a gas flame to char the edges. Place on a plate, and cover with a towel to steam. (If working on an electric stovetop, heat the tortillas on a warmed pan, and cover to steam.) Serve family style. Place the veggies in a serving dish. Discard the bay leaf and liquid from the black beans, and place in a bowl. Set out the tortillas, guacamole, cheese, and salsa.

NOTES

Add chicken to this recipe, if you like. Try the marinade from the Chicken Gyros with Tzatziki (page 136). Keep the marinade the same, or swap out lemon for the lime and lemon pepper for cracked pepper. Cook the chicken first before sautéing the vegetables and allow it to rest while you prepare the rest. Slice it, and then add it back to the pan for a second before serving to warm through.

INGREDIENT TIP

We eat so many tortillas that we've invested in a cloth tortilla warmer. If you do, too, I recommend buying one. After heating tortillas directly over a gas flame or in a hot pan, place them in the tortilla warmer to steam. This keeps them from drying out.

This sweet and savory pizza is the fancy version of what we normally make come Friday night. It's usually just shredded mozzarella, a quick tomato paste sauce, and whatever leftover vegetables are in the fridge (see notes for the recipe). But I wanted to give you something with a little magic and find a way to incorporate the art of caramelizing onions. I love to take shortcuts, but not here. Caramelizing onions takes time. The savory notes come from the rosemary white sauce while the sweet notes come from the caramelized onions. For a quicker prep time, make the onions and cream sauce in advance.

Crispy Pizza with Caramelized Onions `MAKE AHEAD` `WEEKEND`

HANDS-ON: **1 HR.**   TOTAL: **1 HR. 30 MIN.**
YIELDS: **2 LARGE PIZZAS**

CARAMELIZED ONIONS

2 teaspoons olive oil

1 sweet onion, cut into ¼-inch slices

¼ teaspoon kosher salt

1 teaspoon balsamic vinegar

CREAM SAUCE

½ cup heavy cream

½ cup chicken stock

1 tablespoon unsalted butter

1 clove garlic, minced

1 tablespoon unbleached all-purpose flour

¼ teaspoon kosher salt

1 sprig of fresh rosemary, roughly chopped

CRUST

¼ cup unsalted butter

½ cup plus 1 tablespoon water

2 cups unbleached all-purpose flour

1 teaspoon kosher salt

1 teaspoon SAF instant yeast (see tip on page 203)

TOPPINGS

1¾ cups shredded Gruyère

Olive oil

Fresh rosemary

Crushed red pepper

CARAMELIZE THE ONIONS. In a large skillet on the lowest heat, add the oil and onion. Cook for 10 minutes, and then stir in the salt. Cook for 50 minutes total, stirring every 10 minutes or so. Once the onions have browned, deglaze the pan with vinegar and stir to coat. This can be done a week in advance and stored in an airtight container in the fridge.

MAKE THE CREAM SAUCE. In a liquid measuring cup, measure the cream and stock. Set aside.

IN A SMALL SKILLET over medium, melt the butter. Add the garlic, and cook for 30 seconds. Whisk in the flour to create a roux. Pour in half of the cream mixture, and whisk to combine. Pour in the remaining cream mixture, and whisk again to combine. Turn the heat to low, and add the salt and rosemary. Cook for 3 minutes more, whisking every so often or until sauce resembles a loose gravy. Set aside. This can be made a couple days in advance and reheated for easy spreading.

MAKE THE CRUST. Place the oven rack in the top third of the oven, and preheat to 500°F.

IN A SMALL SAUCEPAN, melt the butter. Stir in the water. Set aside. In a large bowl, stir together the flour, salt, and yeast. Add the butter mixture to the flour mixture; stir together until evenly combined. Knead for 1 to 2 minutes in the bowl or on a lightly floured work surface until smooth. Cut the dough in half and form into two balls. Cover with plastic wrap or spray the dough with water and cover with a towel to keep from drying out.

ON A LIGHTLY FLOURED SURFACE, roll out one dough ball until ⅛-inch thick. If the crust sticks in any parts, add a bit more flour. Place the crust on an unlined baking sheet. Using a fork, prick the crust a couple times to keep it from puffing while baking. Partially bake for 4 to 5 minutes. Remove, and add a thin layer of cream sauce and top with half the cheese and half the caramelized onions. Bake for 4 to 5 minutes more. Garnish with a drizzle of oil and a sprinkle of fresh rosemary. Serve with crushed red pepper. Repeat assembly to make the second pizza.

NOTES

To make the red sauce, stir together 3 tablespoons of tomato paste and 6 tablespoons of water (1:2 ratio), plus a dash of dried oregano and a pinch of kosher salt.

If BBQ sliders mated with black bean tacos, it'd go something like this and take a lot less time. The black beans get a quick coat of your favorite BBQ sauce, while the quick neon pink slaw yields a welcomed crunch. The tangy slaw is saucy enough to carry you over here. Make these tacos year-round by substituting seasonal fruit into the slaw to change things up.

BBQ Black Bean and Quick Slaw Tacos `WEEKDAY`

HANDS-ON: **20 MIN.** TOTAL: **20 MIN.**
YIELDS: **4 TO 6 SERVINGS (12 TACOS)**

QUICK SLAW
- ¼ cup lime juice
- 2 tablespoons high-quality mayonnaise
- 2 teaspoons apple cider vinegar
- ½ teaspoon kosher salt
- 4 cups red cabbage, thinly sliced
- 1 cup shredded green apple, segmented orange, diced pineapple, or diced mango
- 2 thinly sliced green onions
- ¼ cup chopped fresh cilantro

BEANS
- 3 (15-ounce) cans black beans, drained and rinsed
- Scant ½ cup BBQ sauce
- ¾ teaspoon kosher salt

GARNISH
- 12 (6-inch) corn tortillas
- 2 avocados, sliced
- 1 jalapeño, thinly sliced
- Crumbled cotija

MAKE THE QUICK SLAW. In a large bowl, whisk together the lime juice, mayonnaise, vinegar, and salt until evenly combined. Stir in the remaining slaw ingredients and toss to evenly coat. Set aside.

MEANWHILE, HEAT ALL of the bean ingredients in a saucepan on medium-low for 5 minutes.

PREPARE THE GARNISHES. Warm the tortillas. Place directly over a gas flame to char the edges. Place on a plate, and cover with a towel to steam. (If working on an electric stovetop, heat the tortillas on a warmed pan, and cover to steam.)

ASSEMBLE THE TACOS. Top the tortillas with the beans and a generous portion of the slaw, and garnish with a couple avocado slices, jalapeños, and a sprinkle of cotija.

A traditional chicken tikka masala calls for marinated chicken and a bit of forethought. This is purely a pantry dish and comes together in about 30 minutes. If you have cauliflower around, make the Curry Cauliflower (page 181), and add about 15 minutes to the total cook time. I've started layering on the cauliflower like I add necklaces to my favorite plain white tee. It's an easy way to fancy up the ordinary. Though, the only reason I call this ordinary is because we make it so often. Beware—the toasted spices and creamy tomato sauce have wooed a self-proclaimed curry powder-hater (or ten).

Chickpea Tikka Masala

MAKE AHEAD   WEEKDAY

HANDS-ON: **15 MIN.**   TOTAL: **25 MIN.**
YIELDS: **4 SERVINGS**

RICE
1 cup rice
1 tablespoon unsalted butter
¼ teaspoon kosher salt

TOPPING (OPTIONAL)
1 recipe Curry Cauliflower (page 181)

CHICKPEA SAUCE
1 tablespoon olive oil
1 cup diced sweet onion
1 teaspoon kosher salt, divided
3 cloves garlic, minced

1 tablespoon curry powder
½ teaspoon cumin
½ teaspoon cinnamon
2 (15-ounce) cans crushed fire-roasted tomatoes
⅓ cup heavy cream or coconut milk
2 (15-ounce) cans chickpeas, drained and rinsed

GARNISH (OPTIONAL)
Squeeze of lime
Plain whole-milk yogurt
Chopped fresh cilantro
Harissa or Sriracha

MAKE THE RICE. In a small saucepan, make the rice according to the package instructions, adding the butter and salt.

MAKE THE CURRY CAULIFLOWER, if desired.

MAKE THE CHICKPEA SAUCE. Heat a large sauté pan over medium. Once the pan is warm, add the oil and onion. Sauté until the onion is translucent, about 4 minutes. Sprinkle with ¼ teaspoon salt. Add the garlic, and cook for 30 seconds more. Stir in the remaining salt, the curry powder, cumin, and cinnamon, and cook for about 1 minute to toast the spices. Add the tomatoes and cream. (If you'd prefer a smooth sauce, puree the tomato mixture in a blender, and then return it back to the pan.) Add the chickpeas, and simmer for at least 15 minutes over medium to allow the flavors to develop. Taste and add more of the seasonings if necessary.

TO SERVE, divide the rice evenly among 4 bowls. Top evenly with the chickpea sauce. Top with the Curry Cauliflower, lime juice, yogurt, cilantro, and harissa, if desired.

NOTES

You can substitute two 6-ounce skinless, boneless chicken breasts cut into ½-inch cubes in place of the chickpeas. Simmer for 15 to 20 minutes in the sauce or until cooked through.

INGREDIENT TIP

Stock a trusty rice that can be used across recipes. I use one with a 20-minute cook time to keep the overall dinner prep time down.

This bowl is named after those kitchen-sink cookies. It's proof that flavorful dinners can be made from the random bits in your pantry. When you eat this meal, I hope you're reminded of the great potential behind those cabinet doors and that simple food can be so satisfying. A bowl of leafy legumes and vegetables is as good excuse as any to eat a bready side, like buttered naan or fluffy pita. In fact, you'll need it to complete this meal. That and a bottle of wine, too.

Kitchen-Sink Lentil Bowls WEEKDAY

HANDS-ON: **10 MIN.**   TOTAL: **40 MIN.**
YIELDS: **4 SERVINGS**

CARROTS
**Caramelized Roasted
   Carrots (page 178)**

LENTILS
1 cup dried green lentils
3 cups water
½ bay leaf
¾ teaspoon kosher salt

YOGURT TAHINI SAUCE
¼ cup plain whole-milk
   yogurt

2 tablespoons tahini
1½ tablespoons lemon juice
1 clove garlic, minced
¼ teaspoon smoky paprika
¼ teaspoon kosher salt

SERVING
2 cups arugula
2 tablespoons chopped
   fresh curly parsley or
   cilantro (optional)
4 pieces naan or pita,
   warmed

MAKE A BATCH of the Caramelized Roasted Carrots.

MEANWHILE, PREPARE THE LENTILS. Add all of the lentil ingredients to a small saucepan. Bring to a boil, and then reduce to a very low simmer. Cook, uncovered, for about 30 minutes. The lentils are ready when just tender and the water is absorbed.

MEANWHILE, PREPARE THE SAUCE. In a small bowl, stir together all of the sauce ingredients until smooth.

ASSEMBLE THE BOWLS. Divide the lentils evenly among 4 bowls, and top with the arugula and the Roasted Carrots. Add a generous dollop of the sauce. Garnish with the parsley or cilantro for a touch of green, if desired. Serve with the warmed naan or pita (and a bottle of wine).

MINIMALIST TIP

To save on cleaning measuring utensils mid-cooking, measure dry ingredients before wet when the same utensil is called for.

Bibimbap bowls are a Korean dish traditionally made with rice and sautéed vegetables. I've taken a nontraditional approach using quinoa in place of the rice, leaving this bowl extra protein-dense. It comes together quickly with a premade batch of Humble Chuck Roast (page 118) and quick-pickled radishes and carrots in the fridge. Between the sweet and salty beef, pickled vegetables, and pantry sauce, this bowl is rich in flavor despite very little cooking.

Quinoa Bibimbap Bowls

MAKE AHEAD **WEEKEND**

HANDS-ON: **45 MIN.**   TOTAL: **45 MIN.**   YIELDS: **4 SERVINGS**

QUICK-PICKLED RADISHES AND CARROTS
- ¾ cup water
- ½ cup white distilled vinegar
- 2 teaspoons sugar
- 1 teaspoon kosher salt
- ⅛ teaspoon peppercorns
- ¾ cup mixture shredded carrots and radishes

SAUCE
- 2 tablespoons harissa
- 2 teaspoons soy sauce
- 2 teaspoons rice vinegar
- 2 teaspoons honey
- 1 teaspoon sesame oil
- 1 clove garlic, minced

QUINOA
- 2 cups water
- 1 cup uncooked quinoa
- 1 tablespoon salted butter
- ¼ teaspoon kosher salt

GREEN BEANS
- 8 ounces haricots verts (French green beans)
- Kosher salt for salting water

BEEF
- 2 tablespoons soy sauce
- 2 tablespoons water
- 1 tablespoon honey
- 2 cloves garlic, minced
- Thumbtip of peeled fresh ginger, minced
- 1½ cups premade Humble Chuck Roast (page 118)

SUNNYSIDE EGGS
- 2 tablespoons neutral oil
- 4 large eggs

GARNISH (OPTIONAL)
- 1 jalapeño, sliced
- 2 green onions, sliced

MAKE THE QUICK-PICKLED RADISHES AND CARROTS. Bring the water to a boil in a small saucepan. In a pint-sized Ball jar with measurements or a glass bowl, add the vinegar, sugar, salt, and peppercorns. Add the boiling water to the vinegar mixture. Stir until the salt and sugar have dissolved. Submerge the carrots and radishes in the pickling solution and let sit for at least 30 minutes. This can be done up to 3 weeks in advance and stored covered in the refrigerator.

MEANWHILE, MAKE THE SAUCE. Stir together all of the sauce ingredients in a small ramekin. Set aside. This can be made a day or two in advance.

MAKE THE QUINOA. Add all the quinoa ingredients to a small saucepan. Bring to a boil, and then cover, reduce the heat, and simmer for 15 minutes or until the water is absorbed. Fluff the quinoa with a fork.

MAKE THE BEANS. Fill a medium saucepan two-thirds full with water; bring to boil. Add the beans; liberally salt the water. Cook for 5 minutes. Drain.

MAKE THE BEEF. Add the soy sauce, water, and honey to the leftover pan from the beans; heat on medium. Once hot, stir in the garlic and ginger; cook for 30 seconds. Stir in the beef; cook until heated through, about 3 minutes. Remove the pan from the heat.

COOK THE EGGS. Heat a 10-inch nonstick skillet on medium-low. Once warm, add the oil. Crack the eggs into separate corners, using a silicone spatula to pull in the whites. If the whites begin to bubble, turn the heat down further or pull the pan off the heat for a second. Cook for 1 minute, and then spoon the oil in the pan over the whites until cooked through. Carefully remove the eggs from the pan. Set aside.

ASSEMBLE THE BOWLS. Divide the quinoa, beef, beans, and eggs among 4 bowls. Spoon the pickled vegetables over each including a generous spoonful of the vinegar mixture. Drizzle with the sauce and garnish, if desired.

NOTES

Not all quinoa cook times are created equal. Stock a variety that takes about 15 minutes to cook. Darker quinoas tend to require more time and liquid to cook through.

MINIMALIST TIP

Use a box grater or mandoline to shred the carrots quickly. See The Essential Tools (page 19) for more notes on efficient box graters.

Soba bowls have been greeting us on the busiest weeknights since before our little one came into the world. They also greet us when the fridge is nearly empty. Somehow there's always enough ingredients in the fridge and pantry to squeak out one of these bowls, even if it means skipping the ginger and green onions. I've made other soba bowls over the years, but I always come back to this one. The peanut-coconut sauce has me wrapped around its finger. And I'm just fine with that. Sitting down to this bowl never gets old. During the colder months of the year, switch over to the Thai-Spiced Rice Bowls (page 152).

Soba Bowls with Peanut Sauce

WEEKDAY

HANDS-ON: **20 MIN.**   TOTAL: **20 MIN.**
YIELDS: **4 SERVINGS**

SOBA MIXTURE

Kosher salt for salting
   water

9 ounces soba noodles
   (3 wrapped portions)

¾ cup frozen peas

¾ cup frozen shelled
   edamame

SAUCE

½ cup light coconut milk

¼ cup natural creamy
   peanut butter

3 tablespoons soy sauce

1 tablespoon lime juice

Thumbtip of peeled
   fresh ginger (optional)

Squeeze of honey

GARNISH

2 medium carrots, shredded

¼ cup chopped fresh
   cilantro

¼ cup chopped peanuts

2 green onions, sliced

Sesame seeds

Sriracha or harissa
   (optional)

MAKE THE SOBA MIXTURE. Fill a large saucepan two-thirds full with water; bring to boil. Liberally salt the water just before adding in the noodles, peas, and edamame. Cook the soba noodles according to the package instructions. Drain and rinse under cold water until the noodles are cold to the touch.

MEANWHILE, MAKE THE SAUCE. In a high-powered blender or food processor, blend all the sauce ingredients on high until smooth. The sauce will be noticeably salty. Set aside, and prepare the garnishes.

ASSEMBLE THE BOWLS. Divide the soba mixture evenly among 4 bowls. Top each with 2 tablespoons of the sauce, a small handful of carrots, 1 tablespoon of cilantro, peanuts, green onion, and a sprinkle of sesame seeds. Serve with Sriracha, if desired, and additional sauce.

NOTES

If you prefer the carrots to be slightly softer than their raw version, add them to the boiling mixture in the last minute of cooking.

INGREDIENT TIP

Buy soba noodles wrapped in 3-ounce portions for mindless measuring.

Vinaigrettes are often underutilized when it comes to pasta. But with their high olive oil ratio and depth of flavor, they are the perfect quick sauce to pasta. On a busy weeknight, I'm known for cooking pasta in a pinch and topping it with whatever vinaigrette I have around. Instead of making a salad, I pile one on top. The greens wilt only slightly under the heat of the noodles. See notes for variations. Leftovers serve well as a chilled pasta salad.

Sun-Dried Greek Pasta WEEKDAY

HANDS-ON: **20 MIN.**   TOTAL: **20 MIN.**
YIELDS: **4 TO 6 SERVINGS**

PASTA
½ teaspoon kosher salt plus
   more for salting water
4 cups short-grain pasta

VINAIGRETTE
½ cup olive oil
¼ cup sun-dried tomatoes
1½ tablespoons white wine
   vinegar
2 cloves garlic, smashed

1 teaspoon Dijon mustard
½ teaspoon dried oregano
¼ teaspoon kosher salt

SALAD
3 cups baby spinach
½ cup thinly sliced red
   onion
½ cup pitted and sliced
   kalamata olives
½ cup crumbled feta

COOK THE PASTA. Fill a large saucepan two-thirds full with water; bring to a boil. Liberally salt the water just before adding in the noodles. Cook the pasta according to the package instructions until al dente.

MAKE THE VINAIGRETTE. In a high-powered blender or food processor, blend all of the vinaigrette ingredients on high until mostly smooth. This yields ¾ cup. It can be made 3 weeks in advance and stored covered in the fridge. If the vinaigrette hardens in the fridge, run under warm water, and shake to combine.

PREPARE THE SALAD. Slice the vegetables. Set aside.

ASSEMBLE THE PASTA. Return the cooked pasta to the pan along with ½ teaspoon of the salt. Pour in half the vinaigrette and stir together. Taste and add additional vinaigrette and salt as needed. Distribute the pasta evenly among the plates and top with the spinach, onion, olives, and feta. The greens will slightly wilt from the warmth of the noodles.

NOTES

Use the vinaigrette for salads or in place of the pesto in the Chicken Pesto Sandwiches (page 142). Or, stir in a couple tablespoons of pesto and cream, in addition to the vinaigrette, for a slight variation.

MINIMALIST TIP

If you're making a sauce
that will eventually be
blended, don't spend
time finely dicing and
mincing. You can roughly
chop in this instance.

There was a time, right after becoming a family of three, that our grocery buying habits slipped away from us completely. I was left with a decently stocked pantry, a nearly empty fridge, and a baby on my hip to figure out dinner. A couple recipes throughout the book bloomed from those days, like this one. We always seemed to have pasta noodles, cans of tomatoes and tomato paste, cloves of garlic, and sweet onions. Since we rarely left the house, I reached for vodka to make dinner taste like a date from our prebaby days. And it did, even if we ended up eating it cold some nights.

Quick Vodka Sauce Pasta WEEKDAY

HANDS-ON: **20 MIN.**   TOTAL: **20 MIN.**
YIELDS: **3 TO 4 SERVINGS**

PASTA
Kosher salt for salting water
3 cups short-grain pasta

SAUCE
2 teaspoons olive oil
1 cup sweet roughly diced onion
2 cloves garlic, roughly chopped
½ cup canned fire-roasted tomatoes
½ cup vodka
3 tablespoons tomato paste
¾ teaspoon kosher salt
½ cup heavy cream
¼ cup grated Parmesan

GARNISH
Basil, chiffonade
Shaved Parmesan
Red pepper flakes (optional)

COOK THE PASTA. Fill a large saucepan two-thirds full with water; bring to a boil. Liberally salt the water before adding in the noodles. Cook according to the package instructions until al dente. Drain the pasta, reserving ½ cup of the pasta water in a liquid measuring cup. (If you forget to reserve the pasta water, it happens, use stock.)

MEANWHILE, MAKE THE SAUCE. Heat a small saucepan over medium heat. Once warm, add the oil and onion. Sauté for 4 minutes or until the onion is tender, stirring occasionally. Add the garlic, and cook for 30 seconds more. Stir in the canned tomatoes, vodka, tomato paste, and salt. Turn the heat down to medium-low, and simmer for 5 minutes to cook out the alcohol.

REMOVE THE PAN FROM THE HEAT. Pour the tomato mixture and the cream into a high-powered blender or food processor; blend until smooth. Pour the blended tomato sauce, grated Parmesan, and the reserved pasta water in the large saucepan used to cook the pasta. Cook over medium heat for about 3 minutes or until heated through. Stir in the pasta, and cook for 1 minute more to coat. Taste and add more salt if necessary.

TO SERVE, spoon the pasta mixture evenly into the bowls. Top with the basil, shaved Parmesan, and, if desired, red pepper flakes.

INGREDIENT TIP

All canned tomatoes aren't created equal. I recommend doing a taste test across canned tomatoes in your price range. Eat them straight out of the can. I buy Muir Glen tomatoes, as I find them less acidic and more balanced than most. I love fire-roasted tomatoes, especially for their added depth of flavor straight out of the can, ultimately reducing the overall cook time.

INGREDIENT TIP

Is it possible to tame raw red onions? Yes! Soak them in an ice-cold bath for 10 minutes before serving.

I learned this pesto trick from Justin's, the nut butter company. Use almond butter in place of pine nuts. It yields a creamy, nutty pesto. I'll never go back to stocking pricey pine nuts. This recipe calls for lemon zest, too; it adds a layer of bright, floral notes while also helping to preserve the bright green color. We typically make this recipe during the hot months, when tomatoes taste like they should. If making in the off-season, skip the tomatoes and mozzarella, and add in ½ cup chopped sun-dried tomatoes. You could easily turn this recipe into a creamy pesto by returning the pasta and pesto to the pan and adding in ¼ cup heavy cream and ½ cup stock. Heat for a couple minutes. As you can see, this recipe is very adaptable. Try the Chicken Pesto Sandwiches (page 142) using this same recipe, too. Make the pesto in advance for an ultra-quick prep time or when your basil plant is in need of a trim.

Pesto Garden Pasta

`MAKE AHEAD` `WEEKDAY`

HANDS-ON: **15 MIN.**   TOTAL: **20 MIN.**
YIELDS: **5 TO 6 SERVINGS**

PESTO

2 cups fresh basil leaves
½ cup grated Parmesan
½ cup olive oil
1 tablespoon almond butter
2 teaspoons grated lemon zest (about 1 large lemon)
1 tablespoon lemon juice
2 cloves garlic, smashed
1 teaspoon kosher salt
A couple cracks of pepper

PASTA

Kosher salt for salting water
4 cups short-grain pasta
1 cup grape tomatoes, halved
1 cup yellow cherry tomatoes, halved
¼ cup thinly sliced red onion
8 ounces pearled mozzarella balls, drained

MAKE THE PESTO. In a high-powered blender, blend all the pesto ingredients on high until smooth and creamy. This yields 1 cup. It can be made a week in advance and stored covered in the fridge.

COOK THE PASTA. Fill a large saucepan two-thirds full with water; bring to a boil. Liberally salt the water before adding in the noodles. Cook the pasta according to the package instructions until al dente. Drain.

MEANWHILE, PREPARE THE TOMATOES AND ONION. Once the pasta is done, drain and place the pasta in a large serving bowl. Add about three-fourths of the pesto, tomatoes, red onion, and mozzarella balls; toss to combine. Taste and add more pesto and salt as desired. Serve warm.

NOTES

This pesto is on the salty side to carry the weight in this recipe. If using elsewhere, drop the amount in half. This can also be served cold as a pasta salad. Or, turn these components into a grilled cheese using shredded (not pulled) mozzarella, leftover pesto, tomatoes, and red onion. My friend, Kathryne, from the blog cookieandkate.com says the best grilled cheese is made by sprinkling Parmesan on the outsides of the bread and cooking it, yielding a crispy, sharp exterior.

Butternut squash might be my favorite late fall/winter squash. But I only like it one way—pureed. It ends up too soft after a roast or a sauté for my liking. To achieve pureed squash, it traditionally undergoes an hour-long roast to soften. In an effort to reduce that time, I've started steaming butternut cubes. They cook in a fraction of the time. Both cooking options are in the notes below. Start with precooked, pureed squash for an easy dinner preparation. I like to top this pasta with peppery arugula and spicy red pepper flakes to contrast the sweetness of the butternut squash. Make this winter pasta recipe for half the year before switching over to the White Wine Spring Pasta (page 121) for the other half of the year.

Butternut Pasta `MAKE AHEAD` `WEEKDAY`

HANDS-ON: **30 MIN.** TOTAL: **30 MIN.**
YIELDS: **3 TO 4 SERVINGS**

SAUCE
2 teaspoons olive oil
¾ cup chopped sweet onion
2 cloves garlic, minced
1½ cups chicken stock
1½ cups pureed butternut
  squash (see notes)
1 sprig fresh sage
1 teaspoon kosher salt
A couple cracks of pepper
¼ cup grated Parmesan
¼ cup heavy cream

PASTA
Kosher salt for salting
  water
3 cups short-grain pasta

GARNISH
Arugula (optional)
Crushed red pepper
  (optional)
Shaved Parmesan

MAKE THE SAUCE. Heat a large sauté pan over medium. Once warm, add the oil and onion. Sauté for 4 minutes or until the onion is tender, stirring occasionally. Add the garlic, and cook for 30 seconds more. Stir in the stock, butternut puree, sage, salt, and pepper. Simmer on low for 10 minutes to develop flavor, stirring occasionally.

COOK THE PASTA. Meanwhile, fill a large saucepan two-thirds full with water; bring to a boil. Liberally salt the water before adding in the noodles. Cook the pasta according to the package instructions until al dente. Drain.

REMOVE THE SAGE sprig from the sauce, and pour the butternut mixture into a high-powered blender; blend until smooth. Return the sauce to the pan over medium. Add the Parmesan and heavy cream, stirring until smooth. Fold in the cooked pasta, and cook for a minute more. Plate the pasta, and top with a handful of arugula (optional), a sprinkle of crushed red pepper (optional), and a heavy-handed dusting of Parmesan (not optional).

NOTES

To roast the squash, cut it in half, core, drizzle with a bit of oil, and place skin side up on a parchment-lined baking sheet. Roast for 45 minutes to 1 hour at 425°F. The squash is done once it's fork tender. Once cool enough to handle, scoop the squash out of the skin and puree. To steam the squash, peel, core, and cut it into ½-inch cubes. Place the cubes in a steamer basket and steam over medium for 12 minutes. Remove from the heat with the lid still on and allow to sit for 5 minutes more, and then puree. This can be done a week in advance and stored in the fridge; or store it in a freezer-safe ziplock bag in the freezer for up to 2 months. If freezing, thaw in the fridge overnight or in a bowl of warm water for about 30 minutes.

INGREDIENT TIP

Buy sweet onions for a sweeter onion flavor. I use them almost exclusively outside of the occasional red onion. I also find that sweet onions rarely make my eyes water.

As a minimalist, I pride myself on making just enough for meals. (I'm not going to mention the part about Kev eating a bowl of cereal at 9 p.m. every other night. He tells me he just really likes cereal.) Needless to say, I'm working on making a little more than enough at dinnertimes. Starting with this recipe. Fried rice is always better with leftover, dried-out rice. When meal planning, I add a rice dish the meal or two before Fried Rice Night and make a large batch. Of course, no one likes leftover rice, unless it tastes like this.

Fried Rice MAKE AHEAD WEEKDAY

HANDS-ON: **20 MIN.** TOTAL: **20 MIN.**
YIELDS: **3 TO 4 SERVINGS**

SAUCE
¼ cup soy sauce plus extra for serving

2 tablespoons rice wine

1½ teaspoons sesame oil

STIR-FRY
2 large carrots, thinly sliced into rounds

2 cloves garlic, minced

Half thumbtip of peeled fresh ginger, minced

2 tablespoons unsalted butter, divided

2 large eggs, lightly beaten

3 cups leftover cooked rice

1 cup frozen green peas

1 cup frozen shelled edamame

GARNISH
2 green onions, finely chopped

1 tablespoon sesame seeds

Sriracha or harissa (optional)

PREPARE THE SAUCE. Whisk together all the sauce ingredients in a small bowl. Set aside.

COOK THE STIR-FRY. Prepare the carrots, garlic, and ginger, and set aside. Heat a 10-inch cast-iron skillet or a griddle over medium. Once hot, add one-third of the butter (2 teaspoons) to the pan. Meanwhile, whisk together the eggs in a small bowl. Once the butter has melted, add the eggs and cook until scrambled (see page 62 for perfect scrambled eggs). Remove the eggs to the bowl, and set aside. Add the remaining two-thirds of the butter (4 teaspoons) to the pan. Stir in the carrots, and cook for 2 minutes. Stir in the garlic and ginger, and cook for 30 seconds more. Add the rice, peas, and edamame, and cook for 4 minutes or until thoroughly heated. Stir in the sauce and cooked eggs. Cook for 3 minutes more or until the sauce is absorbed. Garnish with green onions and sesame seeds. Serve with Sriracha, if desired, and extra soy sauce.

NOTES

For a sweeter option, add pineapple or mango as a garnish. To add shrimp, cook 1 cup of peeled, deveined shrimp in the butter just before cooking the eggs. Once cooked through, remove to a bowl, and then add back in just before serving.

Some say you shouldn't marinate salmon longer than an hour, but I like it best after a full workday's soak, ensuring the insides are as flavorful as the outsides. Just before heading out for the day, soak the salmon in a snug dish or ziplock bag so that it's immersed in the salt bath. Something worth noting: The yield on this recipe is a bit broad and maybe unconventional. When serving meat or fish on its own at a meal (and not incorporated), we tend to serve smaller portions. This allows us to buy high-quality meat. A friend once told me, eat meat only if you can afford it. I took her advice. We can afford it in small portions a couple times a week.

Maple-Soaked Salmon

MAKE AHEAD   WEEKDAY

HANDS-ON: **5 MIN.**   TOTAL: **9 HR. 15 MIN.**
YIELDS: **2 TO 4 SERVINGS**

MARINADE	SALMON
⅓ cup soy sauce	2 (6-ounce) wild-caught
¼ cup pure maple syrup	salmon fillets (about
¼ cup water	1-inch thick)
1 teaspoon smoked paprika	

MAKE THE MARINADE. Up to 9 hours in advance, stir together all the marinade ingredients in a snug dish or a freezer-safe ziplock bag. Place the thawed or fresh salmon in the dish. Cover and let the salmon marinate in the fridge for 9 hours (the longer the better).

COOK THE SALMON. Just before serving, place the oven rack in the top third of the oven. Preheat the broiler for at least 5 minutes. Line a baking sheet with parchment paper, and place the salmon on the parchment paper, skin sides down. Broil for 6 to 8 minutes, keeping close watch. The salmon is done when the sides are no longer translucent and the tops look as if they are about to flake. Serve immediately.

INGREDIENT TIP

I prefer regular soy sauce to reduced-sodium, as I find that I need about double the reduced-sodium soy sauce to carry enough saltiness, which is no reduction at all.

INGREDIENT TIP

Cook times will vary depending on the thickness of the fish. This recipe was written using a thin fillet (about ⅜-inch thick). Buy similar-sized fish every time to take the guesswork out of the cook time.

My mom often made Oprah's Unfried Chicken growing up. She'd add a collection of spices—always paprika—and flour in a ziplock bag and shake it until the chicken was liberally coated. It was one of my favorite meals, if only for the crispy coating. I feel the same way about this white fish: It needs dredging in paprika-spotted flour and pan-frying in butter, leaving a crispy armor. The only other thing it needs—a very generous lemon wedge for squeezing.

Pan-Fried White Fish WEEKDAY

HANDS-ON: **15 MIN.**   TOTAL: **15 MIN.**
YIELDS: **2 SERVINGS**

DREDGE

¼ cup unbleached all-purpose flour

¾ teaspoon kosher salt

½ teaspoon dried oregano

¼ teaspoon paprika

¼ teaspoon lemon pepper

FISH

1 tablespoon salted butter

2 (3-ounce) white fish fillets (such as tilapia or sole)

2 lemon wedges

ASSEMBLE THE DREDGE. In a shallow bowl or plate, stir together all the dredge ingredients.

MAKE THE FISH. Melt the butter in a large skillet over medium. The butter will brown but should not burn. Turn the heat down if so. While the butter melts, evenly dredge the fish fillets.

ADD THE FILLETS TO THE PAN, and cook for 2 to 3 minutes on each side or until the fish flakes easily when pressed with the back of a fork. Remove the fillets from the pan. Serve with the lemon wedges and squeeze just before eating.

NOTES

If doubling or tripling the recipe, cook the fillets in batches to keep from overcrowding the pan. Or, cook the fish on a long cast-iron griddle.

This chicken is not meant to be presented whole. In fact, I've never understood why we present the bird that way only to be carved up moments later. And in most situations around here, it's rare that we serve a large hunk of meat with dinner. When we do, it's incorporated into a dish or stirred into a salad. That's how this efficiency chicken was born. This cooking method steams the chicken, keeping it plenty moist and salty without having to undergo a 24-hour brine. Cooking the whole chicken also lends loads of flavor—from the skin, the bones, and the fat. This recipe is neutral so that it can be added to a variety of recipes. Add herbs, citrus, and garlic if serving alone. To use up the remainder of the carcass (and for an easier cleanup) after you remove the meat from the pan, top off the Dutch oven with water to make a bone stock. (See notes for the stock recipe.) Store the chicken in the fridge for the week or in smaller portions in the freezer for later.

Dutch Oven Whole Chicken

MAKE AHEAD   WEEKEND

HANDS-ON: **20 MIN.**   TOTAL: **1 HR. 30 MIN.**
YIELDS: **ABOUT 4 CUPS OF PULLED CHICKEN**

1 tablespoon kosher salt	3 tablespoons olive oil
A couple generous cracks of pepper	1 (4- to 5-pound) whole chicken, thawed

PREHEAT THE OVEN to 350°F.

IN A SMALL BOWL OR RAMEKIN, stir together the salt, pepper, and oil. Set aside.

HEAT A DUTCH OVEN over medium. Meanwhile, pat the chicken dry. Once the pot is warm, add in about one-third of the oil mixture. Immediately place the chicken in the pot, breast and drumstick side up. Paint the chicken with the remainder of the oil mixture. Cover and place in the oven to cook for 1 hour. At the hour mark, check the temperature between the leg and the breast meat. The chicken is ready when the thermometer reads 165°F and the juices run clear. Cook for 5 to 10 minutes more if needed. Once ready, remove from the oven and uncover to rest for at least 10 minutes before carving into the bird, or until cool enough to handle.

PULL THE MEAT from the entire bird. Pour a couple spoonfuls of the leftover liquid over the meat to keep from drying out. Store covered in the fridge for up to 4 days for use in another recipe or in the freezer for up to a month.

NOTES

With the chicken remains, make a stock. Top with about 10 cups water, 2 roughly chopped carrots, half an onion broken into wedges, a couple sprigs of thyme, a handful of parsley, a bay leaf, a generous pinch of salt, and a couple peppercorns. Add a dash of ground turmeric for color, if desired. Bring to a simmer, and then turn the heat down to keep a very low simmer. Cook low and slow for 2 hours. Taste and add more salt if necessary. Pour the liquid through a fine-mesh sieve into mason jars and store covered overnight in the fridge. In the morning, skim the fat solids off the top and discard. Store in the fridge for a week or in the freezer for 3 months.

INGREDIENT TIP

Buy a similar weight chicken every time for easy, autopilot cooking.

INGREDIENT TIP

To change these
enchiladas up, serve
with avocado, the
Quick Slaw (page 83),
and top with pepitas,
if desired.

I'm elated that this recipe title made it to print. Elated that someone found my quirky sense of humor printable. However, the name is so fitting. This quick enchilada sauce comes together by reconstituting Ancho chiles in hot water. The rest of the ingredients get added and blended to make the most amazing (and quickest) enchilada sauce. Best for use on all enchiladas, Chilaquiles (page 73), or Breakfast Tostada (page 70). For an efficient prep time, make the sauce in advance.

Ancho-ladas MAKE AHEAD WEEKEND

HANDS-ON: **30 MIN.**   TOTAL: **1 HR.**   YIELDS: **4 SERVINGS**

ANCHO-LADA SAUCE

2 cups hot water

4 dried Ancho chiles, stemmed and deseeded

¾ cup roughly chopped sweet onion

1 (15-ounce) can fire-roasted tomatoes

4 cloves garlic, smashed

1 tablespoon honey

2½ teaspoons kosher salt

FILLING

1 large bell pepper, sliced

½ large sweet onion, sliced

2 tablespoons olive oil

½ teaspoon kosher salt

2 cups pulled Dutch Oven Whole Chicken (page 106) or rotisserie chicken

1 (15-ounce) can black beans, drained and rinsed

1½ cups grated cheese (mixture of cheddar and Monterey Jack cheese)

2¼ cups Ancho-lada Sauce, divided

8 (6½-inch) whole-wheat tortillas

TOPPINGS

2 tablespoons crumbled cotija

2 tablespoons chopped fresh cilantro

2 tablespoons pepita seeds (optional)

MAKE THE SAUCE. In a high-powered blender, measure the hot water using the ticks on the side of the blender container. Add the chiles and submerge. Let sit for 10 minutes. Once reconstituted, add the remaining sauce ingredients. Blend on high until smooth. This yields 4 cups. It can be made up to a month in advance and stored covered in the fridge.

MAKE THE FILLING. Preheat the oven to 400°F. Preheat a 10-inch cast-iron skillet on medium-high for 5 minutes. Meanwhile, prepare the bell pepper and onion. Add the pepper, onion, oil, and salt; sauté until charred and softened, about 10 minutes.

MEANWHILE, ADD THE CHICKEN, black beans, cheese, and ¼ cup of the Ancho-lada Sauce to a large bowl. Stir in the sautéed pepper and onion. In a 12 x 10–inch enamel baking dish (or similar-sized glass or ceramic dish), add 1 cup sauce to thinly coat the bottom of the pan. Fill each tortilla with ½ cup of the filling. Roll the enchilada and place snuggly in the pan, seam side down. Repeat. These can be prepped up to a day before baking.

TO COOK, pour 1 cup of the sauce down the center of the pan. Spread the sauce towards the edges leaving about 1½-inch clear space. Tent a piece of foil over the pan to create steam. Bake for 20 minutes. Remove the foil. Sprinkle with the cotija and bake for 10 minutes more. Sprinkle with the chopped cilantro and, if desired, the pepita seeds. Serve.

NOTES

We often make a double batch of this recipe—one for now and one for later. It freezes well. Add the sauce to the top before freezing but skip the cheese. Wrap it tightly with foil. Thaw in the fridge the day of, and bake as directed, adding the cheese in the last 5 minutes of baking.

I'm not good at ordering takeout like my friends who keep a list of restaurants in their phone. The reason is, I can be pretty particular about meat. So much so, I'm often mistaken for a vegetarian. One good thing that's come of it: I've gotten pretty good at cooking takeout at home. If you're crazy like me (or not), I think you'll love this salty-sweet dish. Aside from the rice, it comes together in a crowded cast-iron skillet. By the end of cooking, though, it fits in the pan perfectly, which feels like a victory for my minimal mind-set. Of course, if you have a wok, use it in place of the cast-iron skillet. Let's just rename this Stay-in Cashew Chicken, or something like that.

Takeout Cashew Chicken `WEEKDAY`

HANDS-ON: **30 MIN.**   TOTAL: **30 MIN.**
YIELDS: **4 SERVINGS**

RICE

1½ cups rice

1 tablespoon salted butter

½ teaspoon kosher salt

SAUCE

¼ cup honey

3 tablespoons soy sauce

2 tablespoons rice vinegar

2 cloves garlic, minced

STIR-FRY

2 tablespoons cornstarch

½ teaspoon kosher salt

2 (6-ounce) skinless, boneless chicken breast halves, cut into 1-inch cubes

1 tablespoon neutral oil

1 tablespoon sesame oil

3 cups broccoli florets (about 2 heads)

2 large carrots, thinly sliced rounds (about 1 cup)

1 cup frozen shelled edamame

GARNISH

½ cup chopped cashews

2 green onions, sliced

Sriracha or harissa (optional)

MAKE THE RICE. In a small saucepan, cook the rice according to the package instructions, adding the butter and salt.

ASSEMBLE THE SAUCE. Stir together all the sauce ingredients. Set aside.

MAKE THE STIR-FRY. In a medium bowl, combine the cornstarch and salt. Pat the chicken dry, cut into cubes, and add to the cornstarch mixture, tossing to coat. Set aside. Prepare the vegetables.

HEAT A 10-INCH CAST-IRON SKILLET over medium-high. Once warm, add the neutral and sesame oils. Add the chicken, and cook for 4 minutes or until lightly browned but not cooked all the way through. Lower heat to medium, and add the broccoli, carrots, and edamame. The pan will be exceptionally full at first. Cook 5 minutes or until the vegetables are barely tender and the chicken is done, stirring frequently.

POUR THE PREPARED SAUCE over the chicken and vegetables. Cook for a minute more. Taste and add more salt if necessary. Serve over the rice. Garnish with the cashews, green onions, and, if desired, Sriracha.

NOTES

Swap out broccoli for snap peas or cauliflower, or cashews for peanuts.

MINIMALIST TIP

For easy chicken cubing,
use kitchen shears to cut
the chicken.

MENU
5/21 - 5/27

oba Noodle Bowls
hicken Noodle Sou
Salmon + Asian kal
Vodka Pasta
Crispy Pizza + San gr
Chicken Tinga + M
Bánh Mi Salad

PIZZA NIGHT

I grew up eating Pizza Hut pizza every Friday night and watching TGIF with my family. There's nothing close to TGIF on TV now but we still do Pizza Night (see page 80 for the recipe). Leftovers make for the best lunch on Saturday. To do so, preheat the pan over medium-high. Once hot, place the pizza in the pan to crisp up. After 30 seconds to a minute, pour in about 1 tablespoon of water away from the pizza (you can eyeball this), and immediately cover to steam. Turn off the heat. The pizza is ready once the cheese is melty. Crispy crust and melty cheese: It's almost better this way.

Meat during the week just doesn't happen a whole lot around here for multiple reasons. When Kev was in grad school, we cut it out for budgetary reasons. Around that same time, Michael Pollan said, "Eat food, not too much, mostly plants." And so we did. Once our budget loosened a bit, we kept to our plan, adding meat about one to two times a week. Dinner prep was so much faster without meat. Of course I loved that. And yet, I wanted to figure out a way to prepare meat quickly without compromising flavor. It can be done. With leftover Dutch Oven Whole Chicken (page 106), either from the fridge or the freezer, and a quick blender sauce, Chicken Tinga Tacos were born. Nothing gets compromised, making this weekend or weeknight ready. Make the Dutch Oven Whole Chicken in advance.

Chicken Tinga Tacos

MAKE AHEAD   WEEKDAY

HANDS-ON: **20 MIN.**   TOTAL: **20 MIN.**
YIELDS: **3 SERVINGS (10 TO 12 TACOS)**

CHICKEN

1 tablespoon olive oil

1 cup roughly chopped sweet onion

2 cloves garlic, minced

3 tablespoons pureed chipotles in adobo

1 teaspoon dried oregano

½ teaspoon ground cumin

¾ cup canned crushed fire-roasted tomatoes

¼ cup chicken stock

½ teaspoon kosher salt

3 cups shredded Dutch Oven Whole Chicken (page 106) or rotisserie chicken

SERVING

10 (6-inch) corn tortillas

2 ripe avocados, sliced

¼ cup chopped fresh cilantro

½ cup diced red onion

Crumbled cotija

1 lime, cut into wedges

MAKE THE CHICKEN. Heat a large skillet over medium. Once warm, add the oil and onion. Sauté for 4 minutes or until tender, stirring occasionally. Add in the garlic and cook for 30 seconds more. Stir in the chipotles, oregano, and cumin, and toast for 1 minute. Add in the tomatoes, stock, and salt. Bring to a simmer, and cook for 7 minutes. Place the tomato mixture in a high-powered or regular blender, and blend until smooth. Return the blended sauce to the pan over low heat. Add the chicken, and cook for 5 minutes. Taste and add more salt if necessary.

TO SERVE, WARM THE TORTILLAS. Place directly over a gas flame to char the edges. Place on a plate, and cover with a towel to steam. (If working on an electric stovetop, heat the tortillas on a warmed pan, and cover to steam.) Prepare the garnishes. To assemble, top the tortillas with the chicken and garnish with the avocado slices, cilantro, red onion, and cotija. Serve with a lime wedge for squeezing.

Curly parsley is more than
a disposable garnish.
I actually prefer it to flat-
leaf parsley for its subtle
flavor. I've used it in this
recipe and throughout
the book. Feel free to use
whichever you prefer.

When using prepared Humble Chuck Roast (page 118) either from the freezer or fridge, these tacos are fit for the weeknight but taste like the weekend. The pulled beef takes on a whole new life after a quick bath in the chipotles in adobo. But my favorite part about these tacos might be the herby, creamy chimichurri that comes together under the watch of the blender. Serve with optional sides for a large weekend meal: Spanish Rice (page 201) and Refried Black Beans (page 186).

Beef Tacos with Chimichurri

`MAKE AHEAD` `WEEKDAY`

HANDS-ON: **20 MIN.**   TOTAL: **20 MIN.**
YIELDS: **4 SERVINGS (12 TACOS)**

CHIPOTLE BEEF

1 recipe (about 3 cups) premade Humble Chuck Roast (page 118)

½ cup water

2 tablespoons pureed chipotles in adobo

Pinch of kosher salt, as needed

CHIMICHURRI

½ cup fresh cilantro leaves

½ cup fresh curly parsley

¼ cup olive oil

1 green onion, very roughly chopped

1 clove garlic, smashed

1 tablespoon lime juice

1 tablespoon red wine vinegar

1 tablespoon high-quality mayonnaise (optional)

½ teaspoon kosher salt

Dash of red pepper flakes (optional)

TACOS

12 (6-inch) corn or flour tortillas

2 avocados, sliced

1 cup thinly cut spinach (optional)

½ cup diced red onion

1 thinly sliced jalapeño (optional)

Crumbled cotija

Fresh cilantro leaves

MAKE THE CHIPOTLE BEEF. Place all of the beef ingredients in a large saucepan over medium-low. Cook for 5 to 8 minutes or until heated through. Taste and add more salt if necessary.

MAKE THE CHIMICHURRI. Place all the chimichurri ingredients in a high-powered blender, and process until the sauce looks creamy and flecked with green. This yields ½ cup. It can be made a day in advance.

ASSEMBLE THE TACOS. Warm the tortillas. Place directly over a gas flame to char the edges. Place on a plate, and cover with a towel to steam. (If working on an electric stovetop, heat the tortillas on a warmed pan, and cover to steam.) Prepare the vegetable toppings. To serve, generously add the beef to a tortilla and add the desired vegetable toppings. Drizzle with the chimichurri and a sprinkle of cotija and cilantro.

NOTES

Add Quick-Pickled Radishes and Carrots (page 88) or shredded red cabbage for extra crunch.

This cut of meat and recipe is as humble as they come. Unassuming beforehand, and surprisingly spectacular after. The Dutch oven acts as a slow cooker, but works faster. You'll know it's ready when the meat breaks at the nudge of a fork. My neighbor Lucy cooks most of her large cuts of meat this way. They're always the best. I've used a pale beer in this recipe for added flavor. We're not big beer drinkers, but I stock it for this recipe alone. Feel free to use water instead. You can eat this meat as is, but I like to portion it out and freeze for quick dinners. Try it with the Beef Tacos with Chimichurri (page 117) or Quinoa Bibimbap Bowls (page 88).

Humble Chuck Roast

`MAKE AHEAD` `WEEKEND`

HANDS-ON: **15 MIN.**   TOTAL: **2 HR. 45 MIN.**
YIELDS: **ABOUT 3 CUPS SHREDDED BEEF**

1 tablespoon kosher salt	½ cup roughly chopped sweet onion
A couple cracks of pepper	
1 (2-pound) boneless chuck roast	4 cloves garlic, minced
1 tablespoon olive oil	1 cup pale beer or water

PREHEAT THE OVEN to 300°F. In a small ramekin, combine the salt and pepper. Preheat a Dutch oven over medium-high heat.

MEANWHILE, PAT THE BEEF DRY, and sprinkle the top with half of the salt and pepper mixture. Press into the beef. Once the pot is warm, add the oil.

Place the beef where the oil pools, salt side down. Sprinkle the side up with the remaining salt and pepper. Sear for 3 minutes on each side.

MEANWHILE, PREPARE THE ONION AND GARLIC. Toss them in the Dutch oven, and then pour in the beer, and immediately cover. Place the Dutch oven in the oven, and cook for 2½ hours or until the meat begins to fall apart at the nudge of a fork. Uncover and allow to cool for at least 10 minutes or until cool enough to handle. Pull the fat away from the meat and shred. Store covered in the fridge for up to 4 days or freeze in a freezer-safe ziplock bag in 1½-cup increments for up to 1 month.

NOTES

I'm not a big beer drinker but I love the flavor of it in my beef. If you have an extra can on hand, use it here. It's an easy way to add a lot of flavor. If not, water will work, too.

INGREDIENT TIP

When working with meats, measure out your salt and pepper ahead of time so you're not dipping into your salt cellar with meaty hands.

This pasta recipe is salty from the bacon, sweet from the peas and wine, and peppery from the arugula and red pepper flakes. If I'm not serving a side salad, I like to go ahead and top my pasta with greens. They soften slightly from the heat but not to the point of wilty, a texture I don't care for. I love the efficiency of this recipe—reusing pans and cooking asparagus in the leftover bacon fat. It just works.

White Wine Spring Pasta `WEEKDAY`

HANDS-ON: **30 MIN.** TOTAL: **30 MIN.**
YIELDS: **3 TO 4 SERVINGS**

PASTA

3 cups short-grain pasta

Kosher salt for salting water

1 cup frozen peas

BACON + ASPARAGUS

2 slices bacon

1 bunch asparagus (about 1 pound), woody ends removed, and chopped into 2-inch segments

¼ teaspoon kosher salt

WHITE WINE SAUCE

1 tablespoon salted butter

2 cloves garlic, minced

1 tablespoon unbleached all-purpose flour

1 cup sweet white wine (like Moscato)

¼ cup heavy cream

¾ teaspoon salt

A couple cracks of pepper

GARNISH

1 cup arugula

Red pepper flakes (optional)

Grated Parmesan (optional)

COOK THE PASTA. Fill a large saucepan two-thirds full with water; bring to a boil. Liberally salt the water just before adding in the noodles. Cook the pasta according to the package instructions until al dente, stirring in the peas with 4 minutes remaining. Drain, reserving ½ cup pasta water in a liquid measuring cup.

MEANWHILE, COOK THE BACON. In a cast-iron skillet over medium heat, cook the bacon until crispy. Remove and place on paper towels. Once cooled, chop the bacon. Carefully remove some of the leftover fat in the pan with a paper towel and discard. Add the asparagus and salt to the pan; cook for about 5 minutes or until browned, stirring occasionally.

MAKE THE SAUCE. In the saucepan used to cook the noodles, heat the pan over medium and add the butter. Once melted, add the garlic and cook for 30 seconds. Whisk in the flour until evenly combined and cook for another 30 seconds. Pour in the reserved pasta water, wine, and all the remaining sauce ingredients, and whisk to combine. (If you forgot to reserve the water, it happens, use stock.) Cook for about 3 minutes until thickened. Add the pasta and peas back in. Cook for 2 minutes more to coat the noodles. Taste and add more salt if necessary.

TO SERVE, divide the pasta evenly among plates. Top the pasta with the asparagus, bacon, and arugula. Sprinkle with the Parmesan and red pepper, if desired.

NOTES

Make this a vegetarian dish by leaving out the bacon. Instead, cook the asparagus in 1 tablespoon of olive oil.

INGREDIENT TIP

This sounds crazy, but I prefer the texture of frozen peas to fresh peas, so I stock and use them year-round. Frozen produce is picked at the peak of harvest season, so you can trust the flavor. As for asparagus, I typically only buy it in season. To remove the woody ends, break them off where they naturally break.

CHAPTER 4

Burgers, Wraps & Sandwiches

 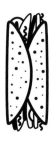

THE BEST SANDWICH might be the simplest one—good deli meat layered between slices of seedy bread, crispy greens, a slice of tomato, and a shmear of dijon mustard and mayo. I left that recipe out, as I imagine you know exactly how to make yours. The sandwiches in this chapter are the special ones we make—usually served at dinnertime or Sunday lunch. Many are inspired by our favorite sandwich shops from around the country—New Haven, CT, to Minneapolis, MN, to Chicago, IL, places we've called home.

Growing up, my mom and dad used a plastic Tupperware mold to shape our burgers. Did you have one, too? I loved the uniformity of it. Surprised? There's a part of me that wants to keep a press like that around. But instead of adding another tool to the collection, I use a rolling pin (or my hands in a pinch) to shape our burgers. I like mine diner-style thin, like a smashed burger, but found smashing them on a hot griddle to be counterproductive to maintaining a juicy burger. If you prefer your burgers thicker, follow the same method, just stack your burger two patties high. Make the Quick-Pickled Cucumbers ahead of time for a shorter prep time.

Diner Burgers `WEEKDAY`

HANDS-ON: **15 MIN.** TOTAL: **35 MIN.**
YIELDS: **4 SERVINGS**

**QUICK-PICKLED
CUCUMBERS**

¾ cup water

½ cup white distilled
vinegar

2 teaspoons granulated
sugar

1 teaspoon kosher salt

⅛ teaspoon peppercorns

¾ cup thinly sliced English
cucumber

A couple sprigs of fresh dill
(optional)

SPECIAL SAUCE

¼ cup high-quality
mayonnaise

2 tablespoons ketchup

1 tablespoon Dijon mustard

2 teaspoons chipotle
pepper in adobo

1 teaspoon pickle juice
from the jar

4 dashes Worcestershire
sauce

BURGERS

⅔ pound ground chuck
(20% fat)

Neutral oil cooking spray

½ teaspoon kosher salt

4 thin potato burger buns

1 ripe tomato, thinly sliced

4 thin slices red onion

MAKE THE QUICK-PICKLED CUCUMBERS. Bring the water to a boil in a small saucepan. In a pint-sized Ball jar with measurements or a glass bowl, add the vinegar, sugar, salt, and peppercorns. Add the boiling water to the vinegar mixture. Stir until the salt and sugar have dissolved. Submerge the sliced cucumbers in the pickling solution and let sit for at least 30 minutes. This can be done up to 3 weeks in advance and stored covered in the refrigerator. Add a couple short sprigs of dill to the pickling solution, if desired.

MAKE THE SAUCE. In a ramekin or small bowl, stir together all the sauce ingredients until smooth, and set aside. This can be made a week in advance.

MAKE THE BURGERS. To prepare the patties, divide the beef into 4 balls. Place the balls in between folded parchment paper. Roll out the patties (or press out using your hands) to about ¼-inch thick. The patties will be thin and large; they'll shrink up to the perfect size while cooking. Heat a 10-inch cast-iron skillet or griddle over medium-high for at least 5 minutes. Once hot, lightly spray the pan with the cooking spray. Add the patties to the pan, cooking in batches if needed, and salt the tops. Cook 1 to 2 minutes on each side or until desired degree of doneness, using a sharp metal spatula to flip. The patties should be charred on both sides. To add cheese, place a thin slice on the patties immediately after the flip and cover the pan to steam the cheese to a just-melted consistency. Spray buns with cooking spray, and toast. To assemble, shmear the top half of the bun with the sauce and top burger with pickles, tomatoes, and red onion. Serve immediately.

NOTES

Serve with Blistered Sweet Potato Rounds (page 193) or Garlicky Potato Wedges (page 190).

INGREDIENT TIP

Chipotles in adobo rarely, if ever, get used whole. When you open a new can, puree them in the blender until smooth. Store covered in a Ball jar for 6 months or longer; the puree lasts forever.

INGREDIENT TIP

Shape plant-based burgers
the same size as the buns.
This will help to keep the
burger intact since the bun
supports it.

When I set out to make a plant-based burger, I wanted it to be protein-dense over carb-dense. Carbs are starchy, which helps plant burger cohesion, so I had some experimenting to do. I landed on quinoa, an egg, smashed black beans, and oat flour as the base, plus some nutty flecks of pecans. I've flavored this burger similar to that of a meat burger. In fact, you might mistake it for one at first glance. This recipe would also make a mighty good Tex-Mex burger, too. Just add cumin and chili powder to the quinoa mixture while it cooks. Top with the Chimichurri (page 117) and sautéed onions or peppers or Quick-Pickled Red Onions (page 145). These burgers freeze really well, too. See notes.

Quinoa Burgers   MAKE AHEAD   WEEKEND

HANDS-ON: **45 MIN.**   TOTAL: **1 HR.**   YIELDS: **6 PATTIES**

QUINOA
¾ cup red quinoa
1½ cups water
½ teaspoon kosher salt

BLACK BEAN MIXTURE
1 (15-ounce) can black beans, drained and rinsed
¼ cup old-fashioned oats
¼ cup pecans
1 tablespoon Worcestershire sauce
½ teaspoon kosher salt

A couple cracks of pepper
1 large egg, whisked
Neutral oil cooking spray or high-heat oil (see method)

FIXIN'S
6 buns
Special Sauce (page 124; optional)
6 crispy lettuce leaves
6 slices ripe tomato
6 thin slices red onion

PREPARE THE QUINOA. Combine all of the quinoa ingredients in a small saucepan. Bring to a simmer over medium heat. Turn the heat to low; cover and cook for about 15 minutes or until just tender. The skinny white ring around the grain will be visible when the quinoa is ready. Let cool to room temperature before assembling the patties. The quinoa can be made a couple days in advance. Note: The quinoa will be on the salty side, which is necessary to carry enough flavor throughout the burger.

PREPARE THE PATTIES. In a large mixing bowl, roughly mash the beans. Set aside. In a high-powered blender or food processor, blend the oats

until a fine powder (flour consistency). Add the pecans to the oats, and blend again until chopped finely. Add the oat mixture, the cooled quinoa, and all the remaining burger ingredients except the cooking spray to the mashed black beans. Stir together until evenly incorporated. Form the black bean mixture into 6 patties, the same width as the buns. If preparing in advance, store the black bean mixture covered in the fridge for up to a day before cooking.

TO PAN-FRY, heat a 10-inch cast-iron skillet or griddle over medium heat for about 10 minutes. Once hot, lightly spray the pan with the cooking spray. Add the patties to the pan, cooking in batches if needed. Cook 3 to 4 minutes on each side. Serve immediately or keep warm in a 250°F oven.

TO DEEP-FRY, add a ½-inch layer of high-heat oil to a 10-inch cast-iron skillet over medium heat. Place the patties in the hot oil, and cook for 3 minutes on each side. Serve immediately or keep warm in a 250°F oven.

TO ASSEMBLE, toast the buns. Top with a quinoa burger, sauce, lettuce, tomato, and onion.

NOTES

Uncooked, shaped patties freeze really well. To freeze, place the patties on a baking sheet in the freezer for about 30 minutes or until hardened. Store in a freezer-safe ziplock bag with as much air removed as possible for up to 2 months. To reheat, use the deep-fry method, cooking for 4 minutes on each side. Cover the pan during the first 4 minutes to also help thaw the patty.

At one of my favorite fancier restaurants in Minneapolis, Spoon and Stable, it's not uncommon for the chefs to explore the same ingredient throughout a dish. It was a grapefruit pavlova that taught me the lesson—grapefruit curd, candied grapefruit, and grapefruit powder. If mindfulness had a flavor, it might be this. Several different iterations of the same ingredient was anything but overkill. It was amazing. This wrap is neither fancy nor sweet, or time-intensive, but I love the two iterations of red peppers—roasted in the hummus and bright and crisp as a meaty vegetable layer. You might question the level of flavor, but every ingredient plays a role, from the floral olive oil to the tangy feta and lemon. This, too, tastes like mindfulness. Make the Roasted Red Pepper Hummus (page 185) ahead of time or use store-bought.

Red Pepper Wraps

MAKE AHEAD   WEEKDAY

HANDS-ON: **10 MIN.**   TOTAL: **10 MIN.**
YIELDS: **4 SERVINGS**

4 (8-inch) whole-wheat tortillas

1 large red bell pepper, sliced

¾ cup baby arugula

½ cup alfalfa sprouts

4 to 6 radishes, thinly sliced

1 avocado, sliced

½ cup Roasted Red Pepper Hummus (page 185) or store-bought

Drizzle of olive oil

1 lemon for squeezing

Sprinkle of crumbled feta

WARM THE TORTILLAS. Place directly over a gas flame to char the edges. Place on a plate, and cover with a towel to steam. (If working on an electric stovetop, heat the tortillas on a warmed pan, and cover to steam.) Prepare the vegetables.

TO SERVE, spread about 2 tablespoons hummus down the center of each tortilla. Layer with the bell pepper, arugula, sprouts, radishes, and avocado. Drizzle with the olive oil and a squeeze of lemon. Sprinkle with the feta. Wrap and serve.

NOTES

This wrap often becomes our weekend lunch. Kev adds deli meat to his, and I keep mine just the way the recipe says. If you'd prefer this in sandwich form, use sturdy bakery bread rubbed with fresh garlic and drizzled with oil. Broil or toast the bread before assembling your sandwich.

High school tasted like chicken lettuce wraps, peppermint mocha Frappuccinos, and blueberry bagels with a shmear of honey-walnut cream cheese. Not all at the same time of course. I've only kept my severe craving for lettuce wraps. I've used lentils in the recipe as a plant-based protein, but feel free to use 1½ cups pulled chicken either from the Dutch Oven Whole Chicken (page 106) or rotisserie chicken for a quick substitution. Serve as a light summer dinner, as an appetizer, or alongside Fried Rice (page 101). Note: This recipe is heavy on vegetable chopping. You can buy slaw if you wish, but I find that freshly cut produce always tastes more like itself.

Lentil Lettuce Wraps `WEEKEND`

HANDS-ON: **45 MIN.**   TOTAL: **45 MIN.**
YIELDS: **3 TO 4 SERVINGS**

SAUCE

4 tablespoons soy sauce

3 tablespoons hoisin sauce

2 tablespoons honey

1 tablespoon rice vinegar

FILLING

½ cup dried green lentils

1½ cups water

½ teaspoon kosher salt

1 tablespoon sesame oil

2 cloves garlic, minced

Thumbtip of peeled fresh ginger, minced

½ cup finely chopped cremini mushrooms

SLAW

2 cups thinly sliced red cabbage

2 large carrots, shredded

3 green onions, sliced and divided

SERVING

¼ cup chopped cashews or peanuts

12 crispy lettuce leaves (like Bibb or iceberg)

Sriracha or harissa (optional)

MAKE THE SAUCE. Whisk together all of the sauce ingredients in a small bowl. Set aside.

MAKE THE FILLING. In a small saucepan, combine the lentils, water, and salt. Bring to a boil. Reduce the heat to low and simmer for 20 to 25 minutes, uncovered, until the lentils are almost cooked through. These can be prepared up to 4 days in advance and stored in the fridge. Meanwhile, prepare the filling vegetables.

PREPARE THE SLAW. Cut all of the slaw ingredients and add to a large bowl, reserving 1 of the cut green onions for garnish.

ONCE THE LENTILS ARE READY, heat a large sauté pan over medium-high. Once warm, add the sesame oil to the pan. Add the garlic and ginger to the pan, and cook for 30 seconds. Add the mushrooms, cooked lentils, and two-thirds of the sauce, reserving the remaining one-third for serving. Turn the heat down to medium, and cook for 3 minutes. Stir in the slaw mixture, and cook for 1 minute more. Remove to a serving bowl and top with the remaining green onions and chopped nuts.

SERVE FAMILY STYLE. Top the lettuce leaves with the filling mixture. Drizzle each wrap with the remaining sauce and Sriracha, if desired.

NOTES

With leftover Bibb lettuce, make the Bacon-Veggie-Tomato Wraps (page 132). With leftover cabbage, make BBQ Black Bean and Quick Slaw Tacos (page 83) or Asian Kale Salad (page 157).

INGREDIENT TIP

I'm not a huge fan of mushrooms, but I find them very palatable when chopped finely and served within the context of other ingredients.

I have vegetable rules for myself. I only eat fresh tomatoes during the summer and early fall. Outside of that, they just don't taste like themselves. Enjoy this wrap during the summer, under the same hot sun that cooked those tomatoes into perfection. Don't be fooled by the title, though. This is a BLT with a couple extra vegetables for added crunch and nutrients, held together by a wrap. Feel free to serve it on toasted bread as well. See notes for make-ahead options. I've listed the alfalfa sprouts as optional, but they add a nice earthy crunch to this familiar combination. I hope they make it onto your wrap, too.

Bacon-Veggie-Tomato Wraps

MAKE AHEAD   WEEKDAY   WEEKEND

HANDS-ON: **15 MIN.**   TOTAL: **15 MIN.**
YIELDS: **4 SERVINGS**

SAUCE

2 tablespoons plain whole-milk yogurt

2 tablespoons high-quality mayonnaise

2 teaspoons Dijon mustard

FILLING

8 slices of crispy cooked bacon

4 (10-inch) whole-wheat tortillas

4 crispy lettuce leaves (like Bibb)

2 ripe tomatoes, halved lengthwise and thinly sliced crosswise

1 large carrot, cut into thin strips

½ cup alfalfa sprouts (optional)

⅛ red onion, thinly sliced

MAKE THE SAUCE. In a small bowl, stir together all of the sauce ingredients until smooth. Set aside.

PREPARE THE FILLING INGREDIENTS. Cook the bacon to desired doneness. See notes below for cooking method and make-ahead options.

TO SERVE, place the tortillas directly over a gas flame to char the edges. Cover to steam. (If working on an electric stovetop, heat the tortillas on a warmed pan, and cover to steam.) Distribute the filling ingredients evenly among the tortillas. Drizzle with 1 tablespoon of the sauce. Wrap and serve.

NOTES

This recipe is fit for making in advance. The carrot and red onion can be cut a week in advance and stored in a container with a bit of water to keep from drying out. Save the tomato cutting until just before serving. Make a large batch of bacon ahead of time and freeze using this low-mess method: Preheat the oven to 400°F. On a parchment-lined baking sheet, place the bacon strips in a single layer. Bake for 10 minutes. Flip, and then bake for 5 minutes more or until the bacon looks as if it's about 1 minute from being done. Remove the bacon onto a paper towel-lined plate to absorb the grease. Store in a freezer-safe ziplock bag in the freezer for up to a month. To reheat the bacon, place on a warmed cast-iron skillet and cook until sizzling, about 3 minutes. Remove to a paper towel and serve.

BURGERS, WRAPS & SANDWICHES

MINIMALIST TIP

Use a pint-sized, wide-mouth mason jar to make and store the quick-pickled onions. Skip measuring cups, and use the notches on the side of the jar to measure instead.

This is not a traditional falafel recipe—fried and made with overnight-soaked chickpeas. The purist in me says that's the only way to make them. But my practical side told me to create a version that uses the canned chickpeas I keep stocked so that I actually make the recipe on a regular basis. The flavor here is very similar, but the texture is altogether different. If I'm being honest, this recipe is a little clunky for a weeknight with all the measuring and cleaning, but here I am on a Monday night making them because a craving hit. For a quicker prep, make the pickled onions and sauce in advance. These baked falafel freeze really well, too. See notes.

Baked Falafel Pitas with Tahini Sauce `MAKE AHEAD` `WEEKEND`

HANDS-ON: **30 MIN.**   TOTAL: **1 HR.**
YIELDS: **5 TO 6 SERVINGS**

FALAFEL

2 (15-ounce) cans chickpeas

¼ cup old-fashioned oats

1 teaspoon cumin

1 teaspoon coriander

Heaping ¾ teaspoon kosher salt

¼ teaspoon baking soda

¼ teaspoon cayenne pepper

½ cup packed fresh cilantro leaves

½ cup packed fresh curly parsley leaves

¼ cup roughly chopped sweet onion

4 cloves garlic, smashed

Neutral oil cooking spray

SAUCE

⅓ cup tahini

¼ cup lemon juice

¼ cup water

½ teaspoon kosher salt

Drizzle of honey to taste

SERVING

3 (6-inch) fluffy pitas, cut in half, or 6 pieces of naan

4 cups mixed greens

Quick-Pickled Red Onions (page 145)

MAKE THE FALAFEL. Preheat the oven to 425°F and line a baking sheet with parchment paper. Rinse the chickpeas in a strainer, shaking off as much water as possible. Set aside.

IN A HIGH-POWERED BLENDER or food processor, blend the oats until a fine powder (flour consistency). Pour into a medium-sized bowl. Stir in the cumin, coriander, salt, baking soda, and cayenne, and set aside. In the blender, combine the cilantro, parsley, onion, and garlic. Pulse to coarsely chop. Add the chickpeas, and pulse on low until a chunky mixture forms (not smooth like hummus), stopping to scrape down the sides every so often. Add the chickpea mixture to the oat mixture in the bowl, and stir until evenly combined. Using a 2 teaspoon-sized spring-release scoop (0.3-ounce scoop/#60 scoop), scoop two balls and shape into a 2-inch patty (yields 18 to 20 patties). Place on the prepared baking sheet. Just before placing in the oven, liberally spray both sides of the patties with cooking spray. Bake for 12 minutes on each side.

MAKE THE SAUCE. Whisk together all of the sauce ingredients until smooth. This can be made up to 2 weeks in advance and stored covered in the fridge.

ASSEMBLE THE PITAS. Place the pitas directly over a gas flame to char the edges. Cover to steam. (If working on an electric stovetop, heat the pitas on a warmed pan, and cover to steam.) Layer each pita evenly with the greens, 3 to 4 falafel, quick-pickled onions, and a liberal drizzle of sauce.

NOTES

Uncooked, shaped patties freeze really well. To freeze, place the patties on a baking sheet in the freezer for about 30 minutes or until hardened. Store in a freezer-safe ziplock bag with as much air removed as possible for up to 2 months. Before baking, spray the patties liberally with cooking spray. Bake at 425°F for 15 minutes on each side. Also, this recipe could easily be turned into a salad, using pita chips instead of pita bread as a salty, crunchy topping. To change things up, top the falafel with the Tzatziki from the Chicken Gyros (page 136) and add tomatoes and cucumber. Serve as lettuce wraps for a naturally gluten-free version.

These gyros coat our hands in tangy tzatziki and fill our bellies all summer long. When stuffed full, they're filling enough on their own for dinner. I like to source the fluffiest pita or naan for these. Find the best. Marinate the chicken ahead of time for a quicker dinner prep. You can do the same with the Tzatziki. I'm not a natural planner. It makes me feel like I've lost all spontaneity in my life. But dinner works only when I plan ahead. And when I do, it feels like it practically makes itself. When possible, find ways to make the everyday work for you, not against.

Chicken Gyros with Tzatziki

`MAKE AHEAD` `WEEKDAY`

HANDS-ON: **35 MIN.** TOTAL: **1 HR. 35 MIN.**
YIELDS: **4 TO 6 SERVINGS**

CHICKEN

1 pound boneless, skinless chicken breast

¼ cup olive oil

2 tablespoons red wine vinegar

2 tablespoons lemon juice

4 cloves garlic, smashed

1½ teaspoons kosher salt

1 teaspoon dried oregano

1 teaspoon lemon pepper

Neutral oil cooking spray

TZATZIKI

½ cup plain whole-milk yogurt

¼ cup diced English cucumber

2 tablespoons chopped fresh dill

1 tablespoon lemon juice

1 small clove garlic, minced

⅛ teaspoon kosher salt

A couple cracks of pepper

SERVING

4 cups thinly chopped romaine

2 ripe tomatoes, thinly sliced

¼ red onion, thinly sliced

¼ cup sliced pepperoncinis

4 to 6 (6-inch) fluffy pitas or naan

¼ cup crumbled feta

MARINATE THE CHICKEN IN ADVANCE. Place the chicken in a freezer-safe ziplock bag and pound out to about ¾-inch thick. Add the remaining chicken ingredients except the cooking spray to the bag. Massage together and place the bag in the refrigerator to marinate for 1 to 8 hours.

MAKE THE TZATZIKI. In a small bowl, stir together all of the tzatziki ingredients. Cover and store in the fridge. This can be made up to 8 hours in advance.

REMOVE THE CHICKEN from the fridge about 15 minutes before cooking to bring to room temperature. Meanwhile, prep the serving vegetables. Set aside.

HEAT A 10-INCH CAST-IRON SKILLET or griddle on medium for 5 minutes. Once hot, lightly spray the pan with cooking spray, and add the chicken to the pan. Cook for about 4 minutes on each side or until a meat thermometer reads 165°F. Remove the chicken from the pan, and let rest for 5 minutes on a cutting board. Cut the chicken into slices.

TO SERVE, place the pita directly over a gas flame to char the edges. Cover to steam. (If working on an electric stovetop, heat the pita on a warmed pan, and cover to steam.) Stuff each pita with the lettuce, chicken, tomatoes, red onion, and pepperoncinis. Drizzle liberally with the tzatziki sauce and sprinkle with the feta.

NOTES

Turn this meal into a salad, serving warmed naan wedges on the side.

INGREDIENT TIP

To use up leftover dill, make Chicken Salad Remix (page 169) or Bright Potato Salad (page 166). See storage tip on page 168.

MINIMALIST TIP

I use this same chicken marinade when making chicken fajitas. In this case, there's no need to reinvent the recipe since they share similar flavor profiles.

THE TASTE OF SIMPLICITY

It was after snowshoeing up a mountain in Colorado that I tasted the sweetness of an almond for the first time. I hope you don't get the idea that I'm a wild adventurer. I'm not that cool. But it's in those spaces—after a long hike, cooking at a campsite, and eating berries straight from the farmers' market—that you get to indulge in the taste of simplicity. It's a flavor I'm prone to forget. Neil Postman wrote a book in the 80s called *Amusing Ourselves to Death*. At the time he was talking about the over-consumption of media and television. I wonder sometimes if we amuse our taste buds to death, too. Can you taste the sweetness of vegetables after a long roast? There's nothing better.

MINIMALIST TIP

A sandwich with buttered bread is a welcomed treat. When adding it to a sandwich, place the buttered side on the interior of your sandwich so that it doesn't rub off on your fingers. For extra flavor, rub a piece of cut garlic over the bread, too.

This sandwich is based off one of my favorites served at a café around the corner from us. It's hard to imagine that a roasted vegetable sandwich could be worthy of making at home, but this sandwich gives its meaty counterparts a run for their money. A crowded baking sheet and plenty of olive oil yields lush almost buttery roasted vegetables. They take on a whole new flavor of their own. Thin slices of deli meat or salty prosciutto would work layered onto the bottom of the sandwich. See notes for roasted vegetable substitutions.

Roasted Vegetable Sandwiches

WEEKDAY

HANDS-ON: **10 MIN.**   TOTAL: **40 MIN.**
YIELDS: **3 TO 4 SERVINGS DEPENDING ON SIZE OF BREAD**

ROASTED VEGETABLES

½ **red onion, cut into 2-inch chunks**

2 **bell peppers, cut into 2-inch chunks**

2 **tablespoons olive oil**

¾ **teaspoon kosher salt**

A **couple sprigs of fresh thyme or ¼ teaspoon dried (optional)**

SANDWICHES

8 **slices of sandwich or ciabatta bread**

Shmear of salted butter (optional)

Shmear of high-quality mayonnaise

Shmear of goat cheese (optional)

2 **cups mixed greens or arugula**

PREHEAT THE OVEN TO 450°F. Add the prepared vegetables to a parchment-lined baking sheet. Toss with the olive oil, salt, and thyme sprigs. Roast for 30 minutes, tossing halfway through.

JUST BEFORE SERVING, toast the bread slices. If using bread that's too thick for a toaster, set under the broiler and toast for a second. Butter the interior of the bread (optional). To assemble the sandwiches, add a shmear of mayo and, if desired, goat cheese to a slice of bread. Top with enough roasted vegetables to cover the bread, mounted at least an inch high. Then top with the greens and the remaining slice of bread. Serve immediately.

NOTES

Feel free to make seasonal substitutions to this sandwich. In total, you should have around 6 cups of vegetables cut into chunks. If using more delicate produce, like summer squash, wait to add it to the baking sheet until the rest of the vegetables are halfway done. If using sturdier produce, like carrots, cut into thinner chunks so that they cook in the same time as everything else.

There was this sandwich shop around the corner from us when we lived in New Haven, CT—home to the best pizza and sandwiches. The shop felt miles away in the heat of the summer during my final month of pregnancy. But I still waddled my way down the street for a sandwich. Their grilled chicken was paper thin. Their house-made focaccia soaked up the pesto in the best possible way, and their greens wilted under the heat of it all. Flecks of sun-dried tomatoes added just enough brightness. They served their sandwich with a shmear of goat cheese, but I always opted for feta. I'll let you decide.

Chicken Pesto Sandwiches

MAKE AHEAD   WEEKDAY

HANDS-ON: **30 MIN.**   TOTAL: **30 MIN.**
YIELDS: **4 SERVINGS**

PESTO

½ recipe Pesto (page 97) or
    about ½ cup store-bought

CHICKEN

1 pound skinless, boneless
    chicken breast

½ teaspoon kosher salt

A couple cracks of pepper

Neutral oil cooking spray

SANDWICHES

1 (8-ounce) loaf focaccia

⅓ cup crumbled feta or a
    shmear of goat cheese

⅓ cup chopped sun-dried
    tomatoes

⅔ cup packed mixed greens

MAKE THE PESTO up to a week in advance, or use leftover or store-bought pesto.

MAKE THE CHICKEN. Heat a 10-inch cast-iron skillet or griddle over medium-high. Meanwhile, add the chicken to a freezer-safe ziplock bag, and pound flat until about ⅜-inch thick. Cut into 4 equal parts. Add the salt and pepper to a small ramekin or bowl. Sprinkle one side of the chicken with half the salt and pepper. Lightly spray the heated pan with cooking spray. Place the chicken salt side down and sprinkle with the remaining salt and pepper. Cook for about 3 minutes on each side or until a meat thermometer reads 165°F. Remove the chicken from the pan, and let rest on a cutting board.

ASSEMBLE THE SANDWICHES. Cut the focaccia into 4 sections. Using a serrated bread knife, carefully cut the sections horizontally in half. On either the top or bottom, liberally spread the prepared pesto. Sprinkle evenly with the feta and sun-dried tomatoes. Top with the greens and the chicken. Place the sandwich on the pan, and cook for about 1 minute on each side. Serve immediately.

NOTES

To change this sandwich up, omit the flecks of sun-dried tomatoes and instead use the sun-dried tomato vinaigrette (page 92) in place of the pesto. Add a little basil to the sandwich if you have it. Or, if you have both the vinaigrette and pesto leftover, stir together for an incredible combination.

INGREDIENT TIP

Don't miss out on
sandwiches because of
the carb overload. Switch
to open-faced sandwiches
and drop to one slice per
serving. Or, buy smaller
loaves of bread that are
about one-third of the size
of a traditional slice.

Tortas, Mexican sandwiches held together by crusty bread, are known for being messy yet extremely flavorful. I'm serving this torta like a Minnesotan would, which they learned from their Nordic ancestors: open-faced with a fork and knife. This recipe is compiled from multiple recipes throughout the book. If they're not already sitting in your fridge, prep the pickled onions and Refried Black Beans ahead of time for an easy assembly. Make the sweet potato rounds just before serving so that they hold their crispy blistered edge.

Open-Faced Sweet Potato Tortas

`MAKE AHEAD`   `WEEKEND`

HANDS-ON: **45 MIN.**   TOTAL: **45 MIN.**
YIELDS: **4 SERVINGS**

QUICK-PICKLED RED ONIONS
- ¾ cup water
- ½ cup white distilled vinegar
- 2 teaspoons granulated sugar
- 1 teaspoon kosher salt
- ⅛ teaspoon peppercorns
- ¾ cup thinly sliced red onion

FILLING
- ½ recipe of Refried Black Beans (page 186)
- Full recipe of Blistered Sweet Potato Rounds (page 193)

CHIPOTLE MAYO
- 1 teaspoon pureed chipotles in adobo
- ¼ cup high-quality mayonnaise

TORTAS
- 4 (½-inch-thick) slices crusty bakery bread
- 1 cup arugula
- 1 sliced avocado
- 1 sliced jalapeño (optional)
- 1 lime, cut into wedges
- 2 tablespoons chopped fresh cilantro
- Sprinkle of cotija

MAKE THE QUICK-PICKLED RED ONIONS. Bring the water to a boil in a small saucepan. In a pint-sized Ball jar with measurements or a glass bowl, add the vinegar, sugar, salt, and peppercorns. Add the boiling water to the vinegar mixture. Stir until the salt and sugar have dissolved. Submerge the sliced onion in the pickling solution and let sit for at least 30 minutes. This can be done up to 3 weeks in advance and stored covered in the refrigerator.

PREPARE A HALF RECIPE of the Refried Black Beans in advance, or use up leftovers from earlier meals. These can also be made while the sweet potatoes roast.

JUST BEFORE SERVING, make a fresh batch of the Blistered Sweet Potato Rounds.

MAKE THE CHIPOTLE MAYO. Stir together all of the chipotle mayo ingredients, and set aside.

TO ASSEMBLE, lightly toast the bread. Shmear each slice of bread with about ¼ cup beans, 1 tablespoon chipotle mayo, 4 to 5 sweet potato rounds, ¼ cup arugula, ¼ of the avocado, 1 to 2 tablespoons of the pickled onions, the jalapeño slices, if desired, a squeeze of lime, ½ tablespoon cilantro, and a sprinkle of cotija. Serve immediately.

NOTES

Use leftover Refried Black Beans to make the Breakfast Tostada (page 70) or serve them alongside the Summer Veggie Fajitas (page 79). Use leftover Quick-Pickled Red Onions to top the falafels (page 135).

CHAPTER 5

Soups & Salads

I PREFER MY SOUPS hearty, with a chew, and topped with plenty of garnishes. I like my salads the same way, substantial and served family style as a meal. For those reasons, don't count this chapter out to fulfill your dinnertime needs. However, these recipes can also act as sides. My favorite thing about this chapter, though, is that these recipes will meet you in the depth of winter and under the blanket of summer's heat.

I love the way that food keeps time.

The base of this chili has a couple ribbons hanging next to its name and two surprising ingredients—cinnamon and chocolate. It yields a deep, warm familiar flavor. This meaty, vegetarian quinoa chili is nearly indistinguishable from its beef-laden counterparts and plenty substantial in the protein department. Of course, you can make this a meat chili by omitting the quinoa and water and adding 1 pound of browned ground beef. About canned tomatoes—I stock Muir Glen, as I find them far less acidic than other brands. If your tomatoes are too acidic, use a bit of sugar or honey to neutralize them.

Quinoa Chili `WEEKDAY`

HANDS-ON: **15 MIN.** TOTAL: **40 MIN.**
YIELDS: **8 SERVINGS**

CHILI

1 tablespoon olive oil

1½ cups diced sweet onion

2¼ teaspoons kosher salt, divided

4 cloves garlic, minced

1½ tablespoons chili powder

1 tablespoon cumin

1 tablespoon unsweetened cocoa powder

1½ teaspoons cinnamon

2 (28-ounce) cans crushed fire-roasted tomatoes

2 (15-ounce) cans kidney beans, drained and rinsed

2 (15-ounce) cans black beans, drained and rinsed

1½ cups water

¾ cup uncooked red quinoa, rinsed

Squeeze of honey (optional)

Squeeze of Sriracha (optional)

GARNISH

Grated cheddar or Monterey Jack cheese

Chopped fresh cilantro

Crumbled pita chips

Diced avocado

HEAT A DUTCH OVEN over medium. Once warm, add the oil to the pan. Add the onion and ¼ teaspoon of the salt to the pan. Sauté for 4 minutes until tender, stirring occasionally. Add the garlic, chili powder, cumin, cocoa powder, and cinnamon, and cook for 30 seconds more. Turn the heat to medium-low, and add the tomatoes, beans, and the remaining 2 teaspoons kosher salt. Stir to combine. Cook for about 10 minutes on a low simmer, stirring occasionally.

ADD IN THE WATER and quinoa and cook covered for 25 minutes more or until the quinoa is tender. You'll know it's ready when the white ring on the quinoa grain is visible. Taste and add more salt if necessary. To add heat, add Sriracha. To cut the acidity, add honey. Serve and garnish as desired.

NOTES

Different variations of quinoa will yield different cook times. Look for the visible white ring on the quinoa grain to detect doneness. For variations that take longer to cook, more water may also be necessary. For added sweetness, stir in sautéed corn from the Chipotle-Garlic Chopped Salad (page 165). If making in advance, omit adding the quinoa and water until just before serving. Reheat the soup and add the quinoa and water, cooking until tender.

INGREDIENT TIP

Toast your spices. When making a spice-heavy dish, like this one, it's best to toast them first to keep them from tasting dusty.

MINIMALIST TIP

Cook your grains
directly in the soup
you're making by
adding additional
liquid (water or broth)
to be absorbed by the
grain as it cooks.

This chicken noodle soup is unique in that it's slightly creamy and subtly sweet, which is what makes it so crave-worthy. It's the result of making the same recipe over so many winters, adding a little of this and deleting a little of that. It's now at a place where it belongs permanently in print, no more revisions (at least not from me). I hope you feel free to put your stamp on it. This recipe steals the cream and white wine from a chicken pot pie I make on very special occasions, while keeping the natural ease of chicken noodle soup. It's quick, creamy (but not too creamy) comfort food meant for the chilliest of nights. I only make this soup with the addition of sweet white wine, like Moscato or Riesling; it adds a robust roundness to the flavor. I hope it makes it into your final cut, too. Use leftover Dutch Oven Whole Chicken and stock (page 106) for a completely homemade version.

Creamy Chicken Noodle Soup

WEEKDAY

HANDS-ON: **20 MIN.** TOTAL: **30 MIN.**
YIELDS: **6 SERVINGS**

1 tablespoon olive oil	4 sprigs fresh thyme
2 cups thinly sliced carrots (about 4 medium carrots)	A couple cracks of pepper
1 cup diced sweet onion	2 cups short-grain pasta
1¼ teaspoons kosher salt, divided	1½ cups shredded Dutch Oven Whole Chicken (page 106) or rotisserie chicken
2 cloves garlic, minced	
2 quarts chicken stock	1 cup frozen peas
1 cup sweet white wine (like Moscato)	½ cup heavy cream

HEAT A DUTCH OVEN over medium. Once warm, add the oil to the pan. Toss in the prepared carrots, onion, and ½ teaspoon of the kosher salt. Sauté for 4 minutes or until tender, stirring occasionally. Add in the garlic and cook for 30 seconds more.

ADD THE STOCK, wine, and thyme. Season with the remaining ¾ teaspoon salt and pepper to taste. Turn the heat to high and bring to a boil.

ADD THE NOODLES to the boiling stock and cook according to the package instructions or until al dente.

IN THE LAST 4 MINUTES of cooking the pasta, stir in the chicken, peas, and cream. Taste and add more salt and pepper if necessary. Test the pasta for doneness. Remove the thyme stems and serve.

NOTES

If you're making this ahead of time and freezing, cook the vegetables and stock, stopping before adding the noodles. Once cooled, add the stock to a freezer-safe ziplock bag and store flat in the freezer for easy stacking. To reheat, thaw, bring to a boil, and pick the recipe back up with adding the noodles to a pot of boiling soup.

At our house, we like our soups with a bit of textural variety. There's something so satisfying about chewing through a mealtime, which is the same reason I can't drink a smoothie alone for breakfast. The base of this soup is a creamy, nutty broth. It's brilliant on its own, but, because of the aforementioned, I prefer it with everything else—cooked rice, crunchy raw vegetables, and herby garnishes. Though we eat this throughout the winter, the vegetables aren't necessarily in season. However, some produce tastes like itself year-round, especially the ones used in this recipe. Feel free to substitute in frozen peas or edamame. During the warmer months, switch over to the Soba Bowls with Peanut Sauce (page 91) for a similar flavor experience.

Thai-Spiced Rice Bowls

`MAKE AHEAD`   `WEEKDAY`

HANDS-ON: **25 MIN.**   TOTAL: **25 MIN.**
YIELDS: **6 SERVINGS**

RICE
1½ cups uncooked rice
1½ tablespoons salted butter
½ teaspoon kosher salt

BROTH
1 teaspoon olive oil
4 cloves garlic, minced
Thumbtip of peeled fresh ginger, minced
1 quart chicken stock
1 (14-ounce) can light coconut milk
¼ cup soy sauce
¼ cup natural creamy peanut butter
1 tablespoon Thai curry paste
Generous squeeze of honey

GARNISH
1 cup matchstick-cut carrots
1 red bell pepper, thinly sliced
½ English cucumber, halved lengthwise and thinly sliced (optional)
¼ cup chopped fresh cilantro
¼ cup chopped dry-roasted peanuts
2 tablespoons chopped fresh mint (optional)
2 green onions, sliced
1 jalapeño, thinly sliced
1 lime, cut into wedges

MAKE THE RICE. In a small saucepan, make the rice according to the package instructions, adding the butter and salt.

MAKE THE BROTH. Heat a medium saucepan over medium. Once warm, add the oil. Add in the garlic and ginger. Cook for 30 seconds, stirring constantly. Add the remaining broth ingredients. Bring to a boil, reduce the heat, and simmer for 10 minutes to develop the flavor.

MEANWHILE, PREPARE THE GARNISHES. To serve, divide the rice evenly among 6 serving bowls. Top each serving evenly with the broth. Garnish as desired.

NOTES

To add chicken, cut 1 pound of chicken into ½-inch chunks (breasts or thighs will work) and cook in the broth for the last 5 to 10 minutes until the internal temperature of the chicken reaches 165°F. Or, use leftover chicken from the Dutch Oven Whole Chicken (page 106) or rotisserie chicken.

INGREDIENT TIP

I prefer English cucumbers, as they are typically seedless and more flavorful. Slice and serve as is. No need to carve out the pesky seeds.

Sweet potatoes can turn
from perfect to mush
very quickly. Check for
fork tenderness as they
cook. For this reason, if
you're making the soup
in advance, add the
sweet potatoes during
the reheating phase.

I like to find ways to brighten up the flavor of winter. Adding a chipotle pepper to soup, or anything for that matter, will instantly boost the profile. This recipe is based off a traditional chicken tortilla soup sans the chicken. With almost every ingredient sitting in the pantry, this soup comes together so fast for the weeknight. If you're pressed for time, add crushed tortilla chips instead of making the strips, but whatever you do, don't skip the squeeze of lime just before serving. It's just the touch of brightness winter (and this soup) needs.

Chipotle Tortilla Soup WEEKDAY

HANDS-ON: **25 MIN.**   TOTAL: **25 MIN.**
YIELDS: **4 SERVINGS**

SOUP

2 teaspoons olive oil

1 cup finely chopped sweet onion

1 cup frozen corn

½ teaspoon kosher salt, divided

2 cloves garlic, minced

1½ tablespoons pureed chipotle peppers in adobo

1 tablespoon tomato paste

½ teaspoon ground cumin

1 quart chicken stock

1 (15-ounce) can black beans, drained and rinsed

1 teaspoon honey

1½ cups ½-inch cubed sweet potato

TORTILLA STRIPS

1 tablespoon olive oil

4 (6-inch) corn tortillas, cut into ¾-inch-thick strips

Kosher salt to taste

GARNISH

1 avocado, diced

1 lime, cut into wedges

¼ cup chopped fresh cilantro

Sprinkle of cotija

MAKE THE SOUP. Heat a large saucepan over medium-high. Once warm, add the oil, onion, and corn. Stir in ¼ teaspoon of the salt. Sauté for 4 minutes until lightly browned, stirring occasionally. Add in the garlic and toast for 30 seconds more. Stir in the chipotles, tomato paste, cumin, and remaining ¼ teaspoon salt. Cook for about 1 minute to toast. Pour in the stock, beans, and honey. Bring to a simmer for 5 minutes. Add the prepared sweet potatoes and cook for 6 to 9 minutes or until the sweet potatoes are just tender. Taste and adjust the salt and honey as necessary.

PREPARE THE TORTILLA STRIPS. Meanwhile, heat a 10-inch cast-iron skillet over medium-high. Once warm, add the oil. Toss in the tortilla strips, and cook for about 10 minutes or until golden and crisp. Sprinkle with the salt to taste.

MEANWHILE, PREPARE THE GARNISHES. To serve, divide the soup evenly among 4 serving bowls. Top each serving with a handful of tortilla strips, diced avocado, a lime wedge, and a sprinkle of cilantro and cotija.

NOTES

To turn this into chicken tortilla soup, add 1½ cups of prepared Dutch Oven Whole Chicken (page 106) or pulled rotisserie chicken at the same time as the sweet potatoes. Add more salt if needed.

INGREDIENT TIP

On its own, kale is nutrient-dense and bitter. I believe a little bit of bitter is a good thing. To help cut the bitterness to the point of palatable, use a mixture of vinegar and honey to neutralize it.

Your version of this salad might include crumbled ramen in place of the kale. This version is a bit more nutrient-dense but every bit as delicious. The dressing does a salty-sweet tango between the citrus, honey, and soy sauce. If you can handle it, don't skip the heat from the jalapeños. You'll notice throughout the book that the heat is usually optional. One of us thinks it is (Kev) and one of us thinks it's not (me). He wins this time. If you stock curly ramen noodles, toss them in for added crunch. Note: Kale, like me, does best with a little rest.

Asian Kale Salad

MAKE AHEAD   WEEKEND

HANDS-ON: **30 MIN.**   TOTAL: **1 HR. 30 MIN.**
YIELDS: **4 DINNER SALADS, 8 SIDE SALADS**

DRESSING

3 tablespoons soy sauce

2 tablespoons rice vinegar

1 tablespoon honey

1 teaspoon orange zest

½ teaspoon sesame oil

3 tablespoons neutral oil

SALAD

8 ounces kale, rinsed, stemmed, and chopped

1 cup thinly sliced red cabbage

2 medium carrots, peeled and shredded

1 large orange, segmented

1 cup frozen shelled edamame, rinsed under hot water to thaw

½ jalapeño, seeded and finely chopped (optional)

GARNISH

½ cup lightly chopped salted peanuts or cashews

¼ cup chopped fresh cilantro

2 green onions, thinly sliced on the diagonal

MAKE THE DRESSING. In a large salad bowl, add all the dressing ingredients except the oils. Pour the oils in a slow steady stream, whisking until emulsified (until the oils and vinegar become one).

AT LEAST AN HOUR BEFORE SERVING, assemble the salad. Prepare the salad ingredients and add all of them to the bowl and toss. Let sit, tossing occasionally until slightly wilted, about 1 hour or up to 8 hours. Top with the garnishes just before serving.

NOTES

For a heartier meal, add Maple-Soaked Salmon (page 102), pulled Dutch Oven Whole Chicken (page 106), or store-bought rotisserie chicken into the salad, or serve as a side.

157

If you've never had a bánh mì, it is a Vietnamese sandwich, typically made with salty-sweet marinated pork. It's tangy, too, from the pickled radishes and carrots, and spicy from the jalapeños. It's all of my favorite flavors housed between a crusty baguette. I've turned this classic sandwich into a lighter, plant-forward salad, fusing in a Tex-Mex avocado crema as the dressing. The honey–soy sauce roasted chickpeas, used in place of the pork, are good on their own as a snack. This salad takes a bit of work when done in a single breadth, but most of it can be made ahead, like the Quick-Pickled Radishes and Carrots, the croutons, and even the Avocado Crema. When prepped in advance, dinner takes no time at all to throw together and tastes this good.

Roasted Chickpea Bánh Mì Salad `MAKE AHEAD` `WEEKEND`

HANDS-ON: **45 MIN.**   TOTAL: **45 MIN.**
YIELDS: **4 DINNER SALADS**

ROASTED CHICKPEAS

2 (15-ounce) cans chickpeas

4 tablespoons soy sauce

3 tablespoons neutral oil

1 tablespoon honey

1 tablespoon lime juice

1 tablespoon rice vinegar

1 clove garlic

Half thumbtip of peeled fresh ginger

QUICK-PICKLED RADISHES AND CARROTS (PAGE 88)

CROUTONS

4 cups ½-inch cubed crusty bakery bread (like a baguette)

Scant ¼ cup olive oil

Pinch of kosher salt

AVOCADO CREMA

½ ripe avocado

2 tablespoons plain whole-milk yogurt

4 to 6 tablespoons water

2 tablespoons lime juice

½ teaspoon kosher salt

TOPPINGS

1 (5-ounce) box mixed greens

½ cup thinly sliced English cucumber

¼ cup roughly chopped fresh cilantro

2 green onions, sliced

1 jalapeño, thinly sliced

PREPARE THE CHICKPEAS. Preheat the oven to 425°F and line a baking sheet with parchment paper. Drain, rinse, and dry the chickpeas and place on the prepared baking sheet. Add all the remaining chickpea ingredients into a high-powered blender or food processor. Blend until smooth. Pour the glaze on the chickpeas, tossing to evenly coat. Roast for 30 minutes or until lightly charred, stirring halfway through.

MAKE QUICK-PICKLED RADISHES AND CARROTS. Follow the instructions on page 88. This can be done up to 3 weeks in advance.

MAKE THE CROUTONS. Heat a 10-inch cast-iron skillet or griddle over medium-high. Once hot, add the cubed bread. Toss with the oil and salt. Cook for about 5 minutes or until toasted with a slight chew remaining in the center. Remove from the heat. This can be done up to 1 week in advance and stored covered at room temperature.

MAKE THE CREMA. In a high-powered blender or food processor, add all the crema ingredients; cover and blend until smooth. Add additional water as needed, 1 tablespoon at a time, to reach a sauce/dressing consistency. This can be made up to 1 week in advance.

PREPARE THE TOPPINGS. To assemble the salad, divide the greens evenly among 4 plates. Top with quick-pickled radishes and carrots, roasted chickpeas, croutons, crema, and the desired toppings. For a zippier flavor, add a tiny spoonful of the pickle juice onto the salad.

NOTES

Turn this recipe into walking tacos by trading out the croutons for crushed sweet potato tortilla chips. Walking tacos are just as they sound, tacos that walk with you. They are often served in a small bag of crushed tortilla chips with all the usual toppings. These are fun to serve at parties. Create a walking taco bar for individual assembly. Serve with about 2 cups of finely chopped greens.

MINIMALIST TIP

Several of the recipes throughout the book call for quick-pickled vegetables. Since they last a couple weeks in the fridge, make a double batch and use for other recipes. Also, don't be afraid to swap out vegetables to use up leftovers you already have on hand.

We serve side salads with so many meals, especially when serving pasta. I used to be against side salads during the week because of the extra work and chopping. This house salad is silly simple and requires very little work, making it weeknight friendly. To save on dishes, I like to make the dressing directly in the salad bowl and toss in the greens just before serving. Salad doesn't keep well, so make just enough. This Balsamic Vinaigrette, though, keeps well at room temperature. Double or triple the recipe and store covered at room temperature for up to two months. Shake to re-emulsify before using.

House Side Salad WEEKDAY

HANDS-ON: **8 MIN.** TOTAL: **8 MIN.**
YIELDS: **6 SIDE SALADS**

BALSAMIC VINAIGRETTE
2 tablespoons balsamic
  vinegar
1 teaspoon Dijon mustard
Pinch of kosher salt
A couple cracks of pepper
¼ cup olive oil

SALAD
1 (5-ounce) box spring mix
  or arugula
2 green onions, sliced
¼ cup salted sunflower
  seeds
¼ cup crumbled feta

TOPPINGS (OPTIONAL)
Dried tart cherries
Matchstick apples or pears

MAKE THE VINAIGRETTE. In a large salad bowl, add all the vinaigrette ingredients except the oil. Pour the oil in a slow steady stream, whisking until emulsified (until the oil and vinegar become one). This yields ⅓ cup.

JUST BEFORE SERVING, add all of the salad ingredients and, if desired, the toppings to the bowl. Toss and serve.

MINIMALIST TIP
Use kitchen shears to cut the green onions for a chop-free salad.

This is our house summer salad. I shared it on my site a couple years ago and have heard from so many that it's become their house summer salad, too. It's tangy and creamy and familiar. It accompanies nearly every pizza and pasta night throughout the season. In fact, we love it so much, we eat it early into fall and at least once during winter, when we're craving the bright, crisp flavors of summer. I hope this recipe makes it into your house, too. Make the dressing and store it in the fridge. Use the salad ingredient list as a guide to assemble a large salad bowl or a single serving— whatever the day calls for.

Italian Summer Salad

MAKE AHEAD   WEEKDAY

HANDS-ON: **10 MIN.**   TOTAL: **10 MIN.**
YIELDS: **20 SALADS (¾ CUP DRESSING)**

ITALIAN VINAIGRETTE
**2 tablespoons grated
  Parmesan**
½ cup olive oil
¼ cup red wine vinegar
¾ teaspoon kosher salt
1 clove garlic, smashed
Generous squeeze of honey
A couple cracks of pepper

SALAD
Greens of your choice
English cucumber, chopped
Cherry tomatoes, halved
Green onions, thinly sliced
Pepperoncinis
Sunflower seeds
Crumbled feta

MAKE THE VINAIGRETTE. In a high-powered blender or food processor, add all the vinaigrette ingredients. Cover and blend until creamy, 15 to 30 seconds. This yields ¾ cup. Store in an airtight container for up to 3 weeks in the fridge. Shake well before serving, as the dressing will separate and sometimes congeal.

PREPARE THE SALAD. Use your discretion on how big or small to make the salad. Add all of the salad ingredients to a bowl. Just before serving, toss the salad with just enough dressing. Serve additional dressing on the table for use as needed.

NOTES

It's not uncommon for homemade dressings to solidify in the fridge. There are no synthetic emulsifying agents to keep this from happening. So when it does, run the closed container under hot water and shake well to reconstitute.

MINIMALIST TIP

To keep cleanup minimal, use a ¼-cup measuring utensil to measure the Parmesan, oil, and vinegar. Start by measuring the dry ingredient first (Parmesan), filling halfway full. There are 4 tablespoons in ¼ cup.

This recipe pays homage to my growing up years in Texas, when the only ethnic food I was truly familiar with was Tex-Mex (which was Texans adding cumin to traditional Mexican recipes). It's still my absolute favorite fusion of flavors and where much of my palate began forming. I go out for Tex-Mex every meal when I travel home to Texas. I can't get enough. While this salad is fit for dinner, I make several of the components at the start of the week and eat on the salad for lunch throughout the week, sometimes adding sautéed peppers and onions in place of the corn.

Chipotle-Garlic Chopped Salad

HANDS-ON: **25 MIN.**   TOTAL: **25 MIN.**
YIELDS: **4 DINNER SALADS**

CHIPOTLE-GARLIC DRESSING

- ½ cup olive oil
- 2 tablespoons pureed chipotles in adobo
- 1 tablespoon ketchup
- 1 tablespoon white wine vinegar
- 1 tablespoon high-quality mayonnaise
- 2 cloves garlic, smashed
- ½ teaspoon kosher salt
- Squeeze of honey (optional)

SAUTÉED CORN

- 2 teaspoons olive oil
- 1½ cups frozen or fresh corn
- ¼ teaspoon kosher salt

SALAD

- 1½ pounds romaine, thinly sliced
- 20 sweet potato tortilla chips
- ½ cup shredded Monterey Jack cheese
- 1 (15-ounce) can black beans, drained and rinsed
- ½ cup sliced grape tomatoes
- 1 avocado, diced
- 3 radishes, thinly sliced
- ¼ cup chopped fresh cilantro

PREPARE THE DRESSING. In a high-powered blender or food processor, add all of the dressing ingredients; cover and blend on high until smooth, about 30 seconds. This yields 1 cup. Store covered in the fridge for up to a month. The dressing will separate and harden in the fridge. Run under warm water and shake to re-emulsify.

SAUTÉ THE CORN. Heat a small skillet over medium-high. Once warm, add the oil and the corn. Cook for 5 minutes, stirring often. Add the salt and continuing cooking for 5 minutes more or until charred, stirring often.

PREPARE THE SALAD INGREDIENTS. Divide them evenly among 4 serving plates or serve family style in a large shallow bowl. Add the corn, tossing to combine. Shake the dressing just before serving and distribute evenly among the salads.

NOTES

For a meat option, add 3 slices of chopped crispy bacon or marinated chicken from the Chicken Gyros with Tzatziki (page 136).

INGREDIENT TIP

We buy avocados in bulk for the price break. I ripen them on the counter and refrigerate them once they start to feel like softened butter. They'll last for a couple weeks in the fridge this way, and I'm never without an avocado when I need one.

MINIMALIST TIP

Sautéing corn to the point of charring always makes for a messy pan. Immediately after cooking, remove the corn to a serving bowl. Place the pan back on the stove and pour in hot tap water. The water will steam the residue left on the pan and make cleanup much easier.

On every summer potluck table or picnic blanket sits a bowl of potato salad. You probably know by now, I'm not afraid of using a little mayonnaise in my recipes. After all, good mayo is made from eggs and oil, which I eat in plenty. And yet, I still like to dilute the mayo with a bit of yogurt. This potato salad is bright in color, flavor, and texture. Find multicolored fingerling potatoes if you can. Purple potatoes are always the best surprise. I'm not a huge fan of celery, so I've replaced that crunch with another crunch, red bell peppers. I'm placing this side dish in the weekend category purely because it tastes like a summer weekend. Have you ever had it on a Tuesday night? If so, change the headnote.

Bright Potato Salad WEEKEND

HANDS-ON: **35 MIN.**   TOTAL: **35 MIN.**
YIELDS: **6 SERVINGS AS A SIDE**

STEAMED EGGS
4 large eggs

SALAD
2 pounds multicolored fingerling potatoes, unpeeled and cut into bite-sized pieces
Kosher salt for salting water
1 cup chopped red bell pepper (about 1 medium)
2 tablespoons finely chopped fresh dill
2 tablespoons finely chopped fresh curly parsley
2 green onions, sliced

DRESSING
¼ cup high-quality mayonnaise
¼ cup plain whole-milk yogurt
1 tablespoon Dijon mustard
1 tablespoon apple cider vinegar
1½ teaspoons kosher salt
2 cloves garlic, minced
A couple cracks of pepper

STEAM THE EGGS. In a saucepan fitted with a steamer basket, add water to just below the bottom of the basket. Bring to a boil for at least 1 minute before adding the eggs in a single layer. Cover and steam for 12 to 14 minutes. Turn off the heat and place the eggs in a bowl of ice water for 5 minutes to quickly chill. Peel and dice. (When steaming eggs for the first time, test an egg at the 12-minute mark for doneness. Make a note about the perfect cook time for your stove. Note: When cooking more than 4, add 1 to 2 minutes to the cook time.) Eggs can be steamed and left in the peel a couple days in advance.

MAKE THE SALAD. Prepare the potatoes. Place the potato pieces in a large sauté pan, and barely cover with water. Salt liberally. Bring to a boil over high. Cover and reduce heat to medium-low to maintain a simmer. Cook for 7 to 9 minutes or until the potatoes are fork tender and still hold their shape. Drain and rinse with cold water. Prepare the rest of the salad ingredients.

MAKE THE DRESSING. Stir together all of the dressing ingredients in a serving bowl. Add the potatoes, eggs, and the remaining salad ingredients to the bowl. Gently fold to combine. Taste and adjust the salt and pepper as necessary. Serve immediately or store covered in the fridge for up to a day.

NOTES

For a pretty presentation, reserve a pinch of all the greens and a couple slices of egg to add as a bright garnish.

MINIMALIST TIP

Steamed eggs are so much easier to peel than boiled eggs. The shell comes right off. Give this method a try.

INGREDIENT TIP

To extend the life of fresh dill, store it in a produce bag from the store, adding a paper towel to catch moisture buildup. Change out the paper towel once damp. Store in the crisper drawer. This method also works for fresh cilantro and curly parsley.

I call this a remix because it's a combination of two of my favorite recipes—Lucy's and Cari's. It was our neighbor Lucy's chicken salad that turned me back onto the use of mayonnaise in chicken salad, and the kitchen in general. I started by making my own, which is just a raw egg, lemon, salt, and oil. These days I buy high-quality mayonnaise from the store (because I'll forever be afraid of making someone ill with my food). Lucy also gets ownership of the dill and garlic—two pivotal flavor-makers in this salad. Don't skip them. The soy sauce addition comes from my mom's friend Cari who made a head-turning chicken salad at my wedding shower. Soy sauce is perfect for thinning out mayo to a lighter dressing consistency, while also carrying the weight of the salt in this recipe.

Chicken Salad Remix

`MAKE AHEAD` `WEEKEND`

HANDS-ON: **10 MIN.** TOTAL: **10 MIN.** YIELDS: **3½ CUPS**

DRESSING

¼ cup high-quality
  mayonnaise

1½ tablespoons soy sauce

1 tablespoon chopped fresh
  dill

2 cloves garlic, minced

A couple cracks of pepper

SALAD

2½ cups pulled Dutch Oven
  Whole Chicken (page
  106) or rotisserie chicken

1 cup halved seedless red
  grapes or ½ cup dried
  tart cherries

¼ cup roughly chopped
  pecans

MAKE THE DRESSING. In a serving bowl, whisk together all the dressing ingredients.

MAKE THE SALAD. Add all of the prepared salad ingredients to the serving bowl, and toss until evenly coated. Taste and adjust the seasonings as necessary.

STORE COVERED IN THE FRIDGE for up to 5 days. Serve over a bed of spinach, on a sandwich, or with pita chips or crackers.

NOTES

Do you have extra dill? Make the Bright Potato Salad (page 166) or Chicken Gyros with Tzatziki (page 136). Add in 2 steamed eggs (page 166) to the chicken salad, if desired.

There's something so elegant yet humble about serving a meal family style—out of the same bowl, from the same tongs. Being a mom, I also like the idea of having no excuse to get up from the dinner table. Maybe I'm dreaming. This recipe is meant to be served as a meal, but don't count it out as a side. The lightened-up Caesar dressing comes from a combination of mayonnaise and yogurt, a common trick I use. I've nixed the anchovies and used olives and Worcestershire sauce from the pantry to carry the saltiness throughout. My mom promised me when I was younger that I'd crave bread over dessert as an adult. She was right. The croutons in this salad are just an excuse to eat bread with dinner. But I'd also like to think this is the perfect light dinner to precede dessert. To more family-style salads and dessert!

Family-Style Chicken Caesar Salad `MAKE AHEAD` `WEEKDAY`

HANDS-ON: **35 MIN.**   TOTAL: **35 MIN.**
YIELDS: **4 DINNER SALADS**

DRESSING
¼ cup grated Parmesan

2 tablespoons high-quality mayonnaise

2 tablespoons plain whole-milk yogurt

2 tablespoons lemon juice or white wine vinegar

1 tablespoon olive oil

2 teaspoons Dijon mustard

2 teaspoons Worcestershire sauce

2 green olives, pitted

1 large clove garlic, smashed

A couple cracks of pepper

CROUTONS
4 cups crusty bakery bread (like a baguette), pulled or cut into ½-inch cubes

¼ cup olive oil

½ teaspoon lemon pepper

Pinch of kosher salt

CHICKEN
¾ pound skinless, boneless chicken breast

½ teaspoon kosher salt

A couple cracks of pepper

Neutral oil cooking spray (optional)

SALAD
1½ pounds thinly sliced romaine lettuce

Scant ½ cup shredded Parmesan

MAKE THE DRESSING. In a high-powered blender or food processor, add all of the dressing ingredients; cover and blend until smooth. This can be made 2 weeks in advance and stored in the fridge.

MAKE THE CROUTONS. Heat a 10-inch cast-iron skillet or griddle over medium-high. Once hot, add the cubed bread. Toss with the oil, lemon pepper, and salt. Cook for about 5 minutes or until toasted with a slight chew in the center. Remove from the heat. This can be done up to 1 week in advance and stored covered at room temperature.

COOK THE CHICKEN. Place the chicken in a freezer-safe ziplock bag. Seal the bag, removing as much air as possible, and pound to about ⅜-inch thick. Add the salt and pepper to a small ramekin or bowl. Sprinkle the top of the chicken with half of the salt and cracked pepper. Spray the pan with the cooking spray if needed. Add the chicken, salt side down. Cook for 3 minutes. Sprinkle the other side with the remaining salt and pepper. Flip and cook for 3 minutes more or until the chicken reaches 165°F. Remove from the pan and slice into strips or cubes.

ASSEMBLE THE SALAD. In a large bowl, add the lettuce and about three-fourths of the dressing. Toss to evenly coat. The lettuce should be lightly coated. Taste and add more dressing if necessary. Set the remaining dressing out on the table for serving. Top with the croutons, chicken, and Parmesan. Serve immediately.

INGREDIENT TIP

If your romaine is looking limp, chop it and place in a bowl (or in a salad spinner) of ice-cold water for 10 minutes. Rinse and dry. It should be crispy!

MINIMALIST TIP

Use up leftover bakery
bread to make croutons.
It's impossible not to eat
salads when homemade
croutons are around.

MINIMALIST TIP

To make the dressing, use a tablespoon for all measurements, filling only one-third full for the maple syrup measurement. (Remember this: There are 3 teaspoons in a tablespoon and 4 tablespoons in ¼ cup.)

Transitioning from summer to fall cooking is always a bit rough for me. It's a different way of cooking and thinking. Hearty, root vegetables require a decent roast or steam before eating. I love the depth of flavor that develops over a long(er) cook time under the care of savory herbs. In fact, I crave it. But even still, it's an adjustment from the ease of summer foods that can be consumed half raw. Whether you're just transitioning into the colder months or deeply immersed under a pile of snow, remember this season, too, has its perks. Namely, that month-old sweet potato on the counter that's hardly aged. I think I'll stay in tonight and make this salad.

Roasted Autumn Sweet Potato Salad WEEKDAY

HANDS-ON: **15 MIN.** TOTAL: **40 MIN.**
YIELDS: **6 SIDE SALADS**

ROASTED VEGETABLES

2 cups ½-inch cubed sweet potato

2 cups ½-inch cubed red onion

3 tablespoons olive oil

4 sprigs of fresh thyme

2 sprigs of fresh sage

1 teaspoon kosher salt

A couple cracks of pepper

CRUSHED CROUTONS

1 tablespoon salted butter

½ cup panko

DRESSING

1½ tablespoons white wine vinegar

1 tablespoon Dijon mustard

1 teaspoon pure maple syrup

Pinch of kosher salt

A couple cracks of pepper

3 tablespoons olive oil

GREENS

1 (5-ounce) box arugula or spinach

½ cup pepitas

¼ cup dried cranberries or tart cherries

¼ cup goat cheese or crumbled feta

Fresh thyme leaves (optional)

PREPARE THE ROASTED VEGETABLES. Preheat the oven to 450°F. Line a baking sheet with parchment paper. Place the prepared potatoes and onion on the baking sheet. Add all the remaining roasted vegetable ingredients to the pan; toss to coat. Bake for 25 to 30 minutes or until lightly charred, stirring halfway through.

MAKE THE CRUSHED CROUTONS. In a 10-inch cast-iron skillet, melt the butter over medium. Add the panko and toast until golden, about 3 minutes. Set aside.

MAKE THE DRESSING. In a serving bowl, whisk together all of the dressing ingredients until emulsified (until the oil and vinegar become one). This can be made 3 weeks in advance and stored at room temperature.

ASSEMBLE THE SALAD. Add all the greens ingredients into the salad bowl along with the roasted vegetables (including the crispy herbs) and crushed croutons. Toss to combine. Serve immediately.

NOTES

Swap out the sweet potato for delicata squash.

Pre-Christmas, winter needs no extra cheer. From the fresh garlands drooping across the porches and down the streetlights, to the smell of pine, to the calendars brimming over, the start of winter is so cheery on its own. But by January 2, it's full on hygge-mode over here—candles flickering, fires lit, extra cups of coffee consumed, and a whole lot of citrus filling the drawers of the fridge and the bowls on the counter. (*Hygge* is the Danish word loosely translated to mean cozy.) Citrus season hits in the dead of winter, and, in Minnesota, there's no brighter gift. This Creamy Citrus Salad finds us on the coldest of nights. If you're not already leaning on citrus in the kitchen, try it. Steal the panko "crushed croutons" from the Roasted Autumn Sweet Potato Salad (page 173) for added crunch.

Creamy Citrus Salad

MAKE AHEAD   WEEKDAY

HANDS-ON: **15 MIN.**   TOTAL: **15 MIN.**
YIELDS: **6 SIDE SALADS**

CITRUS
2 large oranges, any
  variety

DRESSING
2 tablespoons fresh orange
  juice
1 tablespoon white wine
  vinegar
1 tablespoon plain whole-
  milk yogurt
1 teaspoon Dijon mustard
⅛ teaspoon kosher salt

Squeeze of honey
A couple cracks of pepper
¼ cup extra-virgin olive oil

SALAD
1 (5-ounce) box arugula or
  mixed greens
½ cup thinly sliced red
  onion
1 (3-ounce) goat cheese
  log, crumbled, or
  crumbled feta

PREPARE THE CITRUS. Peel the oranges using a sharp paring knife. Begin by cutting off the navel (or base) of the oranges to give yourself a flat edge. Place the flat edges to the cutting board and cut away the peel and the bitter white pith. Segment the oranges by cutting in between the white membranes.

MAKE THE DRESSING. In a small bowl, add all of the dressing ingredients except the oil. Pour the oil in a slow steady stream, whisking until emulsified (until the oil and vinegar become one). This can be made 2 weeks in advance and stored in the fridge.

MAKE THE SALAD. Just before serving, toss together the arugula, onion, and half of the dressing in a large bowl. Top with the prepared citrus, and sprinkle with the cheese. Serve the remaining dressing on the side.

INGREDIENT TIP

When cutting rounded produce (like oranges or potatoes), always cut a flat edge to give yourself a stable cutting surface.

CHAPTER 6

Sides

GROWING UP, our plate was mostly full of sides that I'd eat one at a time, slowly spinning my plate to get to each one. As you've probably noticed, most of the recipes in the book aren't composed that way. All the ingredients end up in the same bowl by the end. But there's always a place for sides—next to a burger or a fillet of fish. Use this chapter as you would a necklace or scarf—as an accessory to your meal.

When cooking sturdy vegetables, I like to think of myself as a manager—how can I bring out the best in them. For too many years, I was bringing out the worst in them—shoving them straight into the oven to burn before the insides softened. They were tough and too chewy. On a whim, I tried steaming them to soften, and then finished them under the hot flame of the oven to caramelize. It brought out their full potential. This recipe is so simple, but it's a good lesson that vegetables are wonderful on their own when well managed. Like these carrots. When you start with good ones, this process draws out the natural sugars, leaving them sweet and caramelly by the end. People always ask me—what did you do to those carrots? Well, now my secret is out—not much.

Caramelized Roasted Carrots WEEKDAY

HANDS-ON: **10 MIN.** TOTAL: **40 MIN.**
YIELDS: **6 SERVINGS**

6 large carrots, peeled, cut into 4-inch sticks, and halved lengthwise	1 tablespoon olive oil
	½ teaspoon kosher salt

PREHEAT THE OVEN to 450°F. Line a baking sheet with parchment paper and set aside.

IN A SAUCEPAN fitted with a steamer basket, add water to just below the bottom of the basket. Bring to a boil. Add the carrots, reduce the heat to medium, and cover to steam for 5 minutes. This will begin the cooking process. Remove the carrots, and place on the prepared baking sheet. Drizzle with the olive oil and sprinkle with the salt. Roast for 15 minutes. Stir and roast for 10 to 15 minutes more or until they begin to char. Taste and sprinkle with additional salt as needed. Serve.

NOTES

Produce varies so much in size. Calling it small or large is a bit obscure, but it's a measurement I've chosen to include in the book for ease. I don't cook with a scale and rarely use one at the grocery store. Like most, I cook with my eyes. Well-trained eyes can work as a mighty efficient scale. That aside, add more salt if the carrots need it or more oil if they are drying out. Your eyes and your gut are two essential tools in the kitchen.

INGREDIENT TIP

Buy organic whole carrots
if you can. The flavor
and texture of the carrot
is incomparable to baby
carrots, a carrot I've never
been a fan of. If you like to
snack on carrots throughout
the week, cut them into strips
and store in water to keep
them from drying out.

With its neutral profile and tree-like branches, cauliflower will hold on to just about any flavor. I cook it the same way I cook Caramelized Roasted Carrots (page 178)—a quick steam followed by a roast. It shortens the overall cook time and yields my ideal texture—tender (not mushy) on the inside and charred on the outside. The curry powder creates a beautiful golden color. We devour these straight off the pan, serve the rest as a side, or as a topper on the Chickpea Tikka Masala bowls (page 84).

Curry Cauliflower WEEKDAY

HANDS-ON: **10 MIN.** TOTAL: **40 MIN.**
YIELDS: **6 SERVINGS**

1 large or 2 small cauliflower heads, cut into small florets (about 5 cups)

2 tablespoons olive oil

2 teaspoons curry powder

½ teaspoon kosher salt

½ teaspoon harissa

⅛ teaspoon ground cumin

PREHEAT THE OVEN to 450°F. Line a baking sheet with parchment paper and set aside.

IN A SAUCEPAN fitted with a steamer basket, add water to just below the bottom of the basket. Bring to a boil. Add the cauliflower, reduce the heat to medium, and cover to steam for 5 minutes. This will begin the cooking process. Remove the cauliflower, and place on the prepared baking sheet. In a small ramekin, stir together all of the remaining ingredients. Drizzle over the cauliflower and toss to evenly coat. Bake for 15 minutes. Stir and bake for 10 to 15 minutes more or until the cauliflower begins to char. Taste and sprinkle with additional salt as needed. Serve.

In college, I gained my Freshman 15 (on my very small frame) after a "career"-ending soccer injury to my knee. Around that same time, I started cooking for myself and landed upon a low-calorie recipe series *The New York Times* had just launched. That's where I stumbled upon this general recipe. Since then, I've never made green beans any other way, outside the annual homemade green bean casserole at Thanksgiving. You can get that casserole recipe with homemade cream of mushroom on my site. It's epic. But we're talking about lighter, everyday things right now, like these lemony green beans laced with honey. And since they come together in 15 minutes, you'll want to try these, too.

Lemony Green Beans WEEKDAY

HANDS-ON: **5 MIN.** TOTAL: **15 MIN.**
YIELDS: **6 SERVINGS**

Kosher salt for salting water

1 pound French green beans (haricots verts), ends snipped

1 tablespoon olive oil

1 tablespoon lemon juice

2 teaspoons honey

1 teaspoon kosher salt

2 tablespoons sliced almonds

2 tablespoons grated or shaved Parmesan

FILL A LARGE SAUCEPAN two-thirds full with water; bring to a boil. Salt the water liberally and add the green beans. Cook for 4 minutes. Drain. Into the same pan, add the cooked beans, oil, lemon juice, honey, and salt. Cook over medium-high for 3 to 4 minutes. Taste and adjust the salt if necessary. Top with the almonds and Parmesan.

NOTES

A note on the green beans: I exclusively buy the French kind (haricots verts) for their long skinny stature, supple crunch when put under fire, and lack of stringiness. Because of this, they take little to no time to prepare. Gone are the long afternoons spent stringing green beans.

INGREDIENT TIP

For easy honey release, lightly spray your measuring utensil with a bit of neutral oil before measuring. The honey will slip right out.

If I haven't convinced you yet that a high-powered blender is the best investment for your kitchen, I think this recipe might do it. Of course, a food processor would work just as well, but you can't make a smoothie in a food processor. Add all of the ingredients into the blender and watch them whirl into a creamy hummus. There's no need to remove the skins from each chickpea when using this workhorse of a machine. A note about canned chickpeas: Some varieties are drier than others. If working with drier beans, add a bit of water to achieve a creamy consistency. We like to serve this hummus as a side with pita chips or vegetables cut into sticks. It also makes for the best shmear on the Red Pepper Wraps (page 128).

Roasted Red Pepper Hummus

`MAKE AHEAD` `WEEKEND`

HANDS-ON: **20 MIN.** TOTAL: **20 MIN.** YIELDS: **2½ CUPS**

ROASTED RED PEPPER
1 medium-sized red bell pepper

QUICK-ROASTED GARLIC
1 large clove garlic, skin intact
2 tablespoons water

HUMMUS
1 (15-ounce) can chickpeas, drained and rinsed
¼ cup tahini

¼ cup lemon juice
2 teaspoons chipotle peppers in adobo
1 heaping teaspoon kosher salt
Pinch of cayenne pepper

TOPPINGS (OPTIONAL)
Olive oil
Sprinkle of herbs (like dried oregano or cilantro)
Sprinkle of red pepper flakes

PREPARE THE RED PEPPER. Set the pepper directly on the burner over a gas flame on medium heat. Toast until blackened on all sides, rotating with tongs, about 10 minutes. Once completely charred, remove from the heat, and cover with foil to steam for 10 minutes. Remove the charred skin, stem, and internal seeds. If you have an electric stovetop, preheat the oven to broil, place the pepper on a baking sheet, and broil for 5 to 10 minutes until charred, using tongs to rotate.

MEANWHILE, MAKE THE QUICK-ROASTED GARLIC. If you like the zingy flavor of raw garlic, skip this step. Place the garlic with the skin intact in a small skillet or 10-inch cast-iron skillet. Cook over medium heat, toasting the garlic on all sides, until the skin is lightly browned, about 5 minutes. Pour 2 tablespoons of water into the pan and immediately cover. Turn off the heat and allow the garlic to steam for 5 minutes or until softened.

MAKE THE HUMMUS. In a high-powered blender or food processor, add all of the hummus ingredients, the roasted red pepper, and the peeled roasted garlic. Begin blending on low to incorporate everything. Turn the speed up to high, blending until completely smooth. Stop and scrape down the sides as needed. If the mixture is too thick, add warm water, 1 tablespoon at a time, and blend until the hummus is smooth. The hummus will thicken a bit as it rests.

TO SERVE, transfer the hummus to a plate or a bowl. Using the back of a spoon, pull riverbeds in the hummus, repeating a couple times to make a bulls-eye pattern. Drizzle good-quality olive oil into the beds and sprinkle with herbs and red pepper flakes, if desired. To store, keep covered in the fridge for up to 2 weeks.

NOTES

To make a plain hummus, omit the red peppers, chipotles, and cayenne pepper.

Black beans stand in as a plant protein in a lot of our meals. They're quick, affordable, and hold on to the flavor you give them. We typically serve them one of two ways—cooked with a couple spices (see Summer Veggie Fajitas, page 79) or smashed into a refried version. I love these refried black beans as a side to a Mexican dinner, topped with a little cotija and red onions. But my favorite part about this recipe is that it becomes the glue to so many other recipes. Leftovers look like Open-Faced Sweet Potato Tortas (page 145), Breakfast Tostada (page 70), or dip. Preparing multiple parts of a meal can feel a bit clunky while you're doing it. But when your labor turns into an entirely new meal, it's worth all the effort.

Refried Black Beans

`MAKE AHEAD`   `WEEKDAY`

HANDS-ON: **20 MIN.**   TOTAL: **20 MIN.**
YIELDS: **6 SERVINGS AS A SIDE (2 CUPS)**

2 teaspoons olive oil	1 tablespoon red wine vinegar
1 cup chopped sweet onion	1 bay leaf
2 cloves garlic, minced	¾ teaspoon kosher salt
2 (15-ounce) cans black beans, drained and rinsed	½ teaspoon ground cumin
1 cup water	⅛ teaspoon cayenne pepper (optional)

HEAT A SMALL SAUCEPAN over medium. Once warm, add the oil and onion. Sauté for 4 minutes or until the onion is translucent and tender, stirring occasionally. Add the minced garlic, and sauté 30 seconds more. Stir in the remaining ingredients. Simmer for 5 to 8 minutes or until the beans have softened.

REMOVE THE BAY LEAF. In a high-powered blender or food processor, pulse the beans until they resemble refried beans. This will only take a second. Taste and adjust the salt if necessary. Serve immediately or store in the fridge for a week.

NOTES

For refried chipotle beans, omit the cayenne and add 1 tablespoon of pureed chipotles in adobo.

The problem with Brussels is that they cook too fast on the outside and not fast enough on the inside when roasted, which was the only way I had been cooking them prior. They were tough, chewy, and unmemorable, making their way out of our rotation. My sister insisted on making Brussels sprouts the last time we visited. And I'm so glad she did. I learned a lesson that you'll also see throughout the book. A lot of things do well with a hit of steam. These sprouts are pan-fried in butter and balsamic vinegar. After a quick cook, they steam beneath the lid of a pan for a few minutes before serving. It's at that point that they develop their melt-in-your-mouth texture without the mush.

Pan-Roasted Brussels Sprouts

WEEKDAY

HANDS-ON: **18 MIN.**   TOTAL: **18 MIN.**
YIELDS: **4 SERVINGS**

1 pound small Brussels
  sprouts, rinsed
1 tablespoon unsalted
  butter
1½ tablespoons balsamic
  vinegar

½ teaspoon kosher salt
A couple cracks of pepper
Shaved Parmesan (optional)

PREPARE THE BRUSSELS SPROUTS by slicing a thin sliver off the stem. You'll want to keep as much of the base as possible to keep the leaves intact. Remove any limp exterior leaves. Heat a large sauté pan over medium. Add the butter to the pan. Once melted, add the vinegar and Brussels to the pan, and sauté for 3 minutes or until lightly browned. Sprinkle with the salt and pepper. Cover and remove the pan from the heat. Let the Brussels steam for 4 minutes. Top with a sprinkle of shaved Parmesan, if desired.

NOTES

To add bacon, cook 2 slices before you cook the Brussels sprouts. Remove the cooked bacon from the pan, and place on a paper towel to drain. Omit the butter and cook the Brussels directly in the bacon fat. Chop the bacon, and sprinkle it on just before serving.

I debated on whether this potato recipe should be in mashed or wedged form. Wedges require less work and fewer dishes. For that reason, they get made far more often than the mashed variety. I lived a couple years of life without fries, and it was just plain boring. Now, I order fries out when the craving hits and make this baked variety when the evening calls for it. For even coating, dirty up a bowl and toss together. Whatever you do, don't skip the Parm. Serve with Diner Burgers (page 124) or Quinoa Burgers (page 127).

Garlicky Potato Wedges

WEEKDAY WEEKEND

HANDS-ON: **10 MIN.** TOTAL: **45 MIN.**
YIELDS: **6 TO 8 SERVINGS**

POTATOES	GARNISH
2 tablespoons olive oil	2 tablespoons chopped fresh curly parsley (optional)
1 clove garlic, minced	
3 pounds russet potatoes (6 to 8 potatoes)	2 tablespoons finely chopped Parmesan
1 teaspoon kosher salt	Ketchup (optional)

MAKE THE POTATOES. Preheat the oven to 400°F. Set out an unlined baking sheet. Combine the oil and garlic in a large bowl. Set aside. Scrub the potatoes and pat dry. Cut each potato in half lengthwise. Then cut each half into 4 (1-inch-thick) wedges. Add the wedges to the oil mixture, and toss to thoroughly coat. Sprinkle with the salt and toss once more. Place the wedges in a single layer on the baking sheet. Bake for 20 minutes. Flip and cook for 15 minutes more.

GARNISH THE POTATOES with the parsley (for color), if desired, and the Parmesan (for flavor). Taste and adjust the salt if necessary. Serve with ketchup, if desired.

INGREDIENT TIP

When looking to achieve an extra-crispy exterior on potatoes, use an unlined baking sheet. Parchment liners tend to trap moisture between the liner and the potato, preventing it from ever getting crisp.

Adding a bit of flour or
cornstarch to your baked
potato rounds will create
a faux-fried crusted finish.
To help achieve this,
also use an unlined pan
(see page 191 for more
information).

Sweet potatoes are often served even sweeter. To me, they're sweet enough on their own. I like to contrast their flavor with salt and heat. Where they need help is in the texture department. Being naturally tender once cooked, I like to coat them in a thin layer of cornstarch to aid in achieving a slight crust, one that blisters in a really hot oven. Serve as a side, ketchup allowed. Or serve as a meaty layer in the Open-Faced Sweet Potato Tortas (page 145). For even cooking, be sure to cut the rounds the same thickness. When cooking at this high of a heat, thinner rounds will burn before thicker rounds finish cooking.

Blistered Sweet Potato Rounds

WEEKDAY WEEKEND

HANDS-ON: **10 MIN.** TOTAL: **35 MIN.**
YIELDS: **4 SERVINGS**

1 ½ **pounds sweet potatoes,
cut into** ¼**-inch-thick
slices**

1 **teaspoon cornstarch**

½ **teaspoon kosher salt**

½ **teaspoon ground cumin**

⅛ **teaspoon cayenne
pepper**

1 **clove garlic, minced**

2 **tablespoons olive oil**

1 **tablespoon chopped fresh
cilantro**

PREHEAT THE OVEN to 450°F. Set out an unlined baking sheet. Slice the potatoes. Set aside.

IN A LARGE BOWL, combine the cornstarch, salt, cumin, cayenne, and garlic. Stir in the olive oil until a paste forms. Add the potato rounds to the paste, and toss to evenly coat. Place the potato rounds in a single layer on the baking sheet. Bake for 12 minutes. Flip and cook for 12 minutes more or until golden. Sprinkle with the fresh cilantro. These are best served hot out of the oven.

193

I'm the product of a Yankee (my dad) and a Southerner (my mom). I grew up with stuffing and cornbread dressing at holidays to appease both palates. But come New Year's Day, my mom's Southern menu was always on the table. She made pork for health, black-eyed peas for luck, and broccoli casserole for prosperity (in place of collard greens), like any good Southerner does. It wasn't until I was a full-fledged adult that I fell in love with collard greens cooked in vinegar, garlic, and a hint of sugar. Wilted greens have never been all that appealing to me, but these sturdy collard greens hold their chew. Collard greens are thick and fibrous like kale. We eat them every January 1st, and the rest of the year, too. Prosperity tastes quite good.

Braised Collard Greens WEEKDAY

HANDS-ON: **10 MIN.** TOTAL: **40 MIN.**
YIELDS: **6 SERVINGS**

2 large bunches of collard greens (about 8 cups chopped)

1 tablespoon olive oil

1 cup diced sweet onion

Pinch of kosher salt

4 cloves garlic, minced

1 quart chicken stock

1 tablespoon granulated sugar

2 tablespoons red wine vinegar

1 teaspoon kosher salt

A couple cracks of pepper

WASH AND DRY THE COLLARD GREENS. Stack the greens on top of each other and roll up as you would a burrito. Chop off the stems and discard. Continue slicing the roll, making ½-inch-wide cuts, as if doing a chiffonade of basil on a larger scale. Make one final cut down the center stem to cut the shreds in half. If needed, wash and dry again using a salad spinner or strainer. Set aside.

HEAT A LARGE SAUTÉ PAN OVER MEDIUM. Once warm, add the oil. Stir in the onion, and sauté until tender, about 4 minutes. Sprinkle with a pinch of salt. Stir in the garlic and cook for 30 seconds more.

ADD IN THE COLLARDS AND ALL REMAINING INGREDIENTS. Bring to a low simmer over medium-low heat. Cover and cook for 20 to 30 minutes, stirring every so often. Collard greens are done once they've turned a deep shade of green and have absorbed about three-fourths of the liquid.

MINIMALIST TIP

To skip cleaning
the utensil, measure
the sugar first and then
the red wine vinegar.

COOK TO A SOUNDTRACK

Can you hear the music playing in the background? I keep Pandora stations at the ready to play on the speakers overhead. It makes mundane tasks, like grating cheese, more tolerable. Movies are best with a soundtrack, so is the everyday. Cozy tastes like homemade mac and cheese and sounds like the Dinner Party station on Pandora. On fajita night, it sounds like Spanish Guitar radio. And during weekend brunch, it sounds like the Early Jazz radio station.

There's an ongoing debate—is it a main dish or a side? As with most recipes, I like to use full-fat everything plus a little butter. So to keep this decadent dish in the regular rotation, we serve it as a side. Though my daughter would vehemently argue that it's a main dish, one that should be served every night. If you'd like to serve this as a main dish, double it at minimum. See notes below for a fancied-up version. No matter which side of the debate you stand on, I think we can all agree that macaroni that comes together fast and in one pot is a very good thing.

Stovetop Mac and Cheese WEEKDAY

HANDS-ON: **20 MIN.**   TOTAL: **20 MIN.**
YIELDS: **4 SERVINGS**

Kosher salt for salting
water

2 cups uncooked elbow
pasta

4 tablespoons unsalted
butter

¼ cup unbleached all-
purpose flour

1½ cups whole milk

1½ teaspoons Dijon
mustard

1 teaspoon kosher salt

Dash of cayenne pepper
(optional)

2 cups shredded cheddar
cheese

FILL A LARGE SAUCEPAN two-thirds full with water; bring to a boil. Liberally salt the water just before adding in the pasta. Cook the pasta according to the package instructions until al dente. Drain.

IN THE SAME PAN, melt the butter over medium. Once melted, whisk in the flour until smooth and cook for 30 seconds. Slowly pour in the milk, whisking to combine. Add the Dijon, salt, and cayenne pepper, if desired. Stir constantly until the sauce thickens, about 3 minutes.

ADD THE CHEESE, whisking until smooth. Heat for 2 minutes more. Stir in the pasta and serve.

NOTES

Want to take this a step further? Place the prepared mac and cheese in an oven-safe pan or in individual ramekins. Top with panko breadcrumbs, a drizzle of olive oil, and a sprinkle of Parmesan and cheddar. Broil until golden. If you're a cheese aficionado like my sister, substitute away. I think she'd use Gruyère, fontina, or something sharp.

INGREDIENT TIP

Most pre-grated cheeses
have anti-caking ingredients
to keep shreds from sticking.
For the purest option, buy
bricks and grate as needed.

INGREDIENT TIP
Stock a semi-quick
cooking all-purpose
rice. I keep a 20-minute
brown rice around for
everyday use.

We don't eat rice as a side unless it's cooked in tomatoes, vegetables, and plenty of spices. I grew up eating Tex-Mex, Texas's version of Mexican food. I always ordered fajitas, which came with a side of Spanish rice and refried pinto beans. Because we can't find anything like Tex-Mex outside the state of Texas, I make it every other meal. To me, it tastes like the weekend. It tastes like all my favorite people gathered around the same table. As a kid, I remember my dad coming home from work, saying, "We should celebrate more." I've adopted that mind-set and tacked it onto the weekend, and to the everyday. It tastes like Tex-Mex served with a side of Spanish Rice and it sounds like Spanish Guitar radio playing on Pandora. Serve as a side on nights when your table is extra-full of people.

Spanish Rice `WEEKEND`

HANDS-ON: **10 MIN.**   TOTAL: **45 MIN.**
YIELDS: **4 TO 6 SERVINGS**

1 teaspoon olive oil	1 cup rice, uncooked
½ cup chopped sweet onion	1 cup chicken stock, plus more as needed
½ cup chopped green bell pepper	½ teaspoon chili powder
1 teaspoon kosher salt, divided	¼ teaspoon ground cumin
2 cloves garlic, minced	Sprinkle of chopped fresh cilantro
1 (15-ounce) can crushed fire-roasted tomatoes	Sprinkle of cotija

HEAT A SMALL SAUCEPAN over medium. Once warm, add the oil. Toss in the prepared onion, bell pepper, and ¼ teaspoon of the salt. Sauté for 4 minutes or until tender, stirring occasionally. Add the garlic and cook for 30 seconds more. Stir in the tomatoes, rice, stock, remaining ¾ teaspoon salt, chili powder, and cumin. Bring to a boil. Cover and reduce to a low simmer. Cook until the liquid is absorbed. The time will vary based on the package instructions, but plan on an additional 10 to 15 minutes of cook time. Check occasionally, stirring and adding more stock or water if needed. Remove from the heat. Taste and adjust the salt if necessary. Garnish with cilantro and cotija.

NOTES

Serve alongside the Summer Veggie Fajitas (page 79), Beef Tacos with Chimichurri (page 117), or BBQ Black Bean and Quick Slaw Tacos (page 83).

A good roll recipe is a good thing to have up your sleeve. It's even better when the recipe works into the natural rhythm of your life. There was a time when I'd block off a whole day to tend to a yeasted bread. My life doesn't beat to that rhythm right now. These buttery rolls take their final rest in the fridge until you're ready for them. Then, they'll steam under a tight sheet of foil in the oven, doubling in size within the first 10 minutes of baking. There's a bit of magic in them. Use this same base recipe to make the Blueberry-Orange Breakfast Rolls (page 47), too.

Make-Ahead Yeast Rolls

MAKE AHEAD   WEEKEND

HANDS-ON: **25 MIN.**   TOTAL: **11 HR.**   YIELDS: **12 ROLLS**

ROLLS

4 tablespoons unsalted butter

2 cups plus 1 tablespoon unbleached all-purpose flour

½ cup whole-wheat pastry flour

2½ teaspoons instant yeast

1½ teaspoons kosher salt

¾ cup whole milk

2 tablespoons sugar

1 large egg, room temperature

GLAZE

1 tablespoon salted butter

Squeeze of orange juice or honey

MAKE THE ROLLS. In a small saucepan, melt the butter on low until half melted. Set aside to continue melting and cooling.

IN A STAND MIXER, add the flours, yeast (see ingredient tip), and salt. Using the paddle attachment on low, mix to combine.

TO THE COOLED BUTTER, add the milk, sugar, and egg, stirring until evenly combined. Pour into the mixer. Using the paddle attachment on medium-low, mix to combine. Switch to the dough hook attachment, and mix on low speed for about 8 minutes. The dough should feel soft but not sticky. If it's noticeably sticky, mix in an additional tablespoon of flour.

COVER THE BOWL with plastic wrap and let rise at room temperature for 2 to 3 hours or until doubled

in bulk. (I prefer using plastic wrap to a towel so that the dough doesn't develop a hard shell. If using a towel, spray the dough lightly with water or oil to keep from drying out.)

PUNCH DOWN THE DOUGH. Remove the dough from the bowl and cut into 12 equally sized pieces. Begin forming into balls by pulling and gathering the dough at the bottom to hide the seam. Place snugly in an 8-inch round pan. Cover with foil and place in the fridge overnight or 12 hours. (If baking the same day, skip the fridge, and allow to double in size, covered, at room temperature, about 1 hour.)

PREHEAT THE OVEN to 375°F. Remove the rolls from the fridge. Bake for 10 minutes with the foil intact and wrapped tightly. Remove the foil and bake 20 minutes longer or until golden and cooked through. Check in between rolls for doneness.

MEANWHILE, MAKE THE GLAZE. In a small saucepan or butter warmer, melt the butter. Stir in the orange juice or honey. Brush the roll tops generously with the glaze after pulling out of the oven. Serve immediately.

NOTES

Room temperature in the winter versus the summer produces two different rise times at my house, even with a 3° temperature difference. In the winter, I often use my oven for rising by preheating it to 200°F for a minute or two just to take the chill off. Turn off the heat, and test the heat with your hand. It should feel slightly warmer (around 70°F to 75°F). Place the bowl inside to rise.

THE MINIMALIST KITCHEN

INGREDIENT TIP

I prefer SAF Instant
Yeast for the fact that it's
instant, no activation in
warm water is required
and it's basically fool-
proof. You'll find it at
specialty kitchen stores
or online. It stores for
1+ years in the fridge.

CHAPTER 7

Drinks

ADMITTEDLY, I never think about drinks until I need one. We subsist on water the majority of the day. For that reason, every drink recipe, outside the cold pressed coffee, comes together as quick as the need arises. You'll find everything from zippy ginger smoothies, to lemonade for a crowd, to single-serving cocktails in this chapter. If drinks are an afterthought for you, too, well then, you'll love these recipes as much as I do.

How you take your coffee is such a personal thing. So personal, I pack my favorite bag of beans, my grinder, and my AeroPress (my current favorite brewing method next to a Chemex) when I travel. Making coffee is a sacred morning ritual for me, the only coffee drinker in the house. It signals the start of the day just as a glass of wine or a cocktail signals the end. I love the rhythm food and drink brings to our days, creating these cozy, intentional moments. I still drink hot coffee on summer mornings, but I like to keep cold brew around. It's how I add a little *hygge* to a really hot afternoon. Cold brew is incredibly easy and an altogether different taste profile. No special tools necessary. See notes on how to vary brew strength.

Cold Brew Coffee

MAKE AHEAD   WEEKDAY

HANDS-ON: **5 MIN.**   TOTAL: **8 HR.**   YIELDS: **3½ CUPS**

1 cup freshly roasted coffee beans, coarsely ground	4 cups drinking water

POUR THE GROUND COFFEE into a medium bowl. Top with the water and stir to combine. Cover and let sit at room temperature overnight or up to 12 hours.

IN THE MORNING, strain the coffee concentrate using the same brewing tools used for hot coffee. For example, a Chemex or French press can be used the same way to strain the concentrate. If using a traditional coffee pot, set a cone with a filter over the opening and pour to strain. Store covered in a large mason jar or pitcher for up to a week.

TO SERVE, fill a small drinking glass or mason jar with ice. Add about ¾ cup of the concentrate, and serve. For a creamy drink, stir in 1 tablespoon of heavy cream, ½ tablespoon of pure maple syrup, and, if desired, a sprig of fresh mint.

NOTES

Since tastes vary so much from person to person, use this recipe as a guide: 1 cup of coffee beans to 4 cups of water. If you find it to be too strong, even with ice, dilute it further with drinking water or cream to reach your desired flavor. If it's not strong enough, use less water. Also, try using different roasts to perfect your cup of cold brew.

I've never been a tea drinker unless you count an Arnold Palmer as drinking tea. Coffee is my beverage of choice. But I do love this green tea on a hot afternoon, sweetened with honey and steeped in mint. It may be unconventional, but I prefer a squeeze of lime in mine, too. This recipe makes a small batch but easily sizes up to fit your pitcher.

House Iced Tea WEEKDAY

HANDS-ON: **5 MIN.**   TOTAL: **15 MIN.**   YIELDS: **4 CUPS**

TEA

2 cups drinking water

3 to 4 tablespoons honey
 (see notes)

½ cup fresh mint leaves,
 washed

4 green tea bags

2 cups ice

GARNISH

Sprig of fresh mint

Squeeze of lime

MAKE THE TEA. Bring the 2 cups of water to a boil in a small saucepan or kettle. Add the honey to a glass pitcher. Pour in the boiling water and stir until the honey dissolves. Add the mint and tea bags and let steep for 10 minutes. Remove the tea bags and mint. Add the ice, and stir until melted.

SERVE CHILLED OVER ICE. Garnish with a sprig of mint and a squeeze of lime. Store covered in the fridge for up to a week.

NOTES

Honey dissolves best in hot liquids, which is why it's added to the hot steeping mixture. I like to keep things just sweet enough by using 3 tablespoons in this recipe. If you prefer things slightly sweeter, go for the extra tablespoon.

Broken down, lemonade is fresh lemon juice sweetened with simple syrup and tamed with water. You can make this the classic way as mentioned. Or you can make it 20 different ways by adding herbs or fruit or both. If you've never made lemonade, you have to try it once. There's no going back. My favorite combination is strawberry-basil lemonade. But then there's thyme lemonade, too. The options are endless.

Fresh-Squeezed Lemonade(s)

WEEKDAY   WEEKEND

HANDS-ON: **15 MIN.**   TOTAL: **15 MIN.**   YIELDS: **6 CUPS**

SIMPLE SYRUP
1 cup granulated sugar
1 cup water

LEMONADE
1 cup lemon juice (6 to
    8 lemons, halved), plus
    more for garnish
4 cups cold water

GARNISH
Thin lemon slices

ADD-INS (OPTIONAL)
Herbs: thyme, mint, basil,
    rosemary
Fruit: berries, cherries,
    watermelon

MAKE THE SIMPLE SYRUP. Add the sugar and water to a small saucepan, and cook over medium until the sugar completely dissolves, but no longer, stirring often. Pour into a pitcher and let cool for 10 minutes.

MAKE THE LEMONADE. While the simple syrup cools, juice the lemons. Set aside. Once the simple syrup has cooled, add in the cold water first, stirring to combine, and then stir in the lemon juice. Taste and dilute with a cup of water if desired. Garnish with thin slices of lemon. Chill the lemonade until ready to serve.

210

VARIATIONS

- To make an herbal lemonade, add a couple sprigs of fresh herbs (basil, thyme, mint, rosemary) to the simple syrup while it cools. Remove before adding to the lemonade. Continue making the recipe as directed. Garnish with a fresh sprig of the herb for a pretty finish and to denote flavor.

- To make a fruity lemonade, puree one cup of fruit (berries, watermelon, cherries), 1 tablespoon honey, and 1 cup water. Pour through a fine mesh sieve and stir into the lemonade.

- To make an Arnold Palmer, mix equal parts lemonade and prepared tea.

- To make it adult-friendly, add a splash of vodka.

INGREDIENT TIP

Even homemade lemonade can be a bit sweet for my taste. I prefer to drink it as an Arnold Palmer—one part lemonade to one part unsweetened tea. The tea dilutes the sweetness without diluting the flavor.

MINIMALIST TIP

Use super-cold water to help cool off the heat of the simple syrup more quickly.

Outside a daily glass of wine (me), we mostly drink water, especially the sparkling variety. Sugary drinks make my blood sugar plummet. But I've found fruit waters sweetened with a little agave nectar, a low glycemic sweetener, leave me feeling refreshed. This drink comes together quickly under the care of a high-powered blender. Make this for a special occasion, a blistering hot afternoon, or whenever you need to use up watermelon before it goes bad.

Watermelon-Lime Agua Fresca

WEEKDAY

HANDS-ON: **15 MIN.**   TOTAL: **15 MIN.**   YIELDS: **4½ CUPS**

4 cups cubed watermelon, seeded

2 cups cold water

¼ cup lime juice

2 tablespoons agave nectar

Thin lime slices

IN A HIGH-POWERED or regular blender, combine all the ingredients and blend on high until smooth. Pour the mixture over a fine-mesh strainer to collect any large bits. Store in the fridge for up to 3 days. Serve over ice with a thin lime slice.

I'm always looking for ways to use up extra coconut milk. One option is to freeze it in smaller portions. (It goes bad pretty fast when left alone in the fridge.) Another option is to add it to smoothies. It's naturally creamy and sweet. In fact, after making this smoothie, you may never make one without coconut milk again. If you need to sneak in extra greens for the day, this smoothie is the perfect vehicle.

Blueberry-Coconut Smoothie

WEEKDAY

HANDS-ON: **5 MIN.**   TOTAL: **5 MIN.**   YIELDS: **3 CUPS**

1 ripe banana
⅔ cup blueberries
⅓ cup old-fashioned oats
⅓ cup spinach (optional)

⅓ cup unsweetened coconut milk
1 tablespoon honey
Tiny pinch of kosher salt
2 cups ice

PLACE ALL THE INGREDIENTS in a high-powered or regular blender, adding in the ice last. Process on medium for about 10 seconds to break up the ice. Finish blending on high until smooth.

NOTES

See notes on page 217 for mastering the perfect smoothie ice ratio.

To keep things simple,
use a ⅓ measuring cup
and a tablespoon for
all the measurements.

During cold season (both the winter and flu variety), we find ourselves drinking this smoothie the most. Our little one is in the process of building up her immune system. We're not so little but seem to be doing the same thing thanks to all the things she brings home. Drinking this smoothie is far tastier than chewing vitamin C tablets, though we do that, too. Use clementines or tangerines but not oranges, as they make for a pulpy smoothie no matter how powerful your blender. See notes for suggestions on achieving the perfect smoothie consistency. An immunity smoothie a day keeps the doctor away. Or something like that.

Immunity Smoothie WEEKDAY

HANDS-ON: **5 MIN.**   TOTAL: **5 MIN.**   YIELDS: **3 CUPS**

4 clementines, peeled

1 ripe banana

1 (6-inch) skinny carrot, peeled

Thumbtip of peeled fresh ginger, grated

¼ cup plain whole-milk yogurt

1 tablespoon honey

Pinch of kosher salt

1½ cups ice

PLACE ALL THE INGREDIENTS in a high-powered or regular blender, adding in the ice last. Process on medium for about 10 seconds to break up the ice. Finish blending on high until smooth.

NOTES

Mastering the ice ratio is key to getting the perfect consistency of a smoothie. There are a couple variables at play—the ice machine and the blender. You'll know you've achieved the perfect consistency when the smoothie burps at the end of a blend. If the smoothie is bubbly at the top, it needs a bit more ice next time. If the smoothie stays put when pouring, it needs less ice.

217

I drink a cup of slowly prepared coffee at the start of the day and often end the day with a glass of wine or a simple cocktail, like this one. I love the rhythm that food and drink naturally bring to the everyday. A Salty Dog is simply a salted Greyhound—a grapefruit vodka drink. I have a thing for citrus cocktails, mostly because the citrus does all the work—from the color to the taste. This drink is thoughtless, which is also a good description of my brain by the end of the day. Serve with a sprig of thyme or rosemary or crushed ice for an extra-beautiful presentation.

Maple Salty Dog WEEKDAY

HANDS-ON: **5 MIN.**   TOTAL: **5 MIN**.   YIELDS: **1 DRINK**

SWEET AND SALTY RIM
1 teaspoon kosher salt
½ teaspoon turbinado
  (coarse) sugar

DRINK
¼ cup plus 2 tablespoons
  grapefruit juice (3 ounces;
  about 1 grapefruit)

¼ cup vodka (2 ounces)
½ teaspoon pure maple
  syrup

GARNISH
Sprig of fresh thyme or
  rosemary (optional)

MAKE THE SWEET AND SALTY RIMS. In a small ramekin, slightly wider than the serving glass, add the salt and sugar. Rub the rim of the glass on a cut grapefruit. Twist the rim in the salt-sugar mixture until coated. Set aside. This makes enough for a couple drinks.

MAKE THE DRINK. Juice the grapefruit. Pour the juice into the prepared glass. Add the vodka and maple syrup, stirring until combined. Top with plenty of ice and garnish with a sprig of thyme, if desired.

218

This drink is a 2:3 ratio—2 parts vodka to 3 parts grapefruit. For easy measuring, use a ¼-cup measuring utensil. Fill 1½ times with the grapefruit juice and once with vodka. This drink can easily be sized up using this ratio. Add about ½ teaspoon of pure maple syrup per drink.

MINIMALIST TIP

Four tablespoons, the
amount of tequila in the
recipe, equals ¼ cup.
To cut down on cleaning,
I forgo using an extra
measuring utensil and
use a tablespoon for all
of the measurements.

I've written this recipe for the lowest common denominator because sometimes Wednesday needs just one serving of a margarita, not a whole pitcher like the weekend. In a lot of ways, a margarita is a simplified, spiked version of lemonade. You could make a simple syrup, but I prefer to keep it even more simple—sweetened with a squirt of agave to your liking. You don't have to be a mixologist or have special equipment to make this drink. It's as easy as one part and two parts. Any measuring utensil will do. Note: This drink starts out strong, but once the ice melts slightly, it evens out to perfection.

Single-Serving Margarita WEEKDAY

HANDS-ON: **5 MIN.**   TOTAL: **5 MIN.**   YIELDS: **1 DRINK**

2 tablespoons fresh-squeezed lime juice (1 ounce)

2 tablespoons orange liqueur (1 ounce; such as Cointreau)

4 tablespoons 100% pure agave tequila (2 ounces)

¼ teaspoon agave nectar or to taste

Tiny pinch of kosher salt

Generous scoop of ice

ADD ALL OF THE INGREDIENTS to a glass, stirring to combine. Taste and add more agave nectar if necessary.

NOTES

I prefer to add the salt straight into my drink, but you could just as easily line the rim. To do so, rub lime or water around the rim, and then dip in flaky kosher salt. You can add lime zest to the salt, if desired. To make a frozen margarita, use the measurements at left. Add ½ cup of ice to a high-powered or regular blender, and whirl until smooth. To make a large batch that serves 4, stir together ½ cup lime juice, ½ cup orange liqueur, 1 cup tequila, and 1½ teaspoons agave nectar. Serve over plenty of ice.

I've talked about planning ahead the entire book, but I'm not naturally a planner. Drinks, especially, are always an afterthought for me. For that reason, you'll find most of the recipes in this chapter to be quick, like this sangria that's ready in a little over an hour. What makes this a winter sangria? The spiced maple syrup mixture yields a warm flavor, though it's still served over ice. To convert this recipe for summertime, see the ingredient tip.

Quick Winter Sangria MAKE AHEAD

HANDS-ON: **10 MIN.**   TOTAL: **1 HR. 10 MIN.**
YIELDS: **6 TO 8 DRINKS**

SPICED MAPLE

Scant ¼ cup pure maple syrup

¼ teaspoon ground cinnamon

Pinch of ground cloves

½ cup fresh orange juice

⅓ cup orange liqueur (such as Cointreau)

1 orange, cut into thin wheels

1 lime, cut into thin slices

SANGRIA

1 (750-milliliter) bottle red wine

SERVING

1 bottle sparkling water (optional)

MAKE THE SPICED MAPLE. In a small saucepan or butter warmer, whisk together all of the spiced maple ingredients. Bring to a simmer over medium, and cook until the spices and syrup become one. Remove from the heat and allow to cool.

MAKE THE SANGRIA. While the spiced maple cooks, pour the wine, orange juice, and liqueur into a pitcher. Add the spiced maple, stirring until evenly combined. Add in the citrus slices. Cover and refrigerate for at least 1 hour before serving.

TO SERVE, fill a glass with ice. Combine 3 parts wine to 1 part sparkling water, if desired.

NOTES

Substitute other citrus like blood oranges, satsumas, or tangerines in place of the orange. Or float cranberries for an extra-pretty presentation.

INGREDIENT TIP

To make a Quick Summer Sangria, omit the spices and skip cooking the maple syrup. Add cut fruit or berries.

I like to have a house salad or two in my repertoire. I feel the same way about cocktails. At one point, I wanted to know how to make every cocktail. But as I've learned with most everything, quality always wins over quantity. I encourage you to keep a couple good cocktail recipes on hand, like this simple drink. It goes down easy. Way too easy. And it's not all that sour, unless you'd like to add an extra squeeze of lemon. If you find any mistakes in the book, please attribute it to this drink, and then make one for yourself to forget about it. Chears! Gotcha. Cheers!

Maple-Bourbon Sour WEEKDAY

HANDS-ON: **5 MIN.**   TOTAL: **5 MIN.**   YIELDS: **1 DRINK**

3 tablespoons (1½ ounces) bourbon

1 tablespoon lemon juice (½ ounce)

½ tablespoon pure maple syrup

2 ice cubes

COMBINE THE BOURBON, lemon juice, and maple syrup in a glass. Stir well. Serve over ice cubes.

NOTES

I'm not sure there's such a thing as leftover bourbon, but if you find yourself in such a situation, try the Bourbon-Blueberry Quick Jam (page 40) to top the Honeyed Ricotta Semifreddo (page 228).

CHAPTER 8

Desserts

I'M KNOWN FOR ending many dinners with something sweet. It's a signal to end the day and close the kitchen. But over the years I've come to like my desserts just sweet enough. Minimalism has touched every part of my life, even my beloved desserts. The recipes that follow will leave you feeling satisfied. Some may even find themselves at the breakfast table or as an afternoon treat. I've snuck in a couple maximalist recipes, too. Because even a minimalist needs to let loose sometimes.

This is not a traditional semifreddo made with a custard or meringue. It's a cross between semifreddo and cheesecake, sweetened only with honey and brought together in a blender. It's a light and welcomed dessert anytime of the year. I've served this with leftover Bourbon-Blueberry Quick Jam and a dusting of sweet lemon panko. If you have them, fresh blueberries offer a wonderful tartness in contrast to the stewed variety. Try the Stewed Tart Cherries (page 52) or something as simple as segmented blood oranges and a sprig of mint as a topping.

Honeyed Ricotta Semifreddo

MAKE AHEAD   **WEEKEND**

HANDS-ON: **15 MIN.**   TOTAL: **8 HR. 15 MIN.**
YIELDS: **8 SERVINGS**

SEMIFREDDO

¾ cup heavy cream

1 (15-ounce) container whole-milk ricotta

4 ounces mascarpone

½ cup honey

1½ teaspoons pure vanilla extract

⅛ teaspoon kosher salt

SWEET LEMON PANKO

1 tablespoon unsalted butter

2 teaspoons granulated sugar

Pinch of kosher salt

¼ cup panko

1 teaspoon lemon juice

TOPPINGS

Bourbon-Blueberry Quick Jam (page 40)

Fresh blueberries

Sprinkle of bee pollen (optional)

MAKE THE SEMIFREDDO at least 8 hours before serving. Line the width of a 9 x 5–inch loaf pan with parchment paper. Set aside.

IN A STAND MIXER with the whisk attachment, beat the heavy cream on high until stiff peaks form. Meanwhile, place all the remaining semifreddo ingredients in a high-powered or regular blender or food processor, and process until smooth.

REMOVE THE MIXER BOWL from the stand, and pour the cheese mixture into the whipped cream in four increments, folding vigorously with a spatula

to incorporate. The mixture will be lush and fluffy. Pour into the prepared loaf pan and smooth the top. Cover with plastic wrap, and freeze at least 8 hours or until set.

MAKE THE SWEET LEMON PANKO. In a small skillet, melt the butter. Stir in the sugar and salt until dissolved. Toss in the panko and cook until lightly golden, about 3 minutes. Remove from the pan and add the lemon juice. Store covered for up to 1 week.

TO SERVE, remove the semifreddo from the freezer, and let stand at room temperature for 5 minutes. Discard the top piece of plastic wrap and run a thin, warmed knife along the edges to release. Invert from the loaf pan onto a serving platter. Cut into 1-inch slices as you'd cut bread. Top with the jam, fresh blueberries, a sprinkle of sweet lemon panko, and, if desired, bee pollen (for color).

TO STORE, remove the semifreddo from the pan, keeping the parchment lining intact. Place in a freezer-safe ziplock bag, removing as much air as possible before sealing, and store in the freezer for up to 2 weeks.

INGREDIENT TIP

We eat with our eyes first. Garnishing is a simple way to create a beautiful presentation. To make garnishing easy, we keep a couple small jars of natural "sprinkles" in the pantry, like bee pollen, shredded coconut, hemp seeds, chia seeds, and pepita seeds. Beyond acting as a garnish, they offer nutritional value as well.

REPETITION IS GOOD PEDAGOGY

The best professors are the ones who repeat themselves. They're not forgetful or nutty, but wise. We learn through repetition at the age of 2 and 62. And once you learn something well, it becomes as involuntary as breathing. I use repetition in my cooking techniques, too, to keep it as mindless as possible—like this pastry folding method used throughout. If something works, let it be.

When working on the pie crust for the book, I wondered if adding a couple more folds into the dough would produce a quick puff pastry. The pie crust was naturally buttery and flaky due to the ratios and method. You can probably guess the outcome if you're reading this recipe. It worked! I only wish I'd thought of it sooner. With baking, pastries especially, I've learned that it takes time to master a technique. There are so many variables at play—yourself, your ingredients, your tools, and the temperature in your house. If you can master one technique, why not use it everywhere else? So I have. Whether you're making biscuits (page 40), scones (page 43), or galette crust (page 242), you can pull from the same memory bank of experiences to make this recipe, too.

Orange-Rhubarb Puff Pastry

`MAKE AHEAD`   `WEEKEND`

HANDS-ON: **25 MIN.**   TOTAL: **1 HR.**   YIELDS: **4 SERVINGS**

CRUST

1 single premade Galette Crust (page 242)

1 large egg, whisked

1 tablespoon turbinado (coarse) sugar

FILLING

1 cup sliced rhubarb (see instructions)

2½ tablespoons granulated sugar

1 tablespoon fresh-squeezed orange juice

GARNISH

1 teaspoon orange zest

Powdered sugar

Vanilla ice cream (optional)

PREPARE THE CRUST. Make a half recipe of the galette crust following the recipe through step 2 or start with a single premade crust from the freezer. If the crust is frozen, allow it to thaw in the fridge for 6 hours before using.

ROLL THE DOUGH out to a rectangle (about 10 x 6–inch). Fold into thirds as you would a letter. Repeat 5 more times, using flour to keep the dough from sticking. The last two rolls will require a bit more elbow grease to roll out. On the final roll, roll the dough into an 10 x 6–inch rectangle (about ¼-inch thick). Trim the edges to create a perfect rectangle, which also helps the pastry to puff. Place the dough on a parchment-lined baking sheet and freeze for 15 minutes. Meanwhile, preheat the oven to 425°F.

PREPARE THE FILLING. Slice the rhubarb into ¼-inch-thick slices, cutting at a 45° angle. Place

the rhubarb in a small bowl, and stir in the sugar and orange juice. Set aside.

REMOVE THE PUFF PASTRY from the freezer. Use a sharp knife to score (do not cut all the way through) a ½-inch border around the edges of the dough. Brush a thin coat of the egg wash over the entire pastry. Sprinkle the border with turbinado sugar. Place 1 rhubarb row in one corner of the interior rectangle, using the scored lines as your guide. Continue adding rhubarb slices in rows (all the slices should point the same way), slightly overlapping each slice with the one next to it, until the interior rectangle is full. Pour any remaining juices over the rhubarb. Bake for 20 to 25 minutes or until the edges are deeply golden and the fruit is cooked through.

ALLOW THE PUFF PASTRY TO REST for at least 15 minutes before serving. (This is best when served within 6 hours of baking.) Sprinkle with the orange zest and dust with the powdered sugar. Add a scoop of vanilla ice cream, if desired.

NOTES

Rhubarb is in season for a short time, but this puff pastry can be made year-round. Actually, one of my favorite ways to serve puff pastry is when it's baked off without any fruit. The fruit tends to weigh down the center. Roll the final dough out into an 8-inch square, and then cut the rolled-out dough into 4 (4-inch) squares. Score a small border around the edges of each dough square. Wash each square with the egg wash; sprinkle turbinado on the exterior edge. Bake until puffed and golden, about 10 to 15 minutes. Before serving, punch down the interior square to use as a bowl for macerated fruit topped with whipped cream. These are best served the same day.

I have a cherry trick, and it requires no pitting. When I started cooking, I only wanted to use fresh ingredients. Nothing frozen. And then I started to notice some of my own habits. I'd freeze pureed pumpkin or the very best strawberries to carry over to the next season. It was an age-old preservation technique. After visiting the tart cherry fields of northern Michigan, I realized that's what they were doing, too. (See the ingredient tip.) So that's my cherry trick—I buy them in the freezer aisle already pitted and cook with them year-round. This crisp is a quick crowd-pleaser. It's one part almond-cherry filling to one part crisp, heavy on the crisp.

Almond–Tart Cherry Crisp

WEEKDAY   WEEKEND

HANDS-ON: **15 MIN.**   TOTAL: **40 MIN.**
YIELDS: **10 SERVINGS**

CHERRIES

5 cups frozen Montmorency tart cherries

¾ cup granulated sugar

¼ cup cornstarch

2 tablespoons water

1 tablespoon unsalted butter

½ teaspoon almond extract

Pinch of kosher salt

CRISP

¾ cup unbleached all-purpose flour

¾ cup old-fashioned oats

½ cup packed brown sugar

½ teaspoon kosher salt

7 tablespoons unsalted butter, room temperature

¼ cup sliced almonds

TOPPING (OPTIONAL)

Vanilla ice cream

PREHEAT THE OVEN to 375°F.

PREPARE THE CHERRIES. Add the frozen tart cherries, sugar, cornstarch, and water to a 10-inch cast-iron skillet, stirring to evenly coat. Place the pan over medium. As the cherries begin to thaw, stir occasionally. Once the mixture thickens to where it just coats the back of a spoon, about 10 minutes, remove from the heat. Stir in the butter, almond extract, and pinch of salt.

PREPARE THE CRISP. In a medium bowl, stir together the flour, oats, brown sugar, and salt. Cut the butter into skinny shreds (as if you were cutting thin slices of cheese) and toss them into the flour mixture to coat. Using your hands, quickly break apart the flour-covered butter into pea-sized pieces until a crumble forms. Add in the sliced almonds and spread on top of the prepared cherries in the pan. Bake for about 12 minutes or until the crisp is lightly golden and the cherries are bubbling. Let cool for at least 10 minutes before serving. Top with a scoop of vanilla ice cream, if desired. Store lightly covered at room temperature for up to 4 days.

INGREDIENT TIP

I like to use frozen tart cherries year-round for a couple reasons. First, fresh cherries are too delicate in structure to make it to market. For that reason, growers process and freeze the cherries within hours from harvest. During the processing, the cherries are pitted. Maybe for that reason alone I love tart cherries. Don't be turned off by the word tart. They're just not as sweet as sweet cherries.

MINIMALIST TIP

To easily clean a high-powered blender, add dish soap to the blender and fill half full with hot water. Make sure the lid is placed snugly on the container before blending on high for about 30 seconds. Rinse and voilà. It's clean!

236

This cake is fit for dessert, an afternoon snack, or even breakfast the next day. Spotted with deep red and orange stone fruit slices, dusted with powdered sugar, and lined with a ribbed edge, the presentation of this cake is as beautiful as the simplicity of the flavor. Sliced almonds undergo a quick toast in the skillet before turning into a fine powder in the blender. This recipe is smart in that you add all the dry ingredients to the blender rather than dirtying up another bowl.

Toasted Almond–Stone Fruit Cake `MAKE AHEAD` `WEEKEND`

HANDS-ON: **30 MIN.** TOTAL: **2 HR. 30 MIN.**
YIELDS: **8 TO 12 SLICES**

1½ cups mixed ripe stone fruit (about 4 apricots and plums total), cut into ½-inch slices

½ cup sliced almonds

1¾ cups unbleached all-purpose flour

1 teaspoon aluminum-free baking powder

½ teaspoon kosher salt

¾ cup unsalted butter, room temperature

1 cup granulated sugar

2 large eggs

1 teaspoon pure vanilla extract

½ teaspoon almond extract

½ cup whole milk

Sprinkle of powdered sugar

PREHEAT THE OVEN to 350°F. Place a 10-inch removable-bottom tart pan with a 2-inch height on a baking sheet. Set aside.

SLICE THE STONE FRUIT. Set aside.

IN A 10-INCH CAST-IRON SKILLET, toast the almonds over medium-low until lightly golden, stirring occasionally, about 3 minutes. Pour into a high-powered blender or food processor, and blend on high into a fine powder. Stop to scrape down the sides as needed. Add the flour, baking powder, and salt to the blender, and blend once more to evenly combine. Set aside.

IN A STAND MIXER fitted with a paddle attachment, cream the butter and granulated sugar on medium-low for about 5 minutes. Mix in all the eggs and extracts on medium speed until evenly combined.

POUR THE MILK into a liquid measuring glass. With the mixer on low speed, alternate adding the milk and flour mixture in three increments, mixing until just combined. Stop mixer and fold with a spatula a couple more times to incorporate.

POUR THE BATTER into the prepared pan, leveling with a spatula. Top with the stone fruit in a mosaic pattern, barely pressing into the cake. Bake for 50 minutes to 1 hour or until cooked through in the center. If the edges brown too quickly, tent foil over the top of the tart pan. Place on a cooling rack to cool for 1 hour. Remove the fluted tart pan. Sprinkle lightly with the powdered sugar, slice, and serve. This is best served within 2 days of making. Store lightly covered at room temperature.

I grew up eating my mom's peach cobbler, which was her mom's peach cobbler. The recipe goes like this: a cup, a cup, a cup, a stick. Their recipe calls for buttermilk, which I rarely stock in the fridge. That's one ingredient I've never been able to successfully use before having to feed it to the kitchen sink. So I've removed it. This recipe calls for the things I keep stocked—heavy cream and butter. The cobbler crumble is spotted with cornmeal, creating an unexpected but welcomed texture. If you have extra thyme or mint on hand, I recommend garnishing with that plus a scoop of vanilla ice cream, too.

Peach Cobbler `WEEKDAY` `WEEKEND`

HANDS-ON: **20 MIN.**   TOTAL: **55 MIN.**
YIELDS: **6 SERVINGS**

PEACHES

- **4 cups fresh peach slices (about 4 large peaches), cut into ½-inch wedges**
- **⅓ cup granulated sugar**
- **1 tablespoon unbleached all-purpose flour**

BISCUIT TOPPING

- **3 tablespoons unsalted butter**
- **⅔ cup unbleached all-purpose flour**
- **⅓ cup cornmeal**
- **⅓ cup granulated sugar**
- **1½ teaspoons aluminum-free baking powder**
- **¼ teaspoon kosher salt**
- **⅓ cup heavy cream**

PREHEAT THE OVEN to 375°F.

PREPARE THE PEACHES. Add all of the peach ingredients to a 12 x 10–inch enamel baking dish (or similar-sized glass or ceramic dish), and stir together. Set aside.

PREPARE THE BISCUIT TOPPING. In a small saucepan, melt the butter on low until half melted. Set aside to continue melting and cooling.

MEANWHILE, IN A SMALL BOWL, stir together the flour, cornmeal, sugar, baking powder, and salt. Pour in the melted butter and cream, and stir together until just combined. Sprinkle the mixture over the peaches, and bake for 22 to 25 minutes or until the cobbler is golden and cooked through. Let cool for at least 10 minutes before serving. This is best served the same day.

NOTES

Serve with a scoop of vanilla ice cream. You can substitute in fresh blackberries or blueberries for a cup of the peaches.

NOTES

If you're serving only one cake, wrap the remaining one in plastic wrap and store in the freezer for up to 2 months. Let thaw for at least 2 hours before serving.

I've always served pavlovas as individual desserts, making tiny nests perfect for holding fruit. But after my 8-year-old neighbor declared these as his next birthday cake, I decided to serve them as such. Pavlovas can be finicky. But with their light texture—crispy on the outside, marshmallowy on the inside—they're worth the attempt, as they melt in your mouth. Typically, pavlovas call for extra-fine sugar, which is somewhere between granulated and powdered sugar. I don't keep it stocked, so I give granulated sugar a quick pulse in the blender which yields the perfect consistency. I've slipped in a little brown sugar, too, adding a subtle caramel flavor, which calms the sweetness. This naturally gluten-free cake can be topped with any fruit salad. Be sure to add a touch of sugar in advance to help the fruit release its natural syrup.

Bronzed Pavlovas

MAKE AHEAD   WEEKEND

HANDS-ON: **15 MIN.**   TOTAL: **1 HR. 50 MIN.**
YIELDS: **10 TO 12 SERVINGS (2 PAVLOVA CAKES)**

PAVLOVAS

3 large egg whites

½ cup granulated sugar

¼ cup lightly packed brown sugar

2 teaspoons cornstarch

Pinch of kosher salt

1 teaspoon white distilled vinegar

½ teaspoon pure vanilla extract

FRUIT SALAD

2 cups chopped fresh pineapple

1 cup chopped peeled kiwi

1 tablespoon granulated sugar

GARNISH

Whipped Cream (page 258)

PREHEAT THE OVEN to 275°F. Line a baking sheet with parchment paper, drawing 2 (6-inch) circles on opposite corners, leaving at least a 1-inch clear space for the pavlovas to expand. Flip the parchment paper over so that the pencil lines are baking sheet side down. Set aside.

MAKE THE PAVLOVAS at least 2 hours before serving. In a stand mixer fitted with a whisk attachment, add the egg whites to the bowl to warm up a bit. Set aside.

IN A HIGH-POWERED BLENDER or food processor, add the sugars, cornstarch, and salt. Pulse on medium-low just until the sugars are fine, not powdered. Set aside.

BEAT THE EGG WHITES at high speed until foamy and soft peaks hold, about 1 minute. Slowly add the sugar mixture to the whipped egg whites, beating until thick and glossy, about 4 minutes. Stop the mixer and scrape down the sides of the bowl. Add the vinegar and vanilla and beat again until stiff peaks hold. The mixture will look like a very thick, glossy buttercream. If it collapses slightly with the fold of a spatula, continue beating until the mixture holds its shape upon a fold.

USING A 4 TABLESPOON-SIZED spring-release scoop (2-ounce scoop/#16 scoop), scoop out the egg white mixture onto the prepared baking sheet. Shape the meringue cakes by pressing the back of a large spoon into the middle and pulling to spread. The cakes will be thick and rustic in appearance. Bake for 1 hour 15 minutes. When done, the pavlovas will be golden in color and a light tap in the middle will be firm. They should also easily peel off the parchment paper. Remove from the oven and carefully pull away the parchment paper. Place on a cooling rack to cool completely before serving, at least 20 minutes. These can be made a day in advance and stored uncovered at room temperature.

MAKE THE FRUIT SALAD just before serving. Stir together all the fruit salad ingredients in a bowl, and let sit to give the fruit a chance to release its juices.

PREPARE THE WHIPPED CREAM just before serving. To assemble, evenly distribute the whipped cream over the cakes. Top with the fruit salad, including any juices. Cut into wedges, and serve.

I'm team galette over team pie because of the ease of it all. Don't worry, there's a banana cream pie a couple pages over with simplified tips of its own. But a galette is what I reach for when a quick dessert is needed. It's rustic and beautiful in its own right, no crimping necessary. The crust recipe yields two, though you'll only need one for this galette. Make the full recipe and save one for later by storing it in the freezer. Or turn it into a puff pastry by following the recipe on page 233. When working with any pastry—from biscuits to pie crust—it's important to keep the ingredients cold. Work quickly when possible and chill the dough if you notice it warming up.

Apple Galette   MAKE AHEAD   WEEKEND

HANDS-ON: **40 MIN.**   TOTAL: **2 HR. 20 MIN.**
YIELDS: **6 TO 8 SERVINGS**

DOUBLE GALETTE CRUST

1 cup unbleached all-purpose flour

¼ cup whole-wheat pastry flour

2 teaspoons granulated sugar

½ teaspoon kosher salt

¾ cup cold unsalted butter

½ cup ice-cold water

FILLING

4 cups apples, peeled, cored, and sliced ⅛-inch thick (about 3 apples or 1½ pounds)

¼ cup packed brown sugar

1 teaspoon unbleached all-purpose flour

1 teaspoon lemon juice

½ teaspoon cinnamon

⅛ teaspoon grated nutmeg

⅛ teaspoon kosher salt

Dash of ground cloves

EGG WASH

1 large egg, beaten

Turbinado (coarse) sugar

GARNISH

Vanilla ice cream or Whipped Cream (page 258; optional)

MAKE THE DOUBLE CRUST. In a medium bowl, whisk together the flours, sugar, and salt. Cut the butter into skinny shreds (as if you were cutting thin slices of cheese) and toss them into the flour mixture to coat. Using your hands, quickly break apart the flour-covered butter into pea-sized pieces. Pour in half the ice-cold water. Use a large fork to bring the dough together. Continue adding water until the dough holds together. Form into a rough rectangle.

ON A LIGHTLY FLOURED SURFACE, roll the dough out into a rectangle (about 14 x 6-inch). Fold into thirds as you would a letter. Repeat 3 more times, using flour to keep the dough from sticking. Cut the dough in half.

TO FREEZE, wrap each dough half in plastic wrap, and freeze for 20 minutes. Freeze the extra dough for later use by placing in a freezer-safe ziplock bag, removing as much air as possible.

MAKE THE FILLING. Preheat the oven to 375°F. Line a baking sheet with parchment paper. Set aside. Prepare the apples. In a large bowl, stir together all of the filling ingredients. Set aside.

ROLL OUT THE CHILLED DOUGH on a lightly floured surface to 13 x 13-inch. Carefully fold the dough into quarters and transfer to the prepared baking sheet. Unfold the dough and center within the pan. Pour the filling and all the liquid into the center of the dough. Spread the filling out, keeping a 2½-inch border. Fold the dough snugly around the filling, making literal folds in the dough to form a circle. Brush the dough with the beaten egg and sprinkle liberally with the turbinado sugar. Bake for 40 to 45 minutes or until the crust is golden and the apples are cooked through. Let sit at least 1 hour before serving. Serve with a scoop of vanilla ice cream or whipped cream, if desired. Store leftovers at room temperature for up to 3 days.

NOTES

Save the remaining crust in the freezer for another galette, the Fresh Spinach Quiche (page 69), the Roasted Banana Cream Pie (page 253), or the Orange-Rhubarb Puff Pastry (page 233).

INGREDIENT TIP

To bring butter to room temperature more quickly, cut it into skinny shreds, exposing as much surface area as possible.

If California were a cookie, I think it'd taste like this—bright. Awakened by excessive amounts of citrus zest, spotted with poppy seeds, and held together by fresh, floral olive oil, this is one of my favorite cookies. I'm not a traditionalist when it comes to making cookies at home. I prefer them to look as if they've just been pulled from the shelf of a bakery case. These cookies are just that. They have a bit of height and are substantial in size. So substantial that one is plenty in a sitting. I love the use of cornmeal in this cookie—for both texture and color.

Citrus–Poppy Seed Cookies

`WEEKEND`

HANDS-ON: **25 MIN.**   TOTAL: **1 HR.**
YIELDS: **12 LARGE COOKIES**

DRY
2¼ cups unbleached all-purpose flour
¼ cup cornmeal
2 tablespoons poppy seeds
½ teaspoon baking soda
¼ teaspoon kosher salt

CREAMING
½ cup unsalted butter, room temperature
1 cup granulated sugar, plus more for sprinkling

1½ teaspoons lemon zest
1½ teaspoons orange zest
¼ cup extra-virgin olive oil
1 large egg
2 tablespoons lemon juice

ROLLING
¼ to ½ cup granulated sugar

PREHEAT THE OVEN TO 350°F. Line a baking sheet with parchment paper or a Silpat. Set aside.

PREPARE THE DRY INGREDIENTS. In a medium bowl, whisk together all the dry ingredients. Set aside.

PREPARE THE CREAMING INGREDIENTS. In a stand mixer fitted with the paddle attachment, cream together the butter, sugar, and zests on medium speed until well combined. Add in the oil, egg, and lemon juice. Continue mixing until pale and evenly combined, about 1 minute, scraping down the sides every so often.

ADD THE DRY INGREDIENTS to the creamed ingredients, mixing on low speed until just combined. The dough will be somewhat dense.

USING A 4 TABLESPOON-SIZED spring-release scoop (2-ounce scoop/#16 scoop), scoop out the dough onto the prepared baking sheet. Carefully roll or liberally sprinkle the cookies with sugar. Bake for 12 to 13 minutes. The cookies will seem like they need a minute longer, but take them out anyways. Let cool on the pan for 1 minute before transferring to a cooling rack to cool completely, about 20 minutes. Store in an airtight container for up to 3 days.

NOTES

If you don't have any oranges around, use 1 tablespoon of lemon zest.

245

If you've made The Very Best Scrambled Eggs (page 62), you'll know this lesson—things continue to cook long after departing from their heat source. This is particularly true of cookies. Most people cook them until they look and feel done. And after a 10-minute rest, they're crispier than a cracker and overcooked on the insides. If you break into these cookies fresh out of the oven, they'll look underbaked. Give them 20 minutes and break into them again. Perfection. The crispy shell locks in the heat and cooks them to completion outside the oven. Err on the side of early with cookies. If you make this recipe again and again, you'll figure out the perfect time for your oven. Because every oven is a bit different, get to know yours, and you'll have a happy relationship. Or at least perfectly cooked cookies.

Chocolate Chip Cookies `WEEKDAY`

HANDS-ON: **15 MIN.**   TOTAL: **45 MIN.**
YIELDS: **18 COOKIES**

WET	DRY
7 tablespoons unsalted butter	1 cup unbleached all-purpose flour
½ cup packed brown sugar	½ cup whole-wheat pastry flour
¼ cup turbinado (coarse) sugar	½ cup chocolate chips
1 large egg, room temperature	¾ teaspoon kosher salt
1 teaspoon pure vanilla extract	½ teaspoon aluminum-free baking powder
	¼ teaspoon baking soda

PREHEAT THE OVEN TO 350°F. Line a baking sheet with parchment paper or a Silpat and set aside.

BEGIN PREPARING THE WET INGREDIENTS. In a small saucepan, melt the butter on low until half melted. Set aside to continue melting and cooling.

PREPARE THE DRY INGREDIENTS. Stir together all of the dry ingredients in a bowl.

ADD ALL THE REMAINING WET INGREDIENTS to the cooled butter mixture, stirring until evenly combined. Pour the wet mixture into the dry mixture, and stir until just combined. The dough will be fairly dense.

USING A 2 TEASPOON-SIZED spring-release scoop (0.3-ounce scoop/#60 scoop), scoop two balls and roll together for each cookie. Place on the prepared baking sheet. Bake for 10 to 11 minutes. When done, the cookies will have a web of crackles across the top. They will appear soft, but will harden up as they cool. Let cool on the pan for 1 minute before transferring to a cooling rack to cool completely, about 20 minutes. Store in an airtight container for up to 4 days or in a freezer-safe ziplock bag in the freezer for a month.

NOTES

Adding the sugars into the melted butter helps to dissolve the granules and remove the grittiness from the final cookie.

INGREDIENT TIP

To ensure a pretty final cookie, turn over 1 to 2 chocolate chips to reveal the flat round side, pressing the pointy side into the top of the cookie.

INGREDIENT TIP

We use a lot of coconut around here as a garnish and in recipes. For that reason, we stock two unsweetened varieties—large flaked and shredded. That may seem excessive for a minimalist kitchen, but it's best to stock what you actually use on a daily basis, and get rid of the rest.

A well-stocked pantry is one of your best resources, for more than when the power goes out—it fuels the everyday. These oatmeal dough bites are some of the magic that can come from grabbing a little bit of this and a little bit of that from the pantry and throwing it into the blender. You're left with protein-packed cookie dough bites for a wholesome post-lunch or afternoon treat. Store in the freezer for at-the-ready convenience. Note: These are not fit for on-the-go, as they become too warm and soft.

Pantry Oatmeal Dough Bites

MAKE AHEAD   WEEKDAY

HANDS-ON: **20 MIN.**   TOTAL: **30 MIN.**
YIELDS: **38 BALLS**

DOUGH BITES

2 cups packed large flaked unsweetened coconut

1½ cups old-fashioned oats

¼ cup dried currants or raisins

¼ cup chocolate chips

½ cup almond butter

½ cup honey

¼ cup hemp seeds

1 teaspoon pure vanilla extract

¼ teaspoon kosher salt

¼ teaspoon cinnamon

COATING (OPTIONAL)

½ cup unsweetened coconut shreds

MAKE THE DOUGH BITES. In a high-powered blender or food processor, blend the coconut and oats into a fine powder. Add the currants and chocolate chips, and blend again to roughly chop.

POUR THE COCONUT MIXTURE into a large bowl. Add all of the remaining dough bite ingredients. Stir until evenly combined. Place in the freezer for 10 minutes to firm up.

USING A 2 TEASPOON-SIZED spring-release scoop (0.3-ounce scoop/#60 scoop), scoop the dough, rolling between your palms to create a ball. Roll each ball in coconut shreds, if desired. The coconut coating also acts as a barrier from the wet cookie dough texture. Place in a freezer-safe ziplock bag. Store in the freezer for up to 2 months. Let stand for a minute or two at room temperature before eating to warm up a little.

249

I was born with a sweet tooth. It's never gone away, but my preferred level of sweetness has changed vastly. I like my desserts to toe the line of just sweet enough, like these macaroons. Sweetened only with maple syrup and chocolate, they curb my dessert craving without leaving a trail of guilt. They are at their best on day 2 or 3, once they've had enough time to rest and soften up a bit. Mom, these are for you: I know where all the Almond Joys went from our Halloween baskets.

Almond Joy Macaroons

MAKE AHEAD   WEEKDAY

HANDS-ON: **30 MIN.**   TOTAL: **1 HR.**
YIELDS: **16 TINY MACAROONS**

DRY	WET
1¼ cups unsweetened coconut shreds	1 egg white
¼ cup unbleached all-purpose flour	¼ cup pure maple syrup
⅛ teaspoon kosher salt	1 teaspoon almond extract
	DRIZZLE
	¼ cup chocolate chips
	16 almond slivers (optional)

PREHEAT THE OVEN TO 350°F. Line a baking sheet with parchment paper or a Silpat. Set aside.

PREPARE THE DRY INGREDIENTS. In a small bowl, stir together all the dry ingredients. Set aside.

PREPARE THE WET INGREDIENTS. In a stand mixer fitted with the whisk attachment, beat the egg white on high speed until soft peaks form. It will look like a tight foam. Add in the maple syrup and almond extract, and beat again until soft peaks form and ribbons hold for a second as the whisk attachment passes through the bowl. The mixture will be fluffy and have the color of pale caramel. Fold into the dry mixture until evenly combined.

USING A 2 TEASPOON-SIZED spring-release scoop (0.3-ounce scoop/#60 scoop), scoop the dough, being sure to tightly pack each scoop. Release the dough onto the prepared baking sheet, and carefully mold the dough back into the rounded shape if needed. Bake for 10 minutes or until firm to the touch. Remove from the oven. Let cool on the pan for 1 minute before transferring to a cooling rack to cool completely, about 15 minutes.

ONCE COMPLETELY COOLED, prepare the drizzle. In a completely dry small saucepan, melt the chocolate, being sure not to let any water come near it. Water can cause the chocolate to seize and crumble. Pour the melted chocolate into a small ziplock bag, pushing the chocolate into a corner as you would a piping bag. Trim off a tiny corner of the bag and drizzle the chocolate over the macaroons. Place 1 almond sliver on the top of each macaroon, if desired. Allow the chocolate to harden before serving. Store in a single layer in a container with a loose cover for up to a week. Storing the macaroons in an airtight container causes them to soften too much.

INGREDIENT TIP

When you need to fill a piping bag or ziplock bag, place the bag inside a glass and fold the top of the bag over the glass for easy filling.

The ice bath for the pudding will feel a bit clunky and over-the-top. Without it, the banana pudding can't cool fast enough before heading into the fridge, taking it twice as long to chill.

Since this pie isn't a spur-of-the-moment kind of dessert, I questioned whether or not to include it. But even a minimalist needs a maximalist recipe. When you decide to make this, plan ahead and make it for a crowd as it doesn't keep well. To make the process less clunky, bake the crust a day in advance. Let the instructions be your guide. When made in sections, it's 100% doable. Use this filling recipe for banana pudding, and swap out the pie crust for vanilla wafers, topping with whipped cream.

Roasted Banana Cream Pie

`MAKE AHEAD` `WEEKEND`

HANDS-ON: **1 HR. 20 MIN.**   TOTAL: **5 HR.**   SERVES: **12**

CRUST

1 single premade Galette Crust (page 242)

FILLING

3 unpeeled yellow (not speckled) bananas, divided

½ cup granulated sugar

¼ cup cornstarch

¼ teaspoon kosher salt

3 large egg yolks

2 cups whole milk

½ cup heavy cream

2 tablespoons unsalted butter, cut in half

1 teaspoon pure vanilla extract

BLACK BOTTOM (OPTIONAL)

3 tablespoons heavy cream

½ cup chocolate chips

GARNISH

Whipped Cream (page 258)

1 tablespoon shaved chocolate bar or chips

BAKE THE PREPARED CRUST. Roll out the chilled crust to a 13½-inch diameter on a lightly floured surface. (If using frozen dough, thaw completely in the fridge first.) Fold the dough in quarters and place in a 10-inch removable bottom tart pan with a 2-inch height. Unfold and center within the pan. Trim excess and repair any holes with excess dough. To do so, rub a bit of water on the dough to act as glue and carefully press the dough scraps into the existing dough. Place the pan in the freezer to chill for 10 minutes.

MEANWHILE, PREHEAT THE OVEN TO 425°F. Prick the bottom and sides of the dough with a fork. Line the dough with parchment paper and fill with pie weights. Place the pan on a baking sheet; bake for 15 minutes. Remove the parchment and pie weights; bake for 4 minutes more. Set aside at room temperature. It's normal for the crust to shrink a bit. This can be made a day in advance and stored uncovered.

PREPARE THE FILLING at least 3½ hours before serving. Preheat the oven to 400°F. Place 1 unpeeled banana on a parchment-lined baking sheet. Bake for 14 minutes, flipping halfway through or until the peel is black. Peel the banana and place in a high-powered blender or food processor; blend until smooth.

IN A MEDIUM SAUCEPAN, whisk together the sugar, cornstarch, and salt. Add yolks and pour in half the milk, whisking until well combined. Pour in the remaining milk and ½ cup heavy cream, whisking to combine. Cook over medium-high until the mixture starts to boil, whisking occasionally, about 4 minutes. Once large lava bubbles form on the surface, turn the heat down to medium-low while still maintaining the lava bubbles, and cook for 3 minutes more, whisking every couple seconds. Remove from the heat. Stir in the butter and vanilla. Pour the pudding into the blender, and blend for about 5 seconds to smooth out the mixture. Prepare an ice bath. Place a smaller bowl in a larger bowl filled with ice and a bit of cold water, being sure no water can seep in. Pour the pudding into the smaller bowl to cool for 20 minutes, stirring occasionally.

MEANWHILE, PREPARE THE BLACK BOTTOM (optional). In a small saucepan, heat the cream until hot. Remove from the heat; stir in the chocolate chips until smooth. Spread along the bottom of the crust.

SLICE THE REMAINING BANANAS into ¼-inch slices and arrange in a single layer over the chocolate (or the base of the crust if omitting the chocolate). Pour in the cooled filling. Cover the surface with plastic wrap and chill at least 3 hours.

PREPARE THE WHIPPED CREAM just before serving. Gently spread over the pie and garnish with the shaved chocolate. This is best served the same day.

When feeding a baby under the age of one without sugar, I learned to bring out the natural sweetness of things using spices and a pinch of salt. I've applied that same lesson to these cupcakes, using a little less sugar than traditionally called for. They're spicy yet sweet. When you start with really good carrots, they'll add an extra layer of natural sweetness. The mascarpone frosting on these cupcakes is something unexpected. It's light and more grown-up than the heavy cream cheese frosting you're probably used to. It's also sturdy enough to hold swoops. One cupcake will leave you satisfied and happy, as a dessert should.

Two-Bowl Carrot Cupcakes

WEEKEND

HANDS-ON: **30 MIN.** TOTAL: **1 HR.**
YIELDS: **12 CUPCAKES**

DRY

1 cup unbleached all-purpose flour

½ cup whole-wheat pastry flour

1 teaspoon baking soda

1 teaspoon ground cinnamon

¾ teaspoon ground cardamom

½ teaspoon kosher salt

¼ teaspoon freshly ground nutmeg

Dash of ground cloves

WET

¾ cup roughly chopped and peeled carrots (around 2 to 3)

Thumbtip of peeled fresh ginger

1 cup granulated sugar

½ cup olive oil

2 large eggs, room temperature

2 tablespoons heavy cream

1 teaspoon pure vanilla extract

FROSTING

1 cup heavy cream, chilled

¾ cup powdered sugar

½ teaspoon cream of tartar

½ teaspoon pure vanilla extract

Dash of cardamom (optional)

4 ounces mascarpone, chilled

SPRINKLES (OPTIONAL)

Large flaked unsweetened coconut, roughly broken up

Hemp seeds

PREHEAT THE OVEN to 350°F. Line a muffin tin with liners.

PREPARE THE DRY INGREDIENTS. In a small bowl, whisk together all of the dry ingredients. Set aside.

PREPARE THE WET INGREDIENTS. In a high-powered blender or food processor, add the carrots and ginger. Blend on medium-low until shredded. In a medium bowl, whisk together the carrot mixture and all of the remaining wet ingredients until well combined. Pour the dry ingredients into the wet ingredients. Fold together until just combined.

USING A 4 TABLESPOON-SIZED spring-release scoop (2-ounce scoop/#16 scoop), scoop the batter evenly into the lined tin, filling a little less than two-thirds full. Bake for about 22 minutes or until a light press in the middle bounces back. Let cool in the pan for 1 minute before transferring to a cooling rack to cool completely before icing, about 30 minutes.

MAKE THE FROSTING. In a stand mixer fitted with a whisk attachment and a completely clean bowl, add the cream, powdered sugar, cream of tartar, vanilla, and, if desired, cardamom. Beat on high until stiff peaks form, as if you were making whipped cream. Add the mascarpone and beat again just until stiff peaks. The frosting will be light yet spreadable. Note: The cream of tartar is necessary as a stabilizer for this frosting.

EVENLY DIVIDE THE FROSTING in the middle of the cooled cupcakes. Using a butter knife, gently smooth off the top. Lightly sprinkle with the coconut and hemp seeds, if desired. The cupcakes are best after at least a 2-hour rest. Store in an airtight container at room temperature for up to 3 days.

INGREDIENT TIP

If you'd like these to be sweeter, try increasing the spices to accentuate sweetness before adding more sugar.

KIDS IN THE KITCHEN

Warning, I'm jumping on a soapbox. Actually, I probably was standing on one in this shot. I'm super short. Figuratively speaking though, I'm a believer in inviting kids into the kitchen. It's neither an efficient nor minimalist philosophy, but a recommended one. Maybe it's because my life is overly immersed in food, but I believe kids should have a basic cooking knowledge by the time they leave home. Like washing clothes, paying a credit card, and learning to drive, cooking seems like one of those basic survival skills. Don't think too highly of me, I've cried over spilled milk. And I'll probably do it again.

257

I read one parenting book before becoming one. It was *Bringing Up Bébé*. I dog-eared the pages on feeding your children and the recipe for Gâteau au Yaourt, a popular yogurt snacking cake kids in France make. Would you ever guess that the early days (or was it years?) of motherhood were difficult for me? I should have read more books on sleeping. We're past the hard, newborn days and happily stirring together cakes in the kitchen. This cake is one we continually come back to, though I've adapted it to fit in our kitchen. It's simple yet satisfying. For this cake, use a ½-cup measuring utensil for all of the measurements. Call them scoops just like the original recipe: 3 scoops of flour, 2 scoops of sugar, a scoop of yogurt and oil, and a half scoop of milk. It's easy like that. So easy you should invite the kids into the kitchen for this one.

Yogurt Shortcake `WEEKDAY`

HANDS-ON: **25 MIN.**   TOTAL: **1 HR. 30 MIN.**
YIELDS: **8 TO 10 SERVINGS**

CAKE

Neutral oil cooking spray

1½ cups unbleached all-
   purpose flour plus more
   for pan

2 teaspoons aluminum-free
   baking powder

½ teaspoon kosher salt

1 cup granulated sugar

½ cup plain whole-milk
   yogurt

½ cup neutral oil

¼ cup whole milk

2 large eggs

1 teaspoon pure vanilla
   extract

**MACERATED
STRAWBERRIES
(OPTIONAL)**

1½ pounds fresh
   strawberries, sliced
   (about 6 cups)

¼ cup granulated sugar

WHIPPED CREAM

1 cup heavy cream

3 tablespoons powdered
   sugar

PREPARE THE CAKE. Preheat the oven to 350°F. Lightly spray the interior sides of an 8-inch round pan with cooking spray. Use a paper towel to wipe smooth. Add a spoonful of flour and shake around the edges to lightly coat. Discard extra flour. Line the bottom of the pan with parchment paper cut to size. Set aside.

IN A MEDIUM BOWL, whisk together 1½ cups flour (3 scoops), baking powder, and salt. Set aside.

IN A LARGE BOWL, whisk together the sugar (2 scoops), yogurt (1 scoop), oil (1 scoop), milk (½ scoop), eggs, and vanilla until smooth. Set aside.

GENTLY FOLD the dry ingredients into the wet ingredients until just combined. Pour the batter into the prepared pan, and bake for 40 to 45 minutes or until the center of the cake is baked through. Remove the cake from the pan, and let cool at least 30 minutes before serving. The cake can be made a day in advance.

MACERATE THE STRAWBERRIES, if desired, about 30 minutes before serving. In a small bowl, stir together the strawberries and sugar. Set aside.

MEANWHILE, MAKE THE WHIPPED CREAM. In a stand mixer fitted with a whisk attachment, beat the cream and powdered sugar on high until medium-stiff peaks form. Slice the cake and top with the whipped cream and, if desired, strawberries.

INGREDIENT TIP

I love changing up the way I serve whipped cream by adding in something as simple as a splash of vanilla extract or something more noticeable like a dollop of mascarpone or plain yogurt. For a warmer flavor, you can sweeten it with a splash of maple syrup as well. If you ever happen to take your whipped cream to the point of curdling butter, fold in a little more heavy cream to soften.

INGREDIENT TIP

Once the cake is cut, press a piece of plastic wrap onto the exposed cake to keep it from drying out.

I learned to make cakes from baking my way through Warren Brown's *Cake Love,* my go-to book for cakes. What I love most about his cakes—they all follow the same rhythm. I, too, ascribe to this philosophy of repeating rhythms in the kitchen. This cake is a nod to Warren's. The crumb is tight from slowly creaming the butter and tender from barely incorporating the flour into the batter. I've left this a single layer cake with a light coat of frosting. Of course, you could double the recipe if you wish. Watch closely as chocolate cakes have a tendency to dry out if even slightly overcooked.

Chocolate, Chocolate Cake

`MAKE AHEAD` `WEEKEND`

HANDS-ON: **45 MIN**.   TOTAL: **4 HR**.   YIELDS: **8 SERVINGS**

CAKE
Neutral oil cooking spray

¾ cup unbleached all-purpose flour plus more for pan

¼ cup unsweetened cocoa powder

¾ teaspoon aluminum-free baking powder

½ teaspoon kosher salt

¼ cup whole milk

¼ cup heavy cream

2 teaspoons pure vanilla extract

6 tablespoons unsalted butter, room temperature

¾ cup granulated sugar

2 large eggs

CHOCOLATE BUTTERCREAM
6 tablespoons unsalted butter, room temperature

1¼ cups powdered sugar

¼ cup unsweetened cocoa powder

2 tablespoons heavy cream

1 teaspoon pure vanilla extract

Pinch of kosher salt

GARNISH (OPTIONAL)
Unsweetened coconut shreds

Cacao nibs

Pepita seeds

MAKE THE CAKE. Preheat the oven to 350°F. Lightly spray the interior sides of an 8-inch round pan with cooking spray. Use a paper towel to wipe smooth. Add a spoonful of flour and shake around the edges to lightly coat. Discard extra flour. Line the bottom of the pan with parchment paper cut to size. Set aside.

IN A SMALL BOWL, whisk together flour, cocoa powder, baking powder, and salt. Set aside.

IN A LIQUID MEASURING CUP, measure the milk, cream, and vanilla. Set aside.

IN THE BOWL OF A STAND MIXER fitted with the paddle attachment, cream together butter and sugar

on the lowest speed for 3 to 5 minutes. (This will feel odd.) When ready, the butter mixture will begin sticking to the sides of the bowl. Add the eggs, one at a time, scraping down sides after each addition; mix until completely combined.

WITH THE MIXER SPEED STILL ON LOW, add the dry ingredients alternately with the wet ingredients in three additions each. This should take 1 minute. Scrape down the sides of the bowl, and then beat again on medium-high for 5 seconds to develop the batter. Pour the batter into the prepared pan, and smooth the top with a spatula. Bake for 25 to 28 minutes, or until a light finger poke to the top bounces back and a crumb of chocolate remains on a toothpick. Let the cake cool in the pan for 10 minutes before running a thin knife around the edge. Transfer to a cooling rack.

MAKE THE CHOCOLATE BUTTERCREAM. In a stand mixer fitted with the whisk attachment, add all of the buttercream ingredients. Beat on low to incorporate. Once combined, beat on high until pale and fluffy, about 4 minutes. The frosting will be pale in color but will deepen as it rests.

TO FROST THE CAKE, add about two-thirds of the frosting to the top of the cake. Using a spatula, spread the remaining frosting snuggly around the sides of the cake, letting the sides of the cake show. Spinning the cake in a circular motion with your spatula pressing down gently in the center, pull the frosting flat, allowing it to pool at the edges. Pull the spatula around the outside edges once more to connect the sides and top. Lightly sprinkle the top edge with garnishes, if desired. This cake is best after a 2-hour rest. Store covered at room temperature for up to 3 days.

The pudding used in this recipe is a similar base to the pudding in the Roasted Banana Cream Pie (page 253). If you can make one, try the other! I cheat a bit in these recipes by adding a yolk directly into the base and heating, rather than tempering first. I also run the pudding through the blender to rid it of any lumps. To make this pudding, buy good-quality chocolate bars, the kind you'd break off a piece and eat. It makes for easy measuring, too. But my favorite part about this recipe—two puddings are made from one base. It's so smart and simple. Top with fruit, coconut, or crushed cookies. It's a great base for toppings. See notes for more ideas.

Black and White Pudding

MAKE AHEAD   WEEKDAY   WEEKEND

HANDS-ON: **20 MIN.**   TOTAL: **4 HR. 20 MIN.**
YIELDS: **6 SERVINGS**

PUDDING

3.5 ounces dark chocolate, broken into small pieces

1.25 ounces white chocolate, broken into small pieces

⅓ cup granulated sugar

3 tablespoons cornstarch

¼ teaspoon kosher salt

2 cups whole milk

1 large egg yolk

1 cup heavy cream

1 teaspoon pure vanilla extract

GARNISH (OPTIONAL)

¼ cup chopped pistachios

¼ cup large flaked unsweetened coconut

2 tablespoons chopped dark chocolate

PREPARE THE PUDDING at least 4 hours before serving. Place the dark and white chocolates in separate bowls, using a larger bowl for the dark chocolate. Set aside.

COMBINE THE SUGAR, cornstarch, and salt in a large saucepan. Whisk in about ½ cup of the milk and the yolk until smooth. Whisk in the remaining milk and cream. Bring to a boil over medium-high, stirring occasionally, about 4 minutes. Once large lava bubbles form on the surface, turn the heat down to medium-low while still maintaining the lava bubbles, and cook for 3 minutes more, whisking every couple seconds. Remove from the heat. Stir in the vanilla. Pour the pudding into a high-powered blender or food processor, and blend for about 5 seconds to smooth out the mixture.

POUR ONE-THIRD OF THE PUDDING MIXTURE (about ¾ cup) in the white chocolate bowl and the remaining amount in the dark chocolate bowl. Stir each bowl until melted and smooth. Press plastic wrap onto the surface of both puddings and refrigerate until cold, at least 4 hours and up to 1 day.

TO ASSEMBLE, give each of the puddings a good stir. Divide the dark chocolate pudding evenly among 6 small glasses or bowls. Then add the white chocolate pudding on top of each. Just before serving, add garnishes, if desired. Serve immediately or refrigerate, covered without garnishes, up to a day.

NOTES

When raspberries are at their best during summer, add them as a garnish. The tartness of the berry is a nice addition. At Christmastime, stir ¼ cup of crushed peppermint into the white chocolate pudding. Top with crushed chocolate wafer cookies and a pinch more of crushed peppermint. Tip: Use mini candy canes. Leave them in their individual wrappers and use a meat mallet or rolling pin to crush.

Seasonal Produce Guide

When you use fresh fruits, vegetables, and herbs, you don't have to do much to make them taste great. Although many fruits, vegetables, and herbs are available year-round, you'll get better flavor and prices when you buy what's in season. This guide helps you choose the best produce so you can substitute seasonal produce into your favorite recipes all year long.

Spring

FRUITS
Bananas
Blood oranges
Coconuts
Grapefruit
Kiwifruit
Lemons
Limes
Mangoes
Navel oranges
Papayas
Passion fruit
Pineapples
Strawberries
Tangerines
Valencia oranges

VEGETABLES
Artichokes
Arugula
Asparagus
Avocados
Baby leeks
Beets
Belgian endive
Broccoli
Cauliflower
Dandelion greens
Fava beans
Green onions
Green peas
Kale
Lettuce
Mushrooms
Radishes
Red potatoes
Rhubarb
Snap beans
Snow peas
Spinach
Sugar snap peas
Sweet onions
Swiss chard

HERBS
Chives
Dill
Garlic chives
Lemongrass
Mint
Parsley
Thyme

Summer

FRUITS
Apricots
Blackberries
Blueberries
Boysenberries
Cantaloupes
Casaba melons
Cherries
Crenshaw melons
Figs
Grapes
Guava
Honeydew melons
Mangoes
Nectarines
Papayas
Peaches
Plums
Raspberries
Strawberries
Watermelons

VEGETABLES
Avocados
Beans: snap, pole,
  and shell
Beets
Bell peppers
Cabbage
Carrots
Celery
Chile peppers
Collards
Corn
Cucumbers
Eggplant
Green beans
Jicama
Lima beans
Okra
Pattypan squash
Peas
Radicchio
Radishes
Summer squash
Tomatoes

HERBS
Basil
Bay leaves
Borage
Chives
Cilantro
Dill
Lavender
Lemon balm
Marjoram
Mint
Oregano
Rosemary
Sage
Summer savory
Tarragon
Thyme

Fall

FRUITS
Apples
Cranberries
Figs
Grapes
Pears
Persimmons
Pomegranates
Quinces

VEGETABLES
Belgian endive
Bell peppers
Broccoli
Brussels sprouts
Cabbage
Cauliflower
Eggplant
Escarole
Fennel
Frisée
Leeks
Mushrooms
Parsnips
Pumpkins
Red potatoes
Rutabagas
Shallots
Sweet potatoes
Winter squash
Yukon Gold potatoes

HERBS
Basil
Bay leaves
Parsley
Rosemary
Sage
Tarragon
Thyme

Winter

FRUITS
Apples
Blood oranges
Cranberries
Grapefruit
Kiwifruit
Kumquats
Lemons
Limes
Mandarin oranges
Navel oranges
Pears
Persimmons
Pomegranates
Pomelos
Tangelos
Tangerines
Quinces

VEGETABLES
Baby turnips
Beets
Belgian endive
Brussels sprouts
Celery root
Escarole
Fennel
Frisée
Jerusalem artichokes
Kale
Leeks
Mushrooms
Parsnips
Potatoes
Rutabagas
Sweet potatoes
Turnips
Watercress
Winter squash

Metric Equivalents

The information in the following chart is provided to help cooks outside the United States successfully use the recipes in this book. All equivalents are approximate.

COOKING/OVEN TEMPERATURES

	Fahrenheit	Celsius	Gas Mark
Freeze Water	32° F	0° C	
Room Temp.	68° F	20° C	
Boil Water	212° F	100° C	
Bake	325° F	160° C	3
	350° F	180° C	4
	375° F	190° C	5
	400° F	200° C	6
	425° F	220° C	7
	450° F	230° C	8
Broil			Grill

LIQUID INGREDIENTS BY VOLUME

¼ tsp					=	1 ml	
½ tsp					=	2 ml	
1 tsp					=	5 ml	
3 tsp	=	1 Tbsp	=	½ fl oz	=	15 ml	
2 Tbsp	=	⅛ cup	=	1 fl oz	=	30 ml	
4 Tbsp	=	¼ cup	=	2 fl oz	=	60 ml	
5⅓ Tbsp	=	⅓ cup	=	3 fl oz	=	80 ml	
8 Tbsp	=	½ cup	=	4 fl oz	=	120 ml	
10⅔ Tbsp	=	⅔ cup	=	5 fl oz	=	160 ml	
12 Tbsp	=	¾ cup	=	6 fl oz	=	180 ml	
16 Tbsp	=	1 cup	=	8 fl oz	=	240 ml	
1 pt	=	2 cups	=	16 fl oz	=	480 ml	
1 qt	=	4 cups	=	32 fl oz	=	960 ml	
				33 fl oz	=	1000 ml	= 1 l

DRY INGREDIENTS BY WEIGHT

(To convert ounces to grams, multiply the number of ounces by 30.)

1 oz	=	¹⁄₁₆ lb	=	30 g
4 oz	=	¼ lb	=	120 g
8 oz	=	½ lb	=	240 g
12 oz	=	¾ lb	=	360 g
16 oz	=	1 lb	=	480 g

LENGTH

(To convert inches to centimeters, multiply inches by 2.5.)

1 in					=	2.5 cm	
12 in	=	1 ft			=	30 cm	
36 in	=	3 ft	=	1 yd	=	90 cm	
40 in	=					100 cm	= 1 m

EQUIVALENTS FOR DIFFERENT TYPES OF INGREDIENTS

Standard Cup	Fine Powder (ex. flour)	Grain (ex. rice)	Granular (ex. sugar)	Liquid Solids (ex. butter)	Liquid (ex. milk)
1	140 g	150 g	190 g	200 g	240 ml
¾	105 g	113 g	143 g	150 g	180 ml
⅔	93 g	100 g	125 g	133 g	160 ml
½	70 g	75 g	95 g	100 g	120 ml
⅓	47 g	50 g	63 g	67 g	80 ml
¼	35 g	38 g	48 g	50 g	60 ml
⅛	18 g	19 g	24 g	25 g	30 ml

Recipe Index

A

Almonds
Cake, Toasted Almond–Stone Fruit, 237
Crisp, Almond–Tart Cherry, 234
Green Beans, Lemony, 182
Macaroons, Almond Joy, 250
Oatmeal, Soaked Overnight, 57
Ancho-ladas, 109
Apples
Galette, Apple, 242
Oatmeal, Soaked Overnight, 57
Salad, House Side, 161
Tacos, BBQ Black Bean and Quick
Slaw, 83
Avocado
Ancho-ladas, 109
Chilaquiles, 73
Chili, Quinoa, 148
Crema, Avocado, 158
Fajitas, Summer Veggie, 79
Salad, Chipotle-Garlic Chopped, 165
Salad, Roasted Chickpea Bánh Mì, 158
Soup, Chipotle Tortilla, 155
Tacos, BBQ Black Bean and Quick
Slaw, 83
Tacos with Chimichurri, Beef, 117
Tacos, Chicken Tinga, 114
Tortas, Open-Faced Sweet Potato, 145
Tostada, Breakfast, 70
Wraps, Red Pepper, 128

B

Bacon
Bacon, Make-Ahead, 132
Brussels Sprouts, Pan-Roasted, 189
Pasta, White Wine Spring, 121
Quiche, Fresh Spinach, 69
Salad, Chipotle-Garlic Chopped, 165
Tostada, Breakfast, 70
Wraps, Bacon-Veggie-Tomato, 132
Bananas
Oatmeal, Banana-Coconut Baked, 58
Oatmeal, Soaked Overnight, 57
Pie, Roasted Banana Cream, 253
Smoothie, Blueberry-Coconut, 214
Smoothie, Immunity, 217
Bánh Mì Salad, Roasted Chickpea, 158
BBQ Black Bean and Quick Slaw
Tacos, 83

Beef
Bibimbap Bowls, Quinoa, 88
Burgers, Diner, 124
Chipotle Beef, 117
Roast, Humble Chuck, 118
Tacos with Chimichurri, Beef, 117
Biscuits with Bourbon-Blueberry
Quick Jam, 40
Biscuit Topping, 238
Black and White Pudding, 262
Black Beans
Ancho-ladas, 109
Burgers, Quinoa, 127
Chili, Quinoa, 148
Fajitas, Summer Veggie, 79
Refried Black Beans, 186
Salad, Chipotle-Garlic Chopped, 165
Soup, Chipotle Tortilla, 155
Tacos, BBQ Black Bean and Quick
Slaw, 83
Tortas, Open-Faced Sweet
Potato, 145
Tostada, Breakfast, 70
Blueberries
Cobbler, Peach, 238
Jam, Biscuits with Bourbon-Blueberry
Quick, 40
Muffins, Berry Bakery, 44
Rolls, Blueberry-Orange Breakfast, 47
Semifreddo, Honeyed Ricotta, 228
Smoothie, Blueberry-Coconut, 214
Bowls
Lentil Bowls, Kitchen-Sink, 87
Quinoa Bibimbap Bowls, 88
Soba Bowls with Peanut Sauce, 91
Thai-Spiced Rice Bowls, 152
Breads. *See also* Pancakes.
Biscuits with Bourbon-Blueberry
Quick Jam, 40
Croutons, 170
Muffins, Berry Bakery, 44
Rolls, Blueberry-Orange Breakfast, 47
Rolls, Make-Ahead Yeast, 202
Scones, Lemon-Ginger, 43
Broccoli
Chicken, Takeout Cashew, 110
Fajitas, Summer Veggie, 79
Brussels Sprouts, Pan-Roasted, 189
Butternut Pasta, 98

C

Cakes
Chocolate, Chocolate Cake, 261
Cupcakes, Two-Bowl Carrot, 254
Shortcake, Yogurt, 258
Toasted Almond–Stone Fruit Cake, 237
Carrots
Bowls, Kitchen-Sink Lentil, 87
Bowls, Thai-Spiced Rice, 152
Bowls with Peanut Sauce, Soba, 91
Caramelized Roasted Carrots, 178
Cupcakes, Two-Bowl Carrot, 254
Fried Rice, 101
Quick-Pickled Radishes and Carrots, 88
Salad, Asian Kale, 157
Salad, Roasted Chickpea Bánh Mì, 158
Soup, Creamy Chicken Noodle, 151
Stock, Dutch Oven Whole Chicken, 106
Takeout Cashew Chicken, 110
Wraps, Lentil Lettuce, 131
Cashew Chicken, Takeout, 110
Casserole, Not Your Mom's Egg, 74
Cauliflower, Curry, 181
Cherries, Stewed Tart, 52
Cherry Crisp, Almond–Tart, 234
Chicken
Ancho-ladas, 109
Cashew Chicken, Takeout, 110
Dutch Oven Whole Chicken, 106
Gyros with Tzatziki, Chicken, 136
Salad, Family-Style Chicken Caesar, 170
Salad Remix, Chicken, 169
Sandwiches, Chicken Pesto, 142
Soup, Creamy Chicken Noodle, 151
Tacos, Chicken Tinga, 114
Chickpeas
Falafel Pitas with Tahini Sauce, Baked, 135
Hummus, Roasted Red Pepper, 185
Roasted Chickpea Bánh Mì Salad, 158
Tikka Masala, Chickpea, 84
Chilaquiles, 73
Chili, Quinoa, 148
Chimichurri, Beef Tacos with, 117
Chocolate
Buttercream, Chocolate, 261
Cake, Chocolate, Chocolate, 261
Chili, Quinoa, 148
Cookies, Chocolate Chip, 246
Macaroons, Almond Joy, 250

Pie, Roasted Banana Cream, 253
Pudding, Black and White, 262
Coconut
  Macaroons, Almond Joy, 250
  Oatmeal, Banana-Coconut Baked, 58
  Oatmeal Dough Bites, Pantry, 249
  Smoothie, Blueberry-Coconut, 214
Coconut Milk
  Bowls with Peanut Sauce, Soba, 91
  Bowls, Thai-Spiced Rice, 152
  Chickpea Tikka Masala, 84
  Oatmeal, Banana-Coconut Baked, 58
  Smoothie, Blueberry-Coconut, 214
Coffee, Cold Brew, 206
Collard Greens, Braised, 194
Cookies
  Chocolate Chip Cookies, 246
  Citrus–Poppy Seed Cookies, 245
  Macaroons, Almond Joy, 250
Corn
  Salad, Chipotle-Garlic Chopped, 165
  Sautéed Corn, 165
  Soup, Chipotle Tortilla, 155
Croutons, 170

D

Drinks
  Agua Fresca, Watermelon-Lime, 213
  Alcoholic
    Margarita, Single-Serving, 221
    Salty Dog, Maple, 218
    Sangria, Quick Summer, 222
    Sangria, Quick Winter, 222
    Sour, Maple-Bourbon, 225
  Coffee, Cold Brew, 206
  Iced Tea, House, 209
  Lemonade(s), Fresh-Squeezed, 210
  Smoothie, Blueberry-Coconut, 214
  Smoothie, Immunity, 217
Dutch Baby, Blender, 52

E

Eggs
  Casserole, Not Your Mom's Egg, 74
  Chilaquiles, 73
  Frittata, The Evergreen, 65
  Rice, Fried, 101
  Scrambled Eggs, The Very Best, 62
Enchiladas
  Ancho-ladas, 109

F

Fajitas, Summer Veggie, 79
Falafel Pitas with Tahini Sauce,
  Baked, 135

Fish
  Salmon, Maple-Soaked, 102
  White Fish, Pan-Fried, 105
Frittata, The Evergreen, 65

G

Green Beans
  Lemony Green Beans, 182
  Quinoa Bibimbap Bowls, 88
Guacamole, 79

H

Ham
  Sandwich, Monte Cristo Breakfast, 61
Hummus, Roasted Red Pepper, 185

J

Jam, Biscuits with Bourbon-
  Blueberry Quick, 40

K

Kale
  Casserole, Not Your Mom's Egg, 74
  Frittata, The Evergreen, 65
  Salad, Asian Kale, 157

L

Lemon
  Bowls, Kitchen-Sink Lentil, 87
  Cookies, Citrus–Poppy Seed, 245
  Galette, Apple, 242
  Green Beans, Lemony, 182
  Gyros with Tzatziki, Chicken, 136
  Hummus, Roasted Red Pepper, 185
  Jam, Bourbon-Blueberry Quick, 40
  Lemonade(s), Fresh-Squeezed, 210
  Maple-Bourbon Sour, 225
  Pesto, 97
  Salad, Family-Style Chicken Caesar, 170
  Scones, Lemon-Ginger, 43
  Sweet Lemon Panko, 228
  Tahini Sauce, 135
  White Fish, Pan-Fried, 105
  Wraps, Red Pepper, 128
Lentil Bowls, Kitchen-Sink, 87
Lentil Lettuce Wraps, 131

M

Mac and Cheese, Stovetop, 198
Make Ahead
  Ancho-ladas, 109
  Apple Galette, 242
  Asian Kale Salad, 157
  Bacon-Veggie-Tomato Wraps, 132

Baked Falafel Pitas with Tahini Sauce, 135
Beef Tacos with Chimichurri, 117
Berry Bakery Muffins, 44
Black and White Pudding, 262
Blueberry-Orange Breakfast Rolls, 47
Breakfast Tostada, 70
Bronzed Pavlovas, 241
Butternut Pasta, 98
Chicken Gyros with Tzatziki, 136
Chicken Pesto Sandwiches, 142
Chicken Salad Remix, 169
Chicken Tinga Tacos, 114
Chilaquiles, 73
Chocolate, Chocolate Cake, 261
Cold Brew Coffee, 206
Creamy Citrus Salad, 174
Crispy Pizza with Caramelized Onions, 80
Dutch Oven Whole Chicken, 106
Family-Style Chicken Caesar Salad, 170
Fresh Spinach Quiche, 69
Fried Rice, 101
Honeyed Ricotta Semifreddo, 228
Humble Chuck Roast, 118
Italian Summer Salad, 162
Make-Ahead Yeast Rolls, 202
Maple-Soaked Salmon, 102
Not Your Mom's Egg Casserole, 74
Open-Faced Sweet Potato Tortas, 145
Orange-Rhubarb Puff Pastry, 233
Pantry Oatmeal Dough Bites, 249
Pesto Garden Pasta, 97
Quick Winter Sangria, 222
Quinoa Bibimbap Bowls, 88
Quinoa Burgers, 127
Red Pepper Wraps, 128
Refried Black Beans, 186
Roasted Banana Cream Pie, 253
Roasted Chickpea Bánh Mì Salad, 158
Roasted Red Pepper Hummus, 185
Soaked Overnight Oatmeal, 57
Thai-Spiced Rice Bowls, 152
Toasted Almond–Stone Fruit Cake, 237
Mascarpone
  Blueberry-Orange Breakfast Rolls, 47
  Fresh Spinach Quiche, 69
  Honeyed Ricotta Semifreddo, 228
  Two-Bowl Carrot Cupcakes, 254
  Whipped Cream, 258
Mayo, Chipotle, 145
Muffins, Berry Bakery, 44

O

Oatmeal
  Banana-Coconut Baked Oatmeal, 58
  Bites, Pantry Oatmeal Dough, 249

Overnight Oatmeal, Soaked, 57

Oranges

Cookies, Citrus–Poppy Seed, 245

Pancakes, Fluffy Multigrain, 48

Puff Pastry, Orange-Rhubarb, 233

Rolls, Blueberry-Orange Breakfast, 47

Salad, Asian Kale, 157

Salad, Creamy Citrus, 174

Sangria, Quick Winter, 222

P

Pancakes

Dutch Baby, Blender, 52

Multigrain Pancakes, Fluffy, 48

Swedish Pancakes, 51

Pasta

Butternut Pasta, 98

Mac and Cheese, Stovetop, 198

Pesto Garden Pasta, 97

Sun-Dried Greek Pasta, 92

Vodka Sauce Pasta, Quick, 95

White Wine Spring Pasta, 121

Peach Cobbler, 238

Peanut Sauce, Soba Bowls with, 91

Peppers

Ancho-ladas, 109

Ancho-lada Sauce, 109

Chipotle Beef, 117

Chipotle-Garlic Chopped Salad, 165

Chipotle-Garlic Dressing, 165

Chipotle Mayo, 145

Chipotle Tortilla Soup, 155

Red Pepper Wraps, 128

Roasted Red Pepper Hummus, 185

Pesto Garden Pasta, 97

Pies and Pastries

Almond–Tart Cherry Crisp, 234

Apple Galette, 242

Biscuit Topping, 238

Orange-Rhubarb Puff Pastry, 233

Peach Cobbler, 238

Roasted Banana Cream Pie, 253

Pizza with Caramelized Onions, Crispy, 80

Potato Salad, Bright, 166

Potato Wedges, Garlicky, 190

Pudding, Black and White, 262

Q

Quiche, Fresh Spinach, 69

Quick-Pickled Cucumbers, 124

Quick-Pickled Radishes and Carrots, 88

Quinoa

Bibimbap Bowls, Quinoa, 88

Burgers, Quinoa, 127

Chili, Quinoa, 148

R

Radishes

Bowls, Quinoa Bibimbap, 88

Chilaquiles, 73

Quick-Pickled Radishes and Carrots, 88

Salad, Chipotle-Garlic Chopped, 165

Salad, Roasted Chickpea Bánh Mì, 158

Tacos with Chimichurri, Beef, 117

Tostada, Breakfast, 70

Wraps, Red Pepper, 128

Rice

Chickpea Tikka Masala, 84

Bowls, Thai-Spiced Rice, 152

Fried Rice, 101

Spanish Rice, 201

S

Salads and Salad Dressings

Balsamic Vinaigrette, 161

Chicken Caesar Salad, Family-Style, 170

Chicken Salad Remix, 169

Chipotle-Garlic Chopped Salad, 165

Chipotle-Garlic Dressing, 165

Citrus Salad, Creamy, 174

Fruit Salad, 241

House Side Salad, 161

Italian Summer Salad, 162

Italian Vinaigrette, 162

Kale Salad, Asian, 157

Pasta, Sun-Dried Greek, 92

Potato Salad, Bright, 166

Roasted Chickpea Bánh Mì Salad, 158

Slaw, Quick, 83

Slaw Tacos, BBQ Black Bean and Quick, 83

Sweet Potato Salad, Roasted Autumn, 173

Sandwiches

Burgers, Diner, 124

Burgers, Quinoa, 127

Chicken Pesto Sandwiches, 142

Gyros with Tzatziki, Chicken, 136

Monte Cristo Breakfast Sandwich, 61

Open-Faced Sweet Potato Tortas, 145

Pitas with Tahini Sauce, Baked Falafel, 135

Roasted Vegetable Sandwiches, 141

Sauces

Ancho-lada Sauce, 109

Avocado Crema, 158

Chimichurri, 117

Peanut Sauce, 91

Pesto, 97

Special Sauce, 124

Tahini Sauce, 135

Tzatziki, 136

Vodka Sauce, Quick, 95

White Wine Sauce, 121

Yogurt Tahini Sauce, 87

Scones, Lemon-Ginger, 43

Soba Bowls with Peanut Sauce, 91

Soup, Chipotle Tortilla, 155

Soup, Creamy Chicken Noodle, 151

Spinach Quiche, Fresh, 69

Stock, Dutch Oven Whole Chicken, 106

Sweet Potatoes

Blistered Sweet Potato Rounds, 193

Salad, Roasted Autumn Sweet Potato, 173

Tortas, Open-Faced Sweet Potato, 145

T

Tacos

BBQ Black Bean and Quick Slaw Tacos, 83

Beef Tacos with Chimichurri, 117

Chicken Tinga Tacos, 114

Tikka Masala, Chickpea, 84

Tortas, Open-Faced Sweet Potato, 145

Tortilla Soup, Chipotle, 155

Tostada, Breakfast, 70

Tzatziki, Chicken Gyros with, 136

W

Weekday

Almond Joy Macaroons, 250

Almond–Tart Cherry Crisp, 234

Bacon-Veggie-Tomato Wraps, 132

BBQ Black Bean and Quick Slaw Tacos, 83

Beef Tacos with Chimichurri, 117

Black and White Pudding, 262

Blueberry-Coconut Smoothie, 214

Braised Collard Greens, 194

Breakfast Tostada, 70

Butternut Pasta, 98

Caramelized Roasted Carrots, 178

Chicken Gyros with Tzatziki, 136

Chicken Pesto Sandwiches, 142

Chicken Tinga Tacos, 114

Chickpea Tikka Masala, 84

Chilaquiles, 73

Chipotle-Garlic Chopped Salad, 165

Chipotle Tortilla Soup, 155

Chocolate Chip Cookies, 246

Cold Brew Coffee, 206

Creamy Chicken Noodle Soup, 151

Creamy Citrus Salad, 174

Curry Cauliflower, 181

Diner Burgers, 124
Family-Style Chicken Caesar Salad, 170
Fresh-Squeezed Lemonade(s), 210
Fried Rice, 101
Garlicky Potato Wedges, 190
House Iced Tea, 209
House Side Salad, 161
Immunity Smoothie, 217
Italian Summer Salad, 162
Kitchen-Sink Lentil Bowls, 87
Lemony Green Beans, 182
Maple-Bourbon Sour, 225
Maple Salty Dog, 218
Maple-Soaked Salmon, 102
Not Your Mom's Egg Casserole, 74
Pan-Fried White Fish, 105
Pan-Roasted Brussels Sprouts, 189
Pantry Oatmeal Dough Bites, 249
Peach Cobbler, 238
Pesto Garden Pasta, 97
Quick Vodka Sauce Pasta, 95
Quinoa Chili, 148
Red Pepper Wraps, 128
Refried Black Beans, 186
Roasted Autumn Sweet Potato Salad, 173
Roasted Vegetable Sandwiches, 141
Single-Serving Margarita, 221
Soaked Overnight Oatmeal, 57
Soba Bowls with Peanut Sauce, 91
Stovetop Mac and Cheese, 198
Sun-Dried Greek Pasta, 92
Takeout Cashew Chicken, 110
Thai-Spiced Rice Bowls, 152
Very Best Scrambled Eggs, The, 62
Watermelon-Lime Agua Fresca, 213

White Wine Spring Pasta, 121
Yogurt Shortcake, 258

Weekend
Almond–Tart Cherry Crisp, 234
Ancho-ladas, 109
Apple Galette, 242
Asian Kale Salad, 157
Bacon-Veggie-Tomato Wraps, 132
Baked Falafel Pitas with Tahini Sauce, 135
Banana-Coconut Baked Oatmeal, 58
Biscuits with Bourbon-Blueberry
    Quick Jam, 40
Black and White Pudding, 262
Blender Dutch Baby, 52
Blistered Sweet Potato Rounds, 193
Breakfast Tostada, 70
Bright Potato Salad, 166
Bronzed Pavlovas, 241
Chicken Salad Remix, 169
Chilaquiles, 73
Chocolate, Chocolate Cake, 261
Citrus–Poppy Seed Cookies, 245
Crispy Pizza with Caramelized Onions, 80
Dutch Oven Whole Chicken, 106
Evergreen Frittata, The, 65
Fluffy Multigrain Pancakes, 48
Fresh Spinach Quiche, 69
Fresh-Squeezed Lemonade(s), 210
Garlicky Potato Wedges, 190
Honeyed Ricotta Semifreddo, 228
Humble Chuck Roast, 118
Lemon-Ginger Scones, 43
Lentil Lettuce Wraps, 131
Make-Ahead Yeast Rolls, 202
Monte Cristo Breakfast Sandwich, 61

Not Your Mom's Egg Casserole, 74
Open-Faced Sweet Potato Tortas, 145
Orange-Rhubarb Puff Pastry, 233
Peach Cobbler, 238
Quinoa Bibimbap Bowls, 88
Quinoa Burgers, 127
Roasted Banana Cream Pie, 253
Roasted Chickpea Bánh Mì Salad, 158
Roasted Red Pepper Hummus, 185
Spanish Rice, 201
Summer Veggie Fajitas, 79
Swedish Pancakes, 51
Toasted Almond–Stone Fruit Cake, 237
Two-Bowl Carrot Cupcakes, 254

Wraps
Bacon-Veggie-Tomato Wraps, 132
Lettuce Wraps, Lentil, 131
Red Pepper Wraps, 128

Y

Yogurt
Bowls, Kitchen-Sink Lentil, 87
Chickpea Tikka Masala, 84
Muffins, Berry Bakery, 44
Oatmeal, Soaked Overnight, 57
Salad, Bright Potato, 166
Salad, Creamy Citrus, 174
Salad, Family-Style Chicken Caesar, 170
Salad, Roasted Chickpea Bánh Mì, 158
Sauce, Yogurt Tahini, 87
Shortcake, Yogurt, 258
Smoothie, Immunity, 217
Tzatziki, Chicken Gyros with, 136
Wraps, Bacon-Veggie-Tomato, 132

Subject Index

B
baking dish, 19
baking pans, 19
baking utensils, 22–23
Bar Keepers Friend, 18, 19
blender, high-powered, 20
box grater, 19
bread knife, 20
butter warmer, 23
buying in bulk, 26, 27, 29, 30, 32

C
cake pan, 19
can opener, 19
casserole pan, 19
cast-iron skillets, 18, 20
chef's knife, 20, 23
cleanup, 18
containers, clear, 26–27, 30
    OXO Pop Containers, 27
colander, 20
commercial grade, 19
cooking pans, 18
cooking utensils, 20
cookware set, stainless-steel, 18
cooling rack, 19
cutting board, 19

D
dishwasher test, 17
Dutch oven, 18

E
efficiency, 14, 15, 17, 26, 27, 29
enamelware, 19
Essential Tools, The, 16–25
    Baking Pans, 19
    Baking Utensils, 22
    Cooking Pas, 18
    Cooking Utensils, 20
    Gadgets, 19
    Knives, 20
    Nonessentials but Recommended, 23
    Small Appliances, 20

expiration dates, 29, 30

G

gadgets, 17, 19
giveaway bin, 17, 18
grocery shopping, 14, 15, 29, 32, 36
    pantry/bulk shopping, 29, 32
    Shop Your List, Not the Store, 29
    weekly maintenance shopping, 29, 32

H

How to Become a Minimalist, 15
How to Build a Minimalist
    Pantry, 26–27
How to Build a Minimalist Spice
    Cabinet, 30–31
    The Spices I Keep Stocked (list), 30
How to Stock a Minimalist
    Pantry, 28–29

I

Ingredients, The, 32–33 (lists)
Ingredient Tips
    Ancho-lada Sauce, leftover, 72
    Arnold Palmer, 210
    asparagus, 121
    avocados, storing, 165
    cake, storing, 260
    canned tomatoes, 95
    carrots, organic whole, 179
    cheese, grating, 199
    cherries, frozen tart, 234
    chicken, cook times, 107
    chiffonade, 69
    chipotles in adobo, 125
    coconut milk, storing leftover, 58
    coconut, varieties of, 248
    cookies, 247
    cotija cheese, 70
    dill, storing fresh, 168
    eggs, 62
    eggs, bringing to room temperature
        quickly, 53
    enchiladas, varying, 108
    English cucumbers, 152
    fish, cook times, 104
    garnishing, 228, 248
    ham, using leftover, 60
    honey, measuring, 183
    kale, 156
    leftover dill, 136
    measuring ingredients, 183
    meats, working with, 119
    mushrooms, 131
    onions, red, 96

onions, sweet, 99
pancakes, freezing, 48
parsley, curly and flat-leaf, 116
peas, frozen, 121
piping bag, filling, 250
plant-based burgers, 126
potatoes, cooking, 191, 192
produce, cutting rounded, 175
 Quick Summer Sangria, 222
rice, 85, 200
rice yields, 100
romaine, crisping, 170
room temperature butter, 244
sandwiches, minimizing carbs in, 144
soba noodles, measuring, 91
soy sauce, 103
spices, 255
sweet potatoes, cooking in soup, 154
tortilla warmer, 79
whipped cream, 258
Yeast, SAF Instant, 203
ziplock bag, filling, 250
inventory
    of the fridge, 36
    of the pantry, 26, 27
    of your tools, 18

J

junk drawer, 18

K

kitchen shears, 23
knives, 20
Koren, Leonard, 13, 15, 36

L

labels
    container, 27
    spice, 30
lists, 29
    of ingredients, 32–33

M

mason jars, 22, 27
meal planning, 14, 15, 36
    Helpful Tips for Meal Planning, 36
measuring cups, 22
measuring spoons, 22
meat mallet, 23
microplane, 23
microwave oven, 23
minimalist ideals
    Cook to a Soundtrack, 197
    How to Hygge, 67

Kids in the Kitchen, 257
Pizza Night, 113
Repetition Is Good Pedagogy, 231
The Taste of Simplicity, 139
We Meet Again, 55
Minimalist Tips
    berries for quick prep, 45
    blender, cleaning, 236
    box grater, deconstructed, 130
    box graters, 90
    carrots, shredding, 90
    chicken, cubing, 111
    chicken marinade, 137
    chop vegetables the night before, 64
    cleanup, 87, 163, 165, 195, 220,
        223, 236
    croutons, homemade, 171
    eggs, peeling, 167
    garlic, rubbing cut clove over
        bread, 140
    grains, cooking in soup, 149
    green onions, cutting, 161
    kitchen shears, 111, 161
    mandoline, 130
    mason jar, 134
    measuring ingredients, 163, 172, 195,
        215, 219, 220, 223
    measuring utensils, 87
    round biscuit cutter alternative, 41
    sandwich with buttered bread, 140
    sauce ingredients, chopping, 94
    simple syrup, cooling, 211
    skip using an extra bowl, 58
    tart pan, 10-inch removable
        bottom, 69
    vegetables, chopping, 64, 130
    vegetables, quick-pickled, 159
    waffles, turn this recipe into, 49
mixer, 20
mixing bowls, 22
muffin tin, 19

N

"neutral oil," 23
nonstick surface, 18, 19, 20

O

oil sprayer, 23
overbuying, 15, 29

P

pantry, 26–29
parchment paper, 19
paring down, 13, 14, 15, 17–18, 30

paring knife, 20
Protein, A Note About, 35

R

Recipes. The, 34–36
  Make Ahead tags, 35
  The Minimalist Kitchen Recipe
    Anatomy, 35
  Weekday tags, 35
  Weekend tags, 35
refrigerator (fridge), 26, 29, 32
  Stock the Fridge Smartly, 29
reusable silicone baking mat
  (like a Silpat), 19
rules, 26, 27

S

salad spinner, 23
Sample Dinner Plans, 37
scoops, 27

scoops, spring-release, 23
sheet pan, 19
small appliances, 20
spatulas, 17, 20
spices, 27
  expiration dates, 30
  How to Build a Minimalist Spice
    Cabinet, 30–31
  The Spices I Keep Stocked (list), 30
  storing, 30
spoons, cooking, 20
spoons, measuring, 22
stainless-steel cookware set, 18
steamer basket, 20
stockpot, 18

T

tart pan, 19
toaster, 20

tongs, 20
tortilla warmer, 23

U

underbuying, 29

V

vegetable peeler, 19

W

What Is a Minimalist Kitchen, 13–14
What Is Minimalism, 13
whisk, 17, 22
wooden rolling pin, 22, 23
Wunderlist, 29

About the Author

MELISSA COLEMAN hopped around the states as a child, living in North Carolina, Alabama, Colorado, and Texas with her dad, Chris; mom, Elizabeth; sister, Ashleigh; and brother, Matt. She was born with a deep love for food, which eventually turned into learning how to bake in high school and college, where she studied graphic design.

She and Kevin, her husband, met in Intro to Psychology and became really good friends before dating two years later. They married a year after graduating and moved to Chicago for Kevin to begin his doctorate in psychology. Working as a graphic designer, Melissa started her blog, thefauxmartha.com, attending to it at nights and on weekends. She learned how to make scones that rose and cakes that wowed.

Four years later, Kevin matched for his doctoral internship in New Haven, Connecticut. The blog moved with them, and along came Hallie, their daughter. Two years later, they moved to Minneapolis, Minnesota, for Kevin to take a permanent position as a child psychologist. The blog came with them again, documenting dinners and a house build. Melissa eventually took the blog full time, hanging up her role as a graphic designer. Little did she know, design was the fuel behind her recipes and the way she navigated the kitchen.

Acknowledgments

I SWORE I'D NEVER WRITE A BOOK. I also swore I'd never write anything longer than an email after college. I need to stop swearing. Eventually, I started saying I'll never write a book unless one pours out of me. With that, I'd like to start by thanking my editor, Rachel West, who pitched this book to me. Somehow she knew the exact one that would pour out of me. Thank you for taking a chance on me, Rachel. This book is just as much yours as it is mine.

To Kevin (Kev), my husband, my left brain, and my biggest believer—thank you for also saying yes to this book. Thank you for doing a lot of weekends without me. Thank you for letting me hound you after the first and last bite of each recipe. Thank you, too, for making me think about the what-else behind minimalism—the psychology, the whys, and the emotions behind it all. Now it's your turn to write that book I've been nagging you about. I love you.

To Hallie (Hal), my daughter, my tiny sous chef, and my biggest fan—this is for you. It was you who inspired this book. You put a deadline on dinnertime, making me build parameters so that I'd actually cook. I want to give you the gift that my mom gave me—a warm dinner shared around the table every night, even on nights when soccer practice ran late. I hope, too, this book reminds you that you can do hard things, things you swore you'd never do.

To my parents, Chris and Elizabeth, thank you for making a point to eat dinner together every night. Mom, thank you for continuing to let me make the rolls at the holidays, even after the year of the rock-hard rolls (see Make-Ahead Yeast Rolls on page 202 for a foolproof recipe). Dad, thank you for showing me that having a hobby around food is worthwhile. (He's a master at the grill.) I'm not sure I would have found my way here otherwise.

To my sister, Ashleigh, thank you for being one of my biggest cheerleaders throughout my less than predictable path. Thank you, too, for making so many of my recipes to feed the people in your life and for reading over my work when I need a second set of eyes. Even though I'm the older one, you've looked after me like an older sister would.

To Tamara, my mother-in-law, thank you for showing me that making food ahead of time is a worthwhile (and wise) use of time. I'm a smarter cook because of you.

To my extended family—Matt and Stephanie, Rusty and Sandy, Jeff, Lauren and Kalli, Blake, Brooke—thank you for being my people by birth, by marriage, and by choice.

To Mimi, my grandmother, thank you for always reminding me how proud you are of me. There's no better fuel for an artist who sometimes flounders. (Mimi also called me Martha, short for Martha Stewart, growing up for my many domestic interests. Thus thefauxmartha.com was born in late 2008.)

To Lucy, my neighbor, thank you for teaching me how to cook meat to perfection. This book is better because I live across the street from you.

To my blog readers, it will always amaze me that you found me in the first place and that you chose to stay. I hope this book nourishes you in ways that it's nourished my family.

And finally, to the team at Time Inc. Books, thank you for making this book a reality—a very beautiful reality. The list includes Allison Chi, Paden Reich, Anja Schmidt, Margot Schupf, Lacie Pinyan, Matt Ryan, Diane Keener, Lauren Moriarty, Callie Nash, Julia Levy, Marianne Williams, Ivy Odom, Paige Grandjean, Kim Cornelison, Diana Scanlon, Thom Driver, Kay Clarke, Mindi Shapiro, Mary Clayton Carl, Greg DuPree, Caitlin Bensel, Alison Miksch, Jennifer Causey, Scott Rounds, Anna Hampton, Margaret Dickey, Mary Claire Britton, Karen Rankin, Danielle Costa, Amanda Lipnick, Laura Gianino, and Kourtney Sokmen.